Bolt of Fate

BOLT OF FATE

Benjamin Franklin
AND
His Electric Kite Hoax

TOM TUCKER

PublicAffairs

NEW YORK

BOOK DESIGN BY JENNY DOSSIN. TEXT SET IN ADOBE CASLON.

Library of Congress Cataloging-in-Publication Data
Tom Tucker, 1944–
Bolt of fate: Benjamin Franklin and his electric kite hoax/Tom Tucker.—1st ed.
p. cm.
Includes bibliographical references and index.
ISBN 1-891620-70-3
1. Franklin, Benjamin, 1706–1790—Knowledge—Physics.
2. Electricity—Experiments—History.
3. Lightning—Experiments—History.
4. United States—History—Revolution, 1775–1783—Science.
5. Physicists—United States—Biography.
6. Statesmen—United States—Biography.
I.   Title.
QC16.F58T83 2003
530'.092—dc21
[B]
2003043167

FIRST EDITION
1 3 5 7 9 10 8 6 4 2

FOR SUSIE, IN MEMORY

Contents

PART ONE
The Hand

PART TWO
The *Virtuoso*

৵ PART THREE

Citizen of the World

৵ PART FOUR

Household God

Acknowledgments

Many scholars, archivists, and translators have helped me along the way with this book. Special thanks are due John Heilbron, Shilton College, Oxford; Max Hall, Cambridge, Massachusetts; Ellen Kuhfeld, curator of electrical instruments at the Bakken Library and Museum; and Paul Zall, Franklin scholar *emeritus* at the Huntington Library; all of them were generous with time and counsel and criticism as this was written.

Another debt is due the Bakken, which awarded me a grant for research there. I was helped in many ways during and after my visits to the Royal Society Library, the British Library, the American Philosophical Library, and the Library Company of Philadelphia.

Also acknowledgment is due I. Bernard Cohen, *emeritus* Harvard University. He is a scholar who has made invaluable contributions to the study of Franklin's science that have benefited this work—although in the area of lightning science, I differ sharply with him.

I gratefully acknowledge *The Papers of Benjamin Franklin,* the magnificent Yale project that, as this was written, advanced to its 37th volume under the editorship of Ellen Cohn. Leo Lemay's Web site in progress, *Franklin* (www.english.udel.edu/lemay/franklin/), has also been invaluable.

Thanks to many authorities who generously advised me, including: Jay Nelson Sr., Philadelphia, expert on eighteenth-century locks and keys; Michele Majer, New York, authority on eighteenth-century silk fashion; Allen G. Noble, authority on eighteenth-century vernacular style in agricultural architecture and professor at the University of Akron; Mike Wister, direct descendant of Franklin neighbors the Wisters, Philadelphia; Edwin Battison, expert on eighteenth- and nineteenth-century iron working, Windsor, Vermont; Bruce Gill, steeple historian and archivist, Christ Church, Philadelphia; Dale Linson and Richard Beard, Rutherford County, N.C., consultants on American wood; Casey Donohue, meteorologist, NASA Dryden Flight Research Center; Don Burbidge, John Lining specialist, Charleston; Kari Diethorn, chief curator at Independence National Historical Park, Philadelphia; and Vladimir Rakov, lightning authority and professor at the University of Florida, who was also invaluable in reading and criticizing the manuscript.

I need to single out staff members at libraries, archives, and museums who offered splendid help. I gratefully acknowledge Stephanie Morris, Joanna Corden, and Nicola Dawson and others at the Royal Society of London Library; Elizabeth Ihrig, the Bakken; Roy Goodman and Robert Coxe, American Philosophical Library; Martin Hackett and Amey Hutchins of the University of Pennsylvania Archives; Dee Cook, archivist to The Worshipful Society of Apothecaries of London; Sara Weatherwax, the Library Company of Philadelphia; Lisa Ann Libby and Susi Krasnoo at the Huntington Library; Nadine Massias, Bibliothèque de Bordeaux; Robin Francis and staff, Heinz Archive at the National Portrait Gallery, London; Roberta Engleman and staff, Wilson Library at the University of North Carolina at Chapel Hill; Ivan Sparkes, historian in Suffolk, England, and the staff of the Thurrock Public Library; Estela Dukan at the library of the Royal College of Physicians of Edinburgh; Stephan Fölske, archivist at the Berlin–Brandenburgische Akademie der Wissenschaften; Patricia Cossard, the Historical Society of Pennsylvania; Bruce Laverty at the Athenaeum Library, Philadelphia; Kay Carter at Waring Historical Library, Medical University of South Carolina; Claudine Pouret, archivist at Académie Royale des Sciences, Paris; Giancarlo Bisazza, archivist at the Instituto Universitario di Architettura di Venezia; Anna Marika at the Walpole Library, Yale University; Maureen Lasko, University of Chicago Fine Arts Library; St. Julien R. Childs, associate of the archive of the South Carolina Historical Society; William Loos, Buffalo and Erie County Public Library; and Lisa Browar, Indiana University Library.

A number of scholars and experts read and criticized manuscript chapters. I am very grateful to David M. Griffiths, University of North Carolina at Chapel Hill; Roger Hahn, University of California at Berkeley; Max Hall, Cambridge, Massachusetts; David Haycock, junior research fellow, Wolfson College, Oxford; Ellen Kuhfeld, curator of electrical instruments, the Bakken; Michael McVaugh, University of North Carolina at Chapel Hill; Robert Middlekauff, University of California at Berkeley; Richard Sorrenson, formerly at the University of Indiana, now Auckland, New Zealand; and Paul Zall, scholar *emeritus* at Huntington Library. Any errors or misreadings of context remain solely mine.

Many scholars were extraordinarily generous with help in e-mail, personal interview, or telephone interview. My thanks to David Rhees, the Bakken; J. Leo LeMay, University of Delaware; H. Otto Sibum, Max Planck Institute for the History of Science; Richard Sorrenson, Indiana University; David Sturdy, University of Ulster; Andreas Kleinert, Universitaet Halle–Wittenberg; Ellen Cohn and Kate Ohno, *The Papers of Benjamin Franklin*, Yale University; Simon Schaffer, Cambridge University; Sheila Skemp, University of Mississippi; David Philip Miller at the University of New South Wales, Australia; Charles Royster, Mississippi State University; Michel Lopez, Université du Maine; and Penny Batchelor, historian *emeritus* at Independence National Historical Park, Philadelphia.

Thanks to my brilliant and patient translators, who included: Chantal McFadden and additionally Elizabeth Ihrig, French; Olga Poliakova and Vlada Deryabina, Russian; Ursula Thompson, German; and Katherine Dobbins, Latin.

This research was mostly performed remote from archives. At home, Susan Vaughn and Becky Cleland of the Isothermal Community College Library were always helpful, and Isothermal student researchers Marcia King and Debbie Millete made contributions. Ben Sherer also provided research help. My special gratitude goes to Michael Greene of Isothermal, who was a wizard at using interlibrary loan to retrieve items that seemed beyond reach.

Thanks to PublicAffairs for the brilliant efforts of my editor, David Patterson; Executive Editor Paul Golob; and Publisher Peter Osnos. Special thanks to my agent Caron K, who made this happen.

The sifting of evidence two and a half centuries old to discover what happened and what-did-not introduced me to more than a hundred specialists, archivists, and scholars. But over and above all contributors, thanks to Diane Tucker, my home-front enthusiast, editor, researcher, and wife.

AUTHOR'S NOTE

BECAUSE THIS BOOK is intended for an audience of general readers, I have mostly modernized the English spellings and removed the typographical devices of the era. For a bit of the original flavor, this language has been retained in the chapter epigraphs.

PROLOGUE

*If there is no other Use discover'd of Electricity, this, however, is
something considerable, that it may help to make a vain Man
humble.*

               ❧ BENJAMIN FRANKLIN

T HE ROOM WAS NOW DARK, THE FACES THAT HAD GLOWED
earlier in the evening in the flickering light of Benjamin's
electrical successes, had gone home. They were merchants, lawyers,
tradesmen, fops, celebrated beauties, no dukes or princes of course,
but possibly the colonial governor from across the Delaware River.
A mingling of cool lavender scent from the ladies and hot sulphur
or phosphor smell from the tube remained in the closed air of the
room; the sulphur pinched his nostrils. The memory of the bite of
the mysterious force, on his knuckle.

In Benjamin Franklin's residential shop on the north side of
Market Street in Philadelphia, electricity made its appearance. The
phenomenon arrived courtesy of contraptions crafted of mahogany,
metal, and glass, devices that, by rubbing the glass, created electricity. The force arrived with what some witnesses reported as a crack-

ling noise resembling green leaves afire. Sometimes the electricity spit, and at other moments it formed silently and slowly into pencils or brushes of eerie colorings. It flared with brilliance, it softened, it gleamed. When human flesh was electrified, said some, the person radiated with a subtle blue light.

The year was 1746, when electricity had fully arrived as the international rage. "It is all the vogue," wrote one reporter of the astonishing events of that year, "electricity has replaced the quadrille." Static electricity, the same energy elicited by rubbing a cat, was now produced more abundantly by hand-cranked devices in fashionable parlors. A few estimable discoveries may have bubbled up in the carefree flow of parties in Berlin, Paris, and London. The thrilled audiences included kings, dukes, celebrities, great beauties, the Hanoverian princesses, Pope Benedict XIV, and, increasingly, growing numbers of middle people—tradesmen, craftsmen, mechanics, and traveling showmen.

Franklin brought to this fashionable science his skill as a master of English prose. In daily life we continue to use his language to talk about electricity, his literary imagination shaping how we encounter this mysterious force, the terms he coined, *positive* and *negative* and *battery*, for instance, surfacing when we do something as simple as changing a flashlight battery.

But if you ask Americans today about Franklin's contribution to electrical science, memory rarely sparks. You often get a two-part reaction—first an *ah-yes* response of genuine appreciation. Vague, yet warm. But second, the eyes shift sideways, off the mark, trying to grasp something—anything, a stock response in this era when Americans, as one historian phrases it, suffer "historical amnesia." We are the people who vividly recall, for instance, that Washington crossed the Delaware, but for the life of us, we're not sure what he hoped to find on the other side.

We vividly recall Franklin lofting his electric kite—even if we're not sure why he did so. The electric kite demonstration remains arguably the most famous experiment in the history of science. No

American scientific event has been more often depicted by graphic artists. It is the only image of a scientific experiment ever printed on U.S. currency. No image more faithfully attends schoolroom education with a plethora of visualizations dating back to the famed nineteenth-century Currier & Ives calendar picture. And on intellectually higher ground, the kite story has established itself as the icon of man in the Age of Reason triumphing over Nature's deadly phenomenon, the lightning bolt.

This book's purpose is to return to primary sources and discover what actually happened in 1752. On close attention, you begin to notice how much unravels when you start looking at the authentic eighteenth-century sources behind Franklin's electric kite and also his lightning rod. Many traditional assumptions set in place in nineteenth-century narratives and continuing to this day have no eighteenth-century context. Behind the legend is a story of great dramatic intensity.

An important key here is Franklin's personality. We tell our children about the advocate of the Revolution, the Founder of the Republic, the homespun philosopher who counseled us in schoolbooks how to become "healthy, wealthy, and wise," the man of letters whose *Autobiography* is a landmark in the history of self-revelation. We celebrate his rags to riches story and his renown as a politician, printer, retailer, philanthropist, humorist, author, postmaster, almanac-maker, investor, newspaperman, and inventor. But this multifaceted genius had another side: He was also a splendid master of the hoax. This side was not fully explored by scholars until the mid-twentieth century and even since then has remained curiously beyond mainstream notice. Franklin's hoaxes were many, spanning his entire career. These hoaxes were political, literary, career-enhancing, sometimes dangerous, and sometimes playfully humorous. The kite experiment was his scientific hoax.

Franklin had good reason to hoax his contemporaries in science. His early attempts to report his electrical theories abroad were rebuffed. In fairness to the Europeans, no one in his right eighteenth-century mind would have imagined that any advance in any sort of science might be made by a printer at the edge of the civilized world.

Franklin recalled in his *Autobiography* that he had been "stifled" at the Royal Society in London. *Stifled,* a word most often in our time used for the polite suppression of a yawn, but in Franklin's time, commonly used to describe throttling about the neck until dead. In fact, the leading British electrical scientist, William Watson, read aloud an excerpt of Franklin's first electrical letter to the Society, asserting that he himself had already thought up the ideas earlier, a claim that a search of that member's writings fails to document.

Benjamin Franklin's first experience in this international science arena was as a victim of intellectual property theft.

What did happen next?

Theft, stonewalling, laughter. These might have withered away a lesser shopkeeper struggling to claim his place in the world of these elite silk-coat gentlemen. But the Royal Society had never seen anything like Franklin. In the strange, tangled sequence of events that gave birth to electrical science, Franklin sent more experiments across the Atlantic to the *virtuosi* at the Royal Society, some of them joke-insults in the guise of science aimed at the thief. One of these, a potentially deadly experiment involving lightning, was ignored in London. But the proposal found its way to France in translation and was performed (with safety modifications) by men who were novices in electrical science. They succeeded beyond their wildest dreams at Marly, France, in May, 1752; they extolled Franklin in Paris. Almost overnight, Franklin became an Age of Reason celebrity, the toast of Europe, feted in every fashionable salon.

Months later when he learned the astonishing news, to claim an active role, Franklin conceived the story that he had already—secretly—performed a variation on his original proposal: He had flown a kite to bring down electricity from overhead. He simply didn't mention it for three months. The report he wrote added to his eminence as a heroic figure, the man who understood the nature of electricity, the hero who diverted Zeus's thunder into experimental science. At the same time, Franklin announced his invention of the lightning rod, a device that protected life and property by guiding lightning harmlessly through rods and wires into the earth. The printer had conquered the deadly bolt.

To follow Benjamin Franklin in this tale is to uncover a man altering the record, secretly editing the past, ducking questions from legitimate scientists, and anonymously spreading misinformation on his lightning science. The laurel crowned him in 1752. Honors, degrees, awards. But less than a year passed before a scientist at St. Petersburg, Russia—diminished in Franklin histories as a man foolishly unaware—was killed in a lightning experiment. Russian and Estonian sources here opened up reveal the victim to have been a brilliant, very aware scientist, courageous if reckless, and a skilled linguist who had followed Franklin's every word in English. More public relations battlegrounds awaited Franklin on the Continent in the next decade. In 1764 the Académie Royale des Sciences at Paris gave credit for the electric kite to another man. Franklin would take fascinating countermeasures.

The fiction of the electric kite was tempered in the face of resistance. Yet thirty years after the electric parties, by the time of the American Revolution, Franklin's lightning science had evolved into legend and acquired political weight. In Franklin's case, the nurturer of the lightning-science myth was the not-so-innocent subject himself. He multiplied and distributed it with the efficiency he brought to the distribution of his newspaper, *The Pennsylvania Gazette.*

※

During the American Revolution, in London scientists worried about some secret weapon, an electrical apparatus Franklin might have devised. "The natural philosophers in power," wrote Horace Walpole in his journal, "believe that Dr. Franklin has invented a

machine the size of a toothpick case, and materials that would reduce St. Pauls to a handful of ashes."

The real electrical weapon that Benjamin Franklin invented was
himself. Behind the gentle, playful face was a shrewd, tough person
who knew how to use his scientific fame, who wielded his lightning-science celebrity in the hallways at Versailles as briskly as a
Minuteman tamping his musket and marching into battle.

The myth had assumed startling power, to the extent that one
twentieth-century author has written of "the kite that won the revolution." Another author, one of Franklin's recent biographers, states
that Franklin's lightning science was of "crucial importance not only
to science but to the history of the Western World. Nothing less
than America's victory in America's War of Independence three
decades later was to be linked with [it]."

In 1776, an aged Benjamin Franklin was sent to Paris on a seemingly impossible mission. The American rebels faced a crisis, their
funds depleted, the powder arsenals empty, New York had fallen
and Philadelphia would soon be subdued. At this juncture, Franklin
arrived to seek French aid. He brought his lightning celebrity to the
task. He would face many questions from the French. But as the influence of the English crown tottered, as the crafty Versailles politicians scrutinized him, as the American experiment in democracy
seemed about to expire, a central question was: How far could Benjamin Franklin take his electric kite hoax?

The answer thunders to this day.

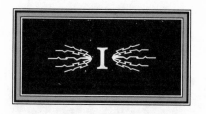

I

The Hand

FRANKLIN IN PARIS, *circa 1777*

A nineteenth-century engraving based on a drawing by C.N. Cochin

(Bakken Library and Museum, Minneapolis)

Almanack-Writer

The first Thing requisite in an Almanack-Writer, is, That he should be descended of a great Family, and bear a Coat of Arms.

> BENJAMIN FRANKLIN

BENJAMIN FRANKLIN CAME OF AGE IN THE PRINT TRADE. All week he lived with it, the *clack* of lead type bits dropped onto the composing bar used by eighteenth-century printers and also the measured *thump* of the press issuing pages to be sewn into hymnbooks and his brother's weekly newspaper the *Courant* and broadsides that would be tacked onto all the pissing posts in Boston.

During five years of indenture, the boy picked up a range of skills. It was a trade that in that era required ideally "a tolerable genius for language" and manual abilities and fix-it skills as well. The mix of competencies would later grace Franklin's entrance into electrical science. It was also the trade that was to lay the foundation of his fortune in Pennsylvania.

On October 6, 1723, however, Benjamin Franklin first appeared in the streets of Philadelphia as a runaway teenager. He arrived as an escapee from indenture. He was seventeen years old. He must have been attractive, the runaway with the moon face, glowing hazel eyes, and square, broad frame. But he was also a sight—grimy from the hundred-mile march and coastal bay ferryings, dirty laundry flapping from his pockets, his financial means diminished to a few coins.

There was the wrinkle on his face seen later in scores of portraits. It was a sly wrinkle descending from the corner of his mouth, revealing humor and a droll generosity at once. But as he walked the strange streets, he was depending on the print trade to survive.

The next morning Franklin presented himself at the shop of Samuel Keimer on Market Street. Nothing about him suggested a journeyman printer to Keimer. No black ink lined Franklin's fingernails—he had been away from the presses several weeks and soused for 30 hours straight by Mid-Atlantic seaboard gales. No stooped shoulders testified to years bent over the press. Nothing about his age was right. So it was not surprising when old Keimer held out the composing stick. A printer? Prove it.

The boy took the stick and set to typesetting a line of poetry supplied by Keimer—a literary dabbler. Franklin must have given a formidable performance. He was hired on the spot. His Philadelphia entrance into the trade had resolved into one simple question: Can you do it?

*

Despite job-seeking success, for half a decade Benjamin Franklin's career in his trade would sputter and stall.

In 1724, comfortably settled into rental lodgings in the Quaker city, the young journeyman printer met Pennsylvania governor William Keith. This silk-coat man urged Franklin to start his own printshop with the governor as a silent partner. Keith promised the eighteen-year-old financial backing and letters of credit needed to go to England and obtain printing equipment. As the scheme developed, the governor buzzed in the youth's ear the need for secrecy. Franklin gave his employer notice, shut down his lodgings, and made the transatlantic crossing, but while at sea, Franklin spoke of his project to fellow passengers who informed him that the governor was famously unreliable. Arriving in London, Franklin found there were no letters of credit.

Stranded, Franklin returned to journeyman status in London's print district. With a friend, he shared a room in an impoverished neighborhood called Little Britain. Even then, he was fascinated by the world of the coffeehouse philosophers at the Royal Society, the great thinkers who charted the travels of planets and measured gravity and identified rare plants. He tried to gain a foothold. He had brought with him a novelty fashioned in the New World, a tiny purse made of asbestos. Franklin's instincts were not that far off the mark. The men of the Society set great value on the curious and bizarre. Franklin contacted the member most famous for his inability to pass up curios, Sir Hans Sloane, the obsessive collector, the vice president at the Society whose personal assembly of fossils, pickled embryos, and pinned butterflies neatly arranged in boxes later formed the basis of the British Museum. Sir Hans bought Franklin's purse—it remains in the inventory of the British Museum to this day—but Benjamin departed without entry to the hallowed meeting rooms. Another member of the Society promised even grander prospects to the young man, an introduction to the Society president, Sir Isaac Newton. The gentleman did not live up to his word.

After eighteen months, Franklin returned to Philadelphia. He had decided to leave printing and went to work as a clerk in a dry goods shop on Water Street, where he learned accounting and "grew in a little time expert at selling." But when the owner died, the heirs took over the store, and the job vanished. Franklin was back in printing.

In June, 1727, Franklin returned to work in Keimer's printshop as foreman. He suspected the old man was using him to instruct new-

comers to the trade with the intent of firing him once the workers
knew enough to handle business. One of the workers, Hugh
Meredith, offered Franklin the chance to form their own partner-
ship, a venture funded at the start by Meredith's father. By 1730,
Meredith made it clear that he wanted to return to agriculture, and
borrowing the money, Franklin bought out Meredith. He was on
his own.

※

  "If a Philadelphian in 1728," wrote Franklin biographer James
Parton, "had been asked to name the business by which, in Philadelphia, a stranger could make a fortune in twenty years, the business of a printer would have been among the very last to occur to
him. There was no good book-store south of Boston, it is true, but
also there was no general regard for books south of Boston."
  When Franklin expanded his printshop operation with the publication in 1729 of his newspaper, *The Pennsylvania Gazette*, no one

PHILADELPHIA

imagined the colonies needed another newspaper. But Franklin's humor surfaced in something even as slight as a police blotter item, twisting a phrase with his odd charm and eliciting a smile or laughter. *The Pennsylvania Gazette* prospered.

In 1732, Franklin entered the almanac market with *Poor Richard's Almanack.* James Parton supplies a nineteenth-century vantage point on the upstart's strategy: "*Poor Richard,* I repeat was a comic almanac. The advertisements which announced its publication were comic; most of the prefaces were comic; the accounts of the eclipses and other natural phenomena were generally comic; the greater part of the verses and proverbs were comic; and those which were not comic, were quaint."

There were already six almanacs oversaturating the market. No need for a new one. But humor was Franklin's entrée. He created a Mr. Richard Saunders (Poor Richard) who was said to have produced this new almanac and, in the preface, the mythical Saunders wrote about his friend Mr. Titan Leeds, who was a very real almanac-maker. Saunders indicated that he had long hesitated to

The artist Peter Cooper painted this image of Philadelphia circa 1720. The view closely resembles the first glimpse Franklin had of his future hometown as the boat approached Market Street Wharf in October of 1723.

begin an almanac out of tender feelings for his friend Titan Leeds.
He explained:

> But this obstacle (I am far from speaking it with pleasure) is soon
> to be removed, since inexorable death, who was never known to
> respect merit, has already prepared the mortal dart, the fatal sis-
> ter has already extended her destroying shears, and that ingenious

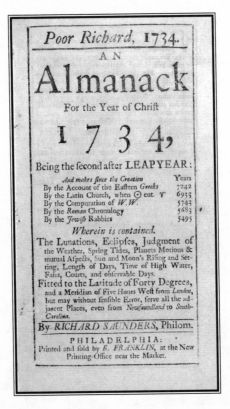

The appearance of the second Poor Richard's Almanack *testified to Frank-*
lin's success. His droll humor and creation of a fictional persona as editor de-
lighted Pennsylvania.

man must soon be taken from us. He dies, by my calculation, made at his request, on October 17, 1733, 3 ho., 29 m., P.M. at the very instant of the ♂ of ☉ and ☿. By his own calculation, he will survive till the 26th of the same month. This small difference between us, we have disputed whenever we have met these nine years past; but at length he is inclinable to agree with my judgement. Which of us is most exact, a little time will now determine.

Upon reading this preface, Titan Leeds was furious. Leeds erupted in print asserting that he had not requested anyone to calculate the sad day of his parting. Saunders was not his friend. In fact, he had never met Richard Saunders.

Next year, poor Leeds remained an easy target again. The fictional Saunders again appeared, concerned about his dear friend, but now unsure if Titan Leeds had died or not.

There is, however, (and I cannot speak it without sorrow), there is the strongest probability that my dear friend is no more; for there appears in his name, as I am assured, an Almanack for the year 1734, in which I am treated in a very gross and unhandsome manner; in which I am called *a false predicter, an ignorant, a conceited scribbler, a fool, and a liar.* Mr. Leeds was too well bred to use any man so indecently and so scurrilously, and moreover, his esteem and affection for me was extraordinary: so that it is to be feared that pamphlet may be only a contrivance of somebody or other, who hopes perhaps to sell two or three year's Almanacks still, by the sole force and virtue of Mr. Leeds's name.

The Leeds/Saunders controversy delighted colonial readers. The brouhaha launched *Poor Richard* as an annual bestseller. In 1735, Saunders reappeared with more bad news.

Having received much abuse from Titan Leeds deceased (Titan Leeds when living would not have used me so!) I say, having received much abuse from the ghost of Titan Leeds, who pretends to be still living, and to write almanacks in spight of me and my predictions, I cannot help saying, that tho' I take it patiently, I take it very unkindly. And whatever he may pretend, 'tis undoubtedly true that he is really defunct and dead.

The presses of Titan Leeds thumped out angry replies. The pious leaden-footed dean of colonial almanac-makers explained that he was not dead at all. And the sharp suspicion that there had never even existed a Richard Saunders occurred to old Leeds, who was neither the first nor last to face this confusion between the real and imaginary when dealing with Benjamin Franklin.

＊

When Franklin tried to gain recognition at the Royal Society, he did not present himself as an almanac-writer. In France, by the winding vagaries of translation, cultural gaps, and bizarre stereotypes at Versailles about America, Franklin sometimes was confused with Poor Richard to great advantage. But in England, neither Franklin nor Peter Collinson introduced him as the free-swinging author of *Poor Richard*. He was presented as businessman, printer, and man of public affairs. Almanac-writer would have been trashier. "Almanacks, how soon cast aside," sighed one lady poet.

＊

When Franklin tried to enter the field of electrical science, he resorted to the strategy that enabled him to break into the almanac field. He tried to do a "Titan Leeds" on William Watson, the Society's leading electrical experimenter. Franklin's original letters to the Royal Society have been lost. The Bowdoin manuscript at the Library of the American Academy of Arts and Sciences in Boston is the earliest draft we have of Franklin's electrical writings. Corrected in his own hand, it gives some idea of what he sent the Royal Society. When James Bowdoin of Boston received the gift manuscript from Franklin in December, 1751, he wrote back, "I take notice that in the printed copies of your letter several things are wanting which are in the manuscript you sent me, particularly what relates to Mr. Watson." What survived as history, edited by Franklin for the printed booklet, was a version with Watson's name—and Franklin's corrections to Watson's mistakes—in significant passages weeded out.

When he began to send letters via Collinson to the Royal Society in 1747, Franklin perhaps hoped that Watson would rush furiously into a debate, just as the hapless Leeds had done. A great public controversy would have ensued. It was a sly gambit, not unlike tempting the fox to punch the lowly tar baby, every assault by the celebrity playing into the newcomer's hands and giving him greater publicity. Franklin was the better writer, as a prose stylist he was light on his feet, and razor-sharp in conceptual matters. But it didn't work that way. Watson was a much shrewder man than Leeds. To gain a foothold at the Royal Society, Franklin was going to have to go through Watson, not around him, not riding piggyback on Watson's shoulders in mockery, not hand in hand in mutual respect, but through, and Franklin's first strategy at breaking through failed completely.

It was all a polite-society transaction, but the truth was: The newcomer would be cudgeled. Watson would cut Franklin off at the knees.

The Party Begins

Philosophy is the darling Science of every Man of Sense, and is a peculiar Grace in the Fair Sex.

                              ❧ BENJAMIN MARTIN

NO ONE KNOWS EXACTLY WHEN BENJAMIN FRANKLIN FIRST got his hands on an electrical tube. Perhaps the year was 1743. It's a date he mentions in his *Autobiography* in recalling electrical experiments at a lecture he attended on a trip home to Boston. He remembered the lecturer as "Dr Spencer, who was lately arrived from Scotland."

"Not very expert," said Franklin describing Spencer.

Historians, however, have found that Franklin likely didn't start experimenting until perhaps late in 1745 when Peter Collinson sent him a glass electrical friction tube and "some account of the use of it." This "account" came not from the world of the scientific *virtuosi* but the world of the Grub Street printers.

✳

The April issue of *Gentleman's Magazine* first came into Franklin's hands near the end of 1745. That issue would have been hawked by boys in the London streets during the first days of May. Sent on by Collinson, it arrived in the colonies six months later. This London review cast a wide editorial net, publishing contributions concerning politics, fashion, commerce, gossip, trivia, poetry, and science. The fateful science article was entitled: *An historical account of the wonderful discoveries, made in Germany, & c concerning Electricity.*

Although the author was not listed, the article had been written by Albrecht von Haller, a Swiss physician and professor of physiology at the prestigious university in Göttingen, Germany. Haller had written his piece in French for publication in a tiny Dutch journal, and the article—in a very poor translation—had found its way into the commercial gristmill of a London printshop. Haller's account offered a bit of history, some science, and, not surprisingly—since *Gentleman's Magazine* aimed at the polite and the would-be polite everywhere—a fashion statement.

Writing about highly theatrical experiments dreamed up by German professors, Haller related that they had discovered "phenomena, so surprising as to awaken the indolent curiosity of the public, the ladies and people of quality, who never regard natural philosophy but when it works miracles." The professor conveyed his contempt. But then as a bit of an eighteenth-century cultural paparazzo himself, Haller proceeded to list the celebrities involved, the Duke and Duchess of Gotha, the royal princess of Prussia, and the Count of Manteufel. "Even Poland itself," concluded the Swiss physiologist emphasizing the excitement, "which is not accounted very polite, was not insensible to these wonders of nature."

Electrical science arrived as the most stunning party ever thrown by scientists. Experiments followed in parlors, mansion halls, ballrooms, and soon after inns, coffeehouses, and taverns. The news had raced ahead of academy publications, borne swiftly by word of mouth, by personal correspondence. The Duchess of Bedford, for instance, wrote to her husband, the Duke, "I supped at the Duchess of Montagu's on Tuesday night, where was Mr. Baker of the RS [Royal Society], who electrified: it really is the most extraordinary thing one can imagine." Two-penny newspapers sold in the streets dashed past the slowly produced scientific journals with the latest electrical news. In England, experimenters hoping to stake an intellectual claim on this frontier published booklets privately at their own expense rather than wait a year for the *Philosophical Transactions* to mark their claim to celebrity.

"The electric shock itself," marveled Joseph Priestley many years later, "if it be conceived attentively, will appear almost as surprising as any discovery that [Sir Isaac Newton] ever made." As the electri-

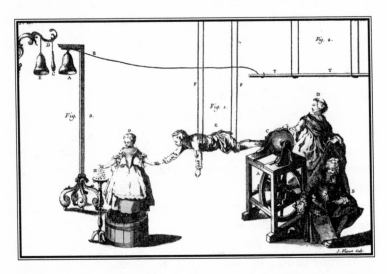

This illustration appears in the 1748 French edition of Experiments and Observations *by William Watson. The man turns the wheel while the woman presses her hand against the glass, creating the charge. The boy suspended by silk cords (nonconductors) receives the charge from his foot, passing it to the girl who stands on a nonconductor. Her electrified hand causes chaff to flutter in the air. Another setup waits behind, a gun barrel (T) to be electrified which by charging the bell (A), alternately attracts and repulses the clapper (C) setting up a merry clatter.*

cal friction machine with its pulleys hummed and squeaked and slapped, the beauties who the year before had touched fingertips with a partner in French dance now hurried to the darkened rooms of philosophy, daring to encounter what the ecstatic French termed *l'expérience du choc électrique*. Belles and beaus joined hands in chains or circles; they conveyed the electric force with their own bodies.

"Could one believe," enthused Haller, "that a lady's finger, that her whale-bone petticoat, should send forth flashes of true lightning, and that such charming lips could set a house on fire?" The German professors had first popularized these delights. Relatively obscure experiments in England during the 1730s had established human flesh as a wonderful conductor. But the Germans abandoned the young boys first used as electrical conductors in these experiments, instead dangling young women from silk ropes, snatching "electric fire" from their bodies. G. M. Bose, professor at the University of Wittenberg, who was known for his "fiery intellect," devised what he called "Venus Electrificata." A related game appeared, the "Electric Kiss," which spread and titillated polite society across the Western world. The language of love became the language of electricity, as the dramatist Richard Sheridan reveals when his character Mr. Faulkner speaks: "If there be but one vicious mind in the set, 'twill spread like a contagion—the action of their pulse beats to the lascivious movement of the jig—their quivering, warm-breathed sighs impregnate the very air—the atmosphere becomes electrical to love, and each amorous spark darts through every link of the chain!"

In 1746, the Man of Pleasure and the Man of Science were one.

The kissing games went on. If you made up and administered the game, you could change the rules. The Electric Kiss offered interesting possibilities.

Electricity defended the maiden. She was suffused with electric fire. Would a man dare kiss one of the charged, tantalizing virgins? What he received was a savage blow before he could taste the honey.

Electricity was chaperone, ward, boundary.

But what if all the electricity accidentally drained off—or not so

G. F. *fc.*

An electrical session illustrated in a book published in Venice in 1746. At the left a man cranks his electrical generator to electrify the young woman suspended by silk ropes on a swing. Some ink problems at the printshop have obscured the teaspoon of brandy in her left hand. The man on the right is setting the brandy afire with a spark from his fingertip. (BAKKEN LIBRARY AND MUSEUM) accidentally drained away, just before your lips touched the maiden? Or what if the boasted shock was just before the kissing reduced to a mere nuzzling commotion? There were sly variations of the kiss available. One device was to bunch up your lips, urging the maiden ahead of time to do the same and then to consummate the rosebud kiss so familiar to the eighteenth century. There are very few nerve ends in that part of the mouth, whereas the contemporary lips-back-sucking kiss of our era would be, with electricity added to the inner-mouth nerve ends, extremely painful.

In the severe moral climate of the New World, these demonstrations were popular. Laughter in the semidark must have seemed sweet music. Despite our current sense of the great contribution Pennsylvania Quakers made to a certain broad mid-American liberality, the walls between the sexes in 1746 rose higher in Philadelphia than we imagine. When the subject was exchanges between men and women, Philadelphians came down harder than their Puritan cousins on the slightest hint of sexual feeling. Some Quakers practiced celibacy *within* marriage. Many couples exercised sexual restraint, producing only two or three children, quite the contrast, for instance, to the Massachusetts family of Franklin's origin with fourteen children. On First Day, when Quakers marched into meeting house, they entered separate doors for men and women and sat in segregation. During the same period, theater was forbidden. To recite lines in a playhouse was a punishable crime.

Yet Franklin's highly theatrical electrical demonstrations went on under the banner of science education. In Franklin's great room, as he fumbled with wire and glass, a young man had the chance to hold the hand of a celebrated beauty, in the interests of science, of course, and even stare into her eyes as the two of them simultaneously convulsed from a deep hidden force and then afterward talked about how it felt.

✸

What else did Haller's article offer besides talk-of-the-town reporting? History, of course. His title said so. But there was not enough historical incident that Franklin might stumble over it in getting to the frontlines of current experimental work. Haller briefly mentioned amber, the mystery fossil, jewel, and decoration of the ancient world, the "stone" of legend, thought to be found only on certain shores of the Baltic Sea. When rubbed, amber becomes electrically charged, able to attract small bits of straw, wood, or metal shavings. In the sixth century B.C., the Greek philosopher Thales, according to hearsay, suggested that amber invisibly exerted force across distance because it was possessed of a soul. Two centuries later, Plato pointed out that magnets and amber both had "wonderful attracting power."

Yet despite some speculations by the Greek philosophers, two thousand years passed before electrical science saw new developments. In 1600, William Gilbert, the physician appointed to Queen Elizabeth, published *De Magnete,* a classic investigation that, in the process of examining magnetism, explored the parallel phenomenon of electricity. Gilbert probed into electricity by resorting to a newfangled method—the experiment. He found that many other objects besides amber could be electrified by rubbing, including diamonds, glass, sulphur, and crystal, and that electricity—unlike magnetism, which only affected certain metals—could exert its force upon nearly "everything subject to our senses, or that which is solid." The royal physician termed the wide-ranging force *electrica,* inspired by the Greek word for amber, *elektron.*

Although Haller's article ignored Gilbert, he did credit the next pioneer, Otto von Guericke, the inventor of the first electrical friction machine. In 1660, the German blacksmith had rubbed a sulphur ball on a frame, using the pressure of his palm to create electrostatics. More than forty years passed, however, before Francis Hauksbee, Sir Isaac Newton's right-hand man at the Royal Society, substituted glass globes and tubes in place of sulphur. The next to appear in Haller's history is Stephen Gray, a disabled tradesman and pensioner in London at the Charter House, a charity institution. Most of Gray's story is lost in the mists of history. "He was the first," writes Haller, "who ventured to electrise men in suspending them on silken cords, and holding near their feet a tube of electrified glass." The vinegary old fellow had dangled charity boys from silk ribbons tied to the roof beams of Charter House, in a curious precursor to the intersection between the eighteenth-century playroom and frontline science that would lead to our electronic future. It was Gray who discovered that the human body had wonderful conducting qualities. Along with investigating conductors, Gray did landmark work studying insulators. He took packing thread, a conductor, and suspended it by silk lines, insulators, thus preventing the electricity from draining away. In effect, Gray channeled electricity with something near the conducting-wire technology we use today.

The last name in Haller's history was Charles Du Fay. In the 1730s the French engineer Du Fay had refined Gray's work, in the process hypothesizing that there were two electricities, one *vitreous* and the other *resinous;* an object charged with *vitreous* electricity repelled all other bodies charged the same, but attracted those charged with *resinous* electricity. Du Fay's assistant, Jean Antoine Nollet, would embrace this theory. It would lead him to a clash with Franklin that would last for decades.

Haller had brought his history of electrical science up to the 1740s. As the Age of Reason was approaching midlife, the *virtuosi* had no idea—for all the socializing hoopla and for all the wild speculations coming out of Germany—how important electricity would become. As one author a few years later wrote a friend at the Royal Society, "I own I thought at first it would have ended in a mere museum."

If you had asked these scientists about true physics before the 1740s, they would have discussed mechanical physics, mathematics, clock-making, and star gazing. Electricity? Something random, miscellaneous, troubled with bizarre and stray investigators such as Gray, a field of inquiry whose insights were separated by gulfs of time on the order of half centuries and even millennia.

This was all in the process of changing.

Haller mentioned several German experiments and offered a picture of gentlemen and ladies standing on cakes of wax used as insulators and other hints. This was enough so that his account may have served as instructions for Franklin, who repeated the experiment.

One of the advantages—for Franklin's purposes—of Haller's article was not what it explained, but what it did not.

An historical account was a boldly liberating work, much bolder than if Haller had fully set forth a program of elaborately linked hypotheses. It is remarkably stripped down in terms of theory. The professor snorted contemptuously at the vortexes of René Descartes, the widely admired cosmic model in fashionable use on the Continent for explaining all natural phenomena. Haller sniffed too at the mystics who were already conjecturing that electricity might be the *Anima mundi* of the ancients, the life force of every living thing. His sarcasm was undisguised: "Are there animal spirits in an iron rod, or a dead carcass?" he asked witheringly. Haller cleared the deck.

As one experimenter in the eighteenth-century comic novel *Tristram Shandy* liked to warn, "Error, Sir, creeps in through small crevices." But error crept in through Big Theories too, especially ones on the order of the Cartesian vortexes. When the Big Theories did not quite fit, the Big Theories begat Sub-Theories. And these theories, subtheories, and elaborate de facto mechanisms were written about in an experimental language comprising unequal parts Greek and Latin and eighteenth-century technospeak and Cartesian jargon—efflatus and afflatus and fluxion.

At the start, Franklin did not have to read through these learned booklets and then push them to the rear of the table. He simply experimented. At the end of his article, even Haller had let himself be carried away, enthusing that electric fire was "as surprising as a miracle."

Franklin would share the exhilaration.

"For my own part," Benjamin wrote Collinson afterward in

March, 1747, "I was never before engaged in any study that so totally engrossed my attention and my time as this has lately done; for what with making experiments when I can be alone, and repeating them to my friends and acquaintance, who, from the novelty of the thing, come continually in crowds to see them, I have, during some months past, had little leisure for anything else."

The Equipment

I think it a great pity that the word Electricity should ever have been given to so wonderful a Phenomenon, which might properly be considered as the first principle in nature.

⋙ JOHN FREKE, 1746

A BIT AFTER MID-DECADE IN THE 1740S, WHEN BENJAMIN Franklin began his experimenting, there were two pieces of equipment used by electrical scientists. One, the electrical friction machine, was often quite expensive and, for all its many developments and improvements, remained easily understood. The other, the Leyden jar, required nothing more than a glass jar lifted from the kitchen, but posed a profound puzzle.

We need to look at both of these apparatus.

＊

Although eighteenth-century electrical machines ranked among the splendors of their age, you don't see many surviving today. A mere handful of museums exhibit them, often in the corner of a remote hallway. Some of these machines, collections of wheels, chains, and wood elegantly crafted by furniture makers, may at first seem akin to Rube Goldberg devices. But, essentially, the machine is as simple as a hammer and nail.

The electrical machine creates static electricity. If you rub a piece of glass, the friction from your hand creates static electricity. The machine does the same. To surpass what the hand alone rubbing glass could achieve, these scientists attached wheel and pulley movements to whirl the glass tube furiously. As the Bishop of Norwich remarked of this wildly spinning experimental world, there was little difference between a turnspit and a philosopher.

Look at an eighteenth-century print, however, showing an "electricising" in a philosophical household and it isn't hard to distinguish the master, the philosopher, from the turnspit servant: The servant turned the crank. It was labor and a bit more art than science, requiring manual adroitness and endurance. An illustration from the era shows one of the huge machines, complete with servant turning a wheel half a head higher than the man: He would have made a vigorous rowing movement, his right foot extended, his left back, rocking back and forth, his head cocked aside so the humidity of his breath would not dissipate the charge building on the glass.

It was tricky, but the problems faced were simple. They could be remedied by better execution or by rubbing the glass with a leather cushion spring-mounted in place of the human hand, or by—as some of the wealthy thought—an additional glass globe or two with more whirling wheels and more servants madly cranking.

✳

The Leyden jar was different. In April of 1745, a cleric who dabbled in electricity first encountered the wonder. The man, Ewald Georg von Kleist of Cammin, likely stumbled upon the landmark discovery by clumsy accident. But Kleist knew his find was important. To protect his claim of priority, he sent letters announcing the news not to one but five eminent German scientists. The cleric wrote so obscurely that none of them could duplicate the effects he described. Poor Kleist would protest afterward to no avail that due credit and honor had passed him by.

Six months later, the independent discovery of the phenomenon at Leyden gave birth to the Leyden jar, the rage of Germany, France, and England. When the news was announced in London in February, 1746, via a letter dispatched with the Belgian experimenter Abraham Trembley who crossed the channel to the Royal Society, it changed a whole field of investigation.

On January 20, 1746, a popular professor at Leyden University, Petrus Musschenbroek, the internationally famous director of the Leyden Theatrum Physicum, had announced the discovery. He wrote to his contact in Paris, the celebrated Cartesian René Réamur at the Académie Royale des Sciences:

> As I see that this sheet. . . is not completely filled, I would like to tell you about a new but terrible experiment, which I advise you never to try yourself, nor would I, who have experienced it and survived by the grace of God, do it again for all the Kingdom of France. I was engaged in displaying the powers of electricity. An iron tube AB was suspended from blue-silk lines; a globe, rapidly spun and rubbed, was located near A, and communicated its electrical power to AB. From a point near the other end B a brass wire hung; in my right hand I held the globe D, partly filled with water, into which the wire dipped; with my left hand E I tried to draw the snapping sparks that jump from the iron tube to the finger; thereupon my right hand F was struck with such force that my whole body quivered just like someone hit by lightning. Generally the blow does not break the glass, no matter how thin it is, nor does it knock the hand away [from the phial]; but the arm and the entire body are affected so terribly I can't describe it. I thought I was done for. But here are some peculiarities. When

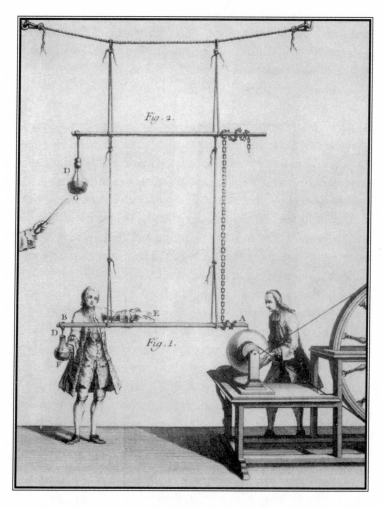

The Leyden jar experiment shown in the annual of the Académie Royale des Sciences at Paris, 1746.

the globe D is made of English glass, there is no effect, or almost none; German glass must be used. Dutch doesn't work either; D does not have to be a globe, a drinking glass will do. . . . I've found out so much about electricity that I've reached the point where I understand nothing and can explain nothing. Well, I've filled this sheet up pretty well.

Today, if you try to find examples of the device that nearly "did in" Musschenbroek, you discover that authentic eighteenth-century Leyden jars are hard to come by. A few survive on display in science museums. The small, wide-necked jar became the preference of the British electricians. The French device of choice was a narrow-necked jar, its cork on top sealed with a wax that over the centuries ages to a smoky, deep red. The French model displayed another curiosity: gold leaf lining the inside of the jar, a sure guarantee that those jars would be lost in the social upheavals to come.

What there is to explain about the Leyden jar, even in our high-tech day, remains simple.

Glass is a good insulator. If you apply a charge to the inside of the glass jar, another charge immediately appears on the outside of the jar. Miraculous, it seems. Benjamin Franklin later identified the charges on opposite sides of the glass as "positive" and "negative." If you put one hand to a wire connected to the inside jar and with your other hand touch the outside, you complete the circuit—and take the celebrated violent snap.

One physicist today compares the discovery of the Leyden jar to the advancement in technology from the firecracker to TNT, calling the Leyden jar "the electrical equivalent of the hand grenade."

As scientists raced for bigger Leyden jar effects, they soon discovered that the thinner the glass, the greater the charge. But these experimenters faced a trade-off—even a good insulator has insulation limits. If you put a strong enough charge on the glass, it will pierce the jar and explode. Inevitably, many experimenters pushed the Leyden jar to its limits, shattering their apparatus. Another rea-

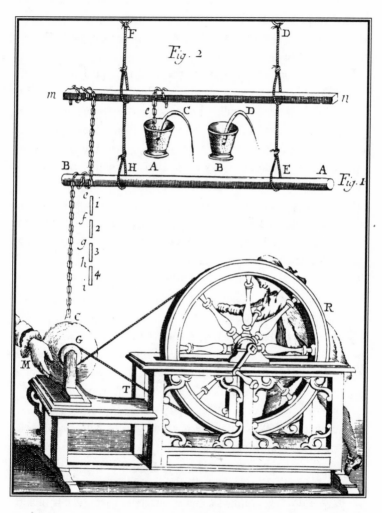

An eighteenth-century electrical friction machine. At M on the left, a hand—perhaps enlarged to emphasize the manual skill involved—presses the revolving glass. The electricity travels up the chain along conducting rods and then charges two Leyden jars, which look to our eyes more like buckets.

son so few authentic Leyden jars survive today is that when the craze for experiments died away, ordinary people put this very ordinary object back on the shelf in the kitchen, minus any precious metal. But more likely, most of them broke.

It is worthwhile to look again at the famous report from Leyden.

At one level the letter is a workman-like professional account, the antithesis of Kleist's murky job. Professor Musschenbroek gives clear directions. But look again—throughout and beneath the functional surface is an under-music. Meanings appear, meanings of the type you find in poems, issues raised with no intention to resolve them in an experiment. Musschenbroek raises curious topics, he alludes to boundaries, some national boundaries, some perhaps not; he mentions survival, survival by divine grace, death by lightning— none of these are denotative in the letter, but in the seven years that follow they will become devastatingly real in the events that connect Benjamin Franklin and a dead scientist in St. Petersburg.

Another issue Musschenbroek raises will become crucial to scientists racing to stake claims of priority; it is ambition—the implication that this experiment might win a kingdom. The kingdom of technological power we have derived from these discoveries? Of course not, rather the kingdom of France, the epitome of cultural empire, the vast stretch of its colonial power across oceans.

This is not a simple scientific instruction.

Paradoxes also abound. One paradox is this: Musschenbroek's letter comes as a warning, but a warning that no one heeds. Another paradox: The author announces one of the grand discoveries of the century while remarking that he's adding these lines merely to fill up the page, a posture assumed again when the report ends. Is he kidding? Is this high science or high comedy? These questions will acquire a disturbing edge in events to come. It is hard to tell in this field of investigation where science involved playing pranks on parlor guests, setting brandy on fire, and pinching women.

Another curiosity of Musschenbroek's report was noted by scientists poring over it in those early weeks. There was no boasting, and despite the odd peccadillo near the end of the letter that English glass had "no effect, or almost none" and that German glass did work, little nationalistic huffing and puffing. The elder statesman of the electrical craze wasn't sharking for reputation. No Dutch hand extended for the drop of a patronage plum. Musschenbroek carefully avoided any wording that staked a claim of ownership.

As the news raced across Europe, attendant rumors buzzed just as quickly that the discovery didn't originate with a celebrated genius, but a clumsy lab assistant. According to some tales, Andreas Cunaeus, a wealthy amateur scientist, a hanger-on at Musschenbroek's lab, made the accidental discovery. None of them knew at the time that earlier the inept minister Kleist of Cammin had stumbled on the same device.

In our era, the term *Leyden jar* has been replaced, first by *condenser,* a term perhaps originally used by Alessandro Volta of Pavia, who suggested a generation later an analogy with chemistry, where the process of condensation in sealed glass jars stores greater amounts of substances by condensing them to liquid form. In the nineteenth century, Michael Faraday introduced the term *dielectric* to describe the configuration of the glass separating the charges, and in the twentieth century electrical specialists introduced the word *capacitor* as a replacement for *condenser.*

The truly complex triumphs achieved with the capacitor in the twentieth century remain engineering ones. Technologists have refined the capacitor, miniaturized the device to micro-size, and installed it in virtually every electronic installation imaginable.

But, if you look at it, it's still just the Leyden jar. The device now uses current electricity rather than static electricity. It's no longer the size of a kitchen jar. But beyond that, its old riddles remain unsolved.

How does electricity in one place create electricity in another?

How does this mysterious force operate at a distance?

Today, the questions still don't have good answers. One contemporary physicist has stated that because engineers have been so successful in manipulating and controlling capacitors, we simply don't have to bother with understanding them.

The static electricity that first prompted these questions, however, remains close at hand today.

✳

To operate a computer is to be near two electricities. Your fingers move above an electronic command center hidden under alphabet and symbol keys. But move the back of your hand near the screen—or any video monitor for that matter—and all the hairs spring erect: You have deserted the realm of *current* electricity, the domesticated electrical force we channel beneath the keyboard, and you suddenly encounter *static* electricity, a wild force, what Michael Faraday in his century called *common electricity,* that power which in winter causes sparks when you rub a cat's fur. It is identical with lightning.

A bolt of lightning is, in essence, an enormous static electrical spark. The cat and the cloud, to different degrees, create the same force. It was this common identity that Franklin illustrated when he wrote of his electric kite.

The race to explain static electricity was open to all comers in the exhilarating 1740s. It was physics for ordinary people. No mathematics required. No special language understood only by experts, no Latin and Greek, no polysyllables. And the puzzles could be understood by most people as well. The space between a charged conductor and the attracted scraps of paper or tiny bits of metal foil used in experiments in the era—How does the force operate across this space?

One answer proposed early on was simple. The force moves through atmospheric molecules. The simple answer was wrong. Perhaps this obvious theory arose in part from an inclination to shrug off more unsettling mysteries. The great Sir Isaac Newton himself had long before offered this solution. But again and again, in the 1740s, in Faraday's time, and later when the quantum physi-

cists have returned to these basic questions, scientists have speculated on this central puzzle.

In our own era, armed with an On/Off button, we trivialize and
demystify this power. But to go back to the still virgin shores of
electricity, to squeeze elbow to elbow in the semidarkness of elegant
parlors next to kings, beauties, and *virtuosi,* and next to men like
Abbé Nollet, William Watson, and Benjamin Franklin, we can
share a sense of what was then a startling wonder.

IV

The Genius
of Nations

For several Years past, Electricity has been my chief Preoccupation.

❧ ABBÉ NOLLET

IN 1746, THE ABBÉ NOLLET WAS A POWER IN FRENCH SCIENCE, a member of the Académie Royale des Sciences at Paris, a favorite in the white-marble splendor at Versailles, the intimate tutor to the royal family in experimental physics. In five years, he would become Franklin's fiercest rival.

A contemporary portrait depicts a man in his forties with broad, sturdy chin and solid cheeks, but small eyes that cant ever slightly left to right, resembling the attention-focusing of a hawk about to swoop. Like Franklin, Nollet rose far above the social station of his birth. Born into a humble farm family at Pimprez, a village sixty miles north of Paris, Nollet had been rescued from the drudgery of a root-farm existence by a local curé who was impressed with the boy's intellectual ability. Nollet was sent to the provincial college at Clermont and later to divinity studies in Paris. The education finally stopped one ceremony short of the priesthood. The young student Nollet soon turned his back on the church, much like the youthful Franklin.

In fact, Franklin and Nollet were alike in many ways. They were tireless experimenters, they were doers, they brought manual skills to silk-coat entertainments, they were shrewd businessmen. But there were differences, too. Nollet had a zest for intellectual debate; Franklin had no taste for confrontation, though immense talent for self-defense secretly performed. Nollet was a spellbinding performer before large audiences; Franklin was a halting, ineffective public speaker.

Their big difference was theory.

The Abbé had established a two-fluid theory of electricity. Franklin argued there was only one. In the heat of his later anti-Franklin campaigns, even as some accused him of spite and jealousy upon the appearance of a newcomer, Nollet always insisted that theory was the crux of the issue.

Today, the Abbé's theory is a bit hard to approach, its antiquated Cartesian terms forbidding. He accepted the two-fluid approach of his mentor, Charles Du Fay, the French aristocrat whose innovations grew out of Stephen Gray's little-noticed efforts. Du Fay had hypothesized the existence of two electricities, *resinous electricity,* so named because it was produced by resin, and *vitreous electricity,* so named because it was produced from glass. The Abbé proposed an *affluent electricity* and an *effluent electricity:* Here was a theory that described electricity as a motion—that when a substance is electrically excited the force flows into it in an affluent stream. When charged bodies repel, the electricity is effluent, the current is flowing out. Along with his theory of movement came a hypothesis of "pores" in all materials. There were two kinds of pores, effluent pores and affluent pores. His theory included cone shapes or vortices, a favorite of Cartesians everywhere, to describe the effluent leaving an electrified body.

His was complicated intellectual baggage that involved the creation of after-the-fact mechanisms to explain electrical effects, but it was appealing to decades of eighteenth-century scientists. Franklin's theory had the advantage of elegance and simplicity. Yet his account had one weakness: He theorized that opposite charges attract and like charges repel, but how could a negative, a lack, repel another lack? The affluent/effluent business presented no such problem. The Abbé's theory explained the Leyden jar in terms of fluids moving through mechanisms. Franklin's theory simply accepted without explaining that electricity acted at a distance.

Central to the debate to follow was the question, could electricity transmit through glass? Franklin said no, willing to let the mystery of electricity appearing on the other side of the Leyden jar's glass remain a wonder. The Abbé's theory eliminated the magic from the explanation. He supplied a mechanism: There were little pores in the glass moving the charge.

The Abbé was an estimable theorist. As early as 1745 he had stated that electricity was a universal force and that the two electricities, for all their back and forth movements, established a balance, a sort of conservation of energy, a prior claim lost sight of by summary histories today that blithely credit Franklin for a wide assembly of discoveries, among them conservation of energy.

Indeed, to this day, both general and specialist histories of science often depict the Abbé as a sort of noodle. But he needs to be seen in context—he had risen up from the bottom in the political environment of the royal court and thrived in a world of shrewd and ruthless competitors. He was applauded by many of the best scientific minds of his era. He was a formidable adversary.

FACING PAGE: *An Abbé Nollet electrical session in Paris, 1746. The electrified boy has been suspended on silk cords. At the right, a woman is about to discharge his nose with her finger. Beneath the boy's left hand, chaff flies, and beneath his right hand, physics papers rustle and are disturbed. Nollet is the man with the electrified glass tube. The Abbé included himself in book illustrations, establishing his visage as a trademark.*   (BAKKEN LIBRARY AND MUSEUM)

The decade spawned the most bizarre and public experiments in the history of science. And Nollet designed many of them. As the approving French king Louis XV beamed down from his grand chair, careful not to roll his head back and lose the curls and powder in his wig, the Abbé unleashed a charge from a Leyden jar through one hundred and eighty palace soldiers, causing them to leap in unison, convulsing instantly like trout snared on a hook. The king smiled at this exercise in discipline. This was sublime theater, so satisfying that seven weeks later Nollet assembled seven hundred Carthusian monks, pairs of the holy men holding each other's hands and each pair joined by iron wire between.

At the Leyden jar's command, the monks leapt for heaven.

✳

The jar also provoked reaction across the Channel in London. William Watson reigned over electrical science in the English-speaking world. Watson, an apothecary who kept a shop in Aldersgate Street, held a coveted membership in the Royal Society, had been elected to its board of directors, the Council, and had been honored in 1745 with the Copley Medal. In the spring, Watson would publish *Experiments and Observations*, a volume that would race through three printings and grace the table of every fashionable mansion west of Covent Garden.

And he was the man who would steal Benjamin Franklin's theory.

Watson is depicted in one surviving oil portrait: a middle-aged man with brown eyes, a large strong nose, a small mouth, and stubborn jaws. The small eyes gaze levelly, he must have been a measurer, a referee between warmly opposed factions who could deftly sidestep the fray. He presses his lips, the perfect picture of caution, competence, responsibility.

Like Benjamin Franklin, Watson was not born into money nor did he start out with connections. Both Franklin and Watson were in many ways self-made, thrown into the workworld in their teens, apprenticed in skills of the hand, mostly self-educated, both voracious readers, economists who rose early in the summer to avail themselves of reading without the expense of candles. Both men entered the scientific arena as masters of English written in a plain style.

Benjamin Franklin and William Watson were also what the time dubbed "associating men"—joiners, networkers. In the colonies, a very youthful Benjamin found his way into the parlors of gentlemen merchants who enjoyed his well-read conversation.

William Watson, the celebrated botanist and electrical scientist, later vice president of the Royal Society. He published sixty-one articles in its prestigious Philosophical Transactions. *This engraving is based on the oil portrait by L.F. Abbot which Watson donated to the Society.*

Botanizing gave Watson an early foothold at the Royal Society, where he made himself invaluable to men of rank and fortune, especially to members of the elite Whig circle of the first Earl Hardwicke and Lord Chancellor of England. Watson would spend weekends as a guest at their manors, advising them in the garden. He brought his experience and encyclopedic knowledge to the rare plants they had acquired at great cost and had shipped in along colonial trade routes. With his discerning eye, Watson looked for fakes and humbugs, noting quality and hardiness to survive, very much the curator as he tamped soil about the roots of some specimen brought in from the banks of the Ganges, as much a curator as some fine arts expert uncrating a Rembrandt in the manor gallery.

When electricity opened up as a field of study, Watson had already established himself as a man to be depended upon in botany. He was very well liked. He had become a member of President Martin Folkes's clique sometimes called the "Junto," that met behind the sacred veil at Rawthmell's, the famous coffeehouse near Covent Garden favored by aristocrats for its curtained seating. Watson had another entrée into these social settings above his own.

It was razor-sharp humor.

His essays reveal the humorist. He shared the quality with Franklin, though the humor of these two scientists flowed in different directions. There was a pointed edge to Watson's wit, always aimed in the other direction, *at* someone. And Watson's laughter always rang in chorus with his associates.

Franklin's humor was different. His wit could flash as suddenly as Watson's but often and very engagingly at himself. His humor could be public or private. And when it was private, Benjamin would walk away poker-faced, never revealing his target.

❋

On an August evening in the summer of 1746, the Duke of Cumberland, the second son of the man who became King George

II, visited the home of William Watson. Cumberland was the hero of the hour, greeted by crowds, their *Huzzah*s echoing in public squares. The Duke had just returned from his sensational victory at Culloden. He had led British forces in routing Bonnie Prince Charles and his troops, many of them Scottish highlanders, turning back what had threatened to become an invasion of London.

When the military man walked into Watson's house, he was twenty-five years old, pupils blue but his eyes reddish from the lifestyle, a pear-shaped man, his flesh already softening and spreading in curiously middle-aged morphing. Cumberland was known for his love of fast horses, available and voluptuous women, excess in food and drink, and a taste for watching bloody pugilistics from the first row. Less well known was his interest in science, first developed during the Duke's childhood when Sir Isaac Newton had cozied his way into evenings with the royal family.

The apothecary and the general, they made for the moment a strange pair. Watson, prim and responsible, the devoted healer. Cumberland, dramatic and excessive, just returned from dealing out wholesale death.

Yet the Duke wasn't out of place in Watson's scientific world. *Violent, theatrical, excessive, brutal, humorous, intellectual,* all the terms that describe the Duke also sum up the electrical science that bloomed in the 1740s.

✳

Watson stood ready with the Leyden jar. Like Nollet, he had moved into an experimental arena of increasingly powerful discharges. His assistants cranked the friction machine until it fully charged the jar. Then the Duke unsheathed his sword. According to a report from that summer, he wasn't carrying around any ordinary piece of ceremonial male jewelry. This was *the* sword from that famous day, and it was also said he had not cleaned the blood off. This was the sword that had been strapped to his side as he had set out on the morning of the slaughter at Culloden, as he wheeled his horse back and stood up in the stirrups and broke into the old Scottish tune in its mournful dialect and mocked his opponents:

Will ye play me fair, Highland Laddie, Highland Laddie?

※

The Duke reached. The sword wavered. The jar could store a vicious kick.

Surely Watson's throat went dry, as he tried to balance the need to display against the welfare of this royal personage.

Before the Duke drove his point home, before he could tap the Leyden jar the spark leaped, a flash, a *snap,* laughter and shouts, the vernacular of the electrical party reasserted itself. The Duke shrugged and grinned, as if in one tilt he'd tossed down a tankard of porter.

Watson sighed with immense relief.

More tricks would have followed, brandy set aflame, gunpowder fired, possibly a woman kissed, more Leyden jars, waiting like Madeira ready to be uncorked.

After his guests departed, Watson must have felt pleased. His prospects had never looked brighter.

I do not exaggerate when I introduce electrification as panacea.

⊱ C. G. KRATZENSTEIN

WHEN WILLIAM WATSON CLIMBED TO THE HEIGHTS IN London during the summer of 1746, he took his place among gentlemen nurturing health care projects.

The Age of Reason traded in healing dreams, in gums and spices and oils and wonderful roots and rare barks and essences of unspeakable origin brought at great expense from Arabia and the Orient and the New World, in promises of diseases banished and life lengthened and sexuality returned and the wound closed. The eighteenth-century colonial ships flooded London with new cures. Merchants filled warehouses, hoping to corner markets and make fortunes.

And now the *virtuosi* with their investments amused themselves at the Society with another "discovery"—electricity. Did the mysterious force have healing powers? The dull eyes of the sickroom looked with longing at the spark in the party room.

In 1745, a medical student at the University of Halle in Germany had published a booklet announcing that his professor, the eminent Dr. Johann Gottlob Krüger, professor of philosophy and medicine, "was the first, whom the idea struck that electrification might be useful in medicine." The young student, Christian Gottlieb Kratzenstein, published *Abhandlung von dem Nutzen der Electricitat.* He reported that the Germans had discovered that electricity applied to the human body speeded the pulse rate and increased perspiration. Kratzenstein claimed that by administering electricity he had cured a young woman whose little finger was contracted. But did he intend for readers to take him seriously?

In reports from the German professors, it is hard to separate high philosophy from low humor of the kind that might be found in an alehouse. "This idea," announces Krüger, "I am going to use in the cure of fat bellies. . . . As fat mostly consists of sulphurous particles the heavy belly will soon melt when these are expelled by electrification. Only I want to whisper something confidential in your ear. The electrification will be of much better effect if you reverse the theatrum and place the person to be electrified not by the globe but by the big wheel and let him turn it."

Regarding the young woman with the crooked little finger: Is not this a traditional image of a young woman wrapping beaus around her little finger, by her beauty commanding whatever she wants? Cure her of this, advised the med student. Shock her.

The idea that electricity might heal moved, however, faster than German university humor. It was fueled by hopes of electrotherapeutic deliverance, and in 1748 the enthusiasm was growing.

Old Krüger himself fueled the flames. The great professor suggested that a balm suffused throughout the body by means of electrification might prevent decay of the human figure. "What reward would be too great for the discoverer?" he asked.

Surely in the dim-lit parlors there was at least one fading beauty who looked at the gleaming friction tube and paid a new attention to the *snaps* at the thought that a Royal Society or Académie Royale des Sciences *virtuoso* might erase the spreading wrinkles and restore the bloom of the rose to her cheek.

＊

As reports of healing and successful medical treatments appeared across Europe, there arose two techniques. One was to transmit healing medicine into the human frame by gentle installments of electricity. The second involved using the violence of a large shock to restore or improve the patient. Both were attended with great claims of success and adherents spoke of them as panaceas.

Universal Cure, the phrase echoed in the newspapers, journals, and diaries of the era, a hope that stirred in people both high and low. It's a concept that today seems a bit foreign, puzzling to hear on the lips of otherwise shrewd observers. There existed the sense that illness might be caused by one essential physical, mental, or spiritual imbalance and might therefore be treated by one simple correction yet to be discovered.

During the same years when electrotherapy was debated, there appeared in English newspapers and magazines the case of the "touching woman" at Middlewich. Bridget Bostock was her name, a domestic servant who earned 35 shillings a year. "Her modus operandi," said one observer, "was touching the patient with 'touching spittle,' and [uttering] *God bless you with faith.*" One writer states she cured "ALL diseases." Another qualified the assertion by saying that there was one disease that she "would not meddle with," likely a sexual ailment that her modesty set off limits. Thousands had been cured by Bostock's spit, touch, and prayers, if you believed the tales, and she took no payment.

There was another long-standing folk-myth of healing that survived even in the Age of Reason, the certainty that the touch of the royal hand had healing powers. Samuel Johnson remembered being taken as a child into the presence of Queen Anne in hopes she would cure his case of scrofula, the disease then called "king's evil."

A *touch* would do it. Just one *touch*. What if the touch was the universal force of electricity?

*

The three tradesmen who were to make advances in electrical theory did not rush to embrace electric healing. Nollet, Watson, and Franklin were experimenters, plain men even when showing off in palaces; they were level-headed and practical. Each of them would contribute a refutation.

Nollet and Watson made newspaper headlines exposing bogus claims.

In 1748, reports had arrived in France from Dr. Gianfrancesco Pivati of Venice, claiming that he had transmitted odors and the powers of drugs via electrical fire. The issue reduced to: Can electricity transmit a smell into the human body? Today, this may seem a ludicrous question. But it was crucial to the argument at hand that an aromatic medicine dissolved into the water of a Leyden jar could transmit its effects via electricity into human flesh. Baffled in repeating the experiment, Nollet journeyed across the Alps to confront the Venetian, who shamefacedly admitted he was unable to repeat the experiment. Nollet vanquished the fraud, was given princely welcomes in Turin, Naples, and Florence and a special audience with Pope Benedict XIV—who had great scientific interests—and then returned triumphant to Paris.

In London, Watson exposed fake reports from Professor Johann Heinrich Winkler of Leipzig, the experimenter known in the German intellectual assemblies as "The Great Winkler." Winkler reported electrifying a man so "that not only his skin and his clothes, but his breath, saliva, and sweat, were impregnated with the smell of the substance included in the glass." Watson found the experiment didn't work and traded letters with a panicked Winkler who saw his international reputation beginning to crumble. After repeated efforts with a blue-chip assembly of Society experts that included one of Winkler's associates for fairness, the gentlemen sniffed nothing. "Must we conclude," offered a scathing Watson, "that our noses are not so good as those of the gentlemen at Leipzig?"

The debunkings in London continued on other fronts. From the Continent came news of the startling discovery that the head of a man would flame with a halo if you electrified him adequately. The correspondent was Professor Georg Matthias Bose of the University of Wittenberg, now bragging that he could create the magical radiance of angels and saints.

Watson, never the man to drag his feet, nominated himself to take the excessive electrical charge, electrifying himself until he reported feeling "a vast number of insects crawling on [my] body at the same time." Among victims of lightning stroke who survive, it is often reported that just before the bolt hits they feel as if many spiders or insects are crawling on their cheeks.

But Watson didn't get a halo.

For a number of months, Watson suffered public embarrassment as several British electrical showmen boasted that they had performed the demonstration. At last, upon prodding from Watson, Bose confessed that his experiment was a mere theatrical trick. He had used an old armor cap with many small sharp points studding it. When electrified, these all glowed in the dark to make the wearer "a canonized Saint."

In Philadelphia, Franklin went about more quietly debunking similar claims. He must have first read of the miracle cures in the newspapers or in the pages of *Gentleman's Magazine*. Peter Collinson tried to fan his interest. "Great numbers of ingenious men," wrote Collinson, "are very earnestly engaged in electrical experimentation applying them to various purposes. I have lately seen a letter from a doctor of physic at Turin, who gives three instances of the electrical power on human bodies by filling the electrical phial with a purgative potion and transferring it into a patient and it had all the effects as if taken into the stomach. The like account has been transmitted from another hand [Dr. Giovanni Batista Bianchi also at Turin]."

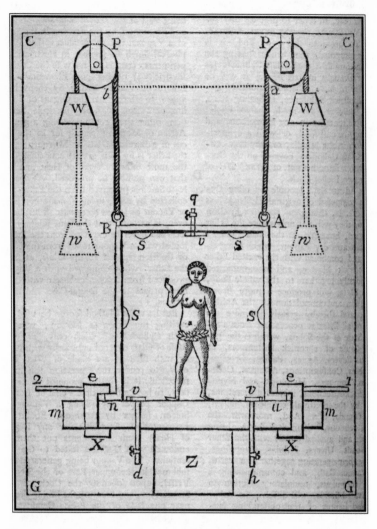

London Magazine *in July, 1747 published this odd proposal for electrical healing, the brainchild of one D. Stephenson. Stephenson called electricity "ethereal fire" and imagined that a nude bath in electricity inside an insulated tank suspended by silk cords would "be attended with extraordinary good effects in the cure of most diseases and topical ailments."*

Franklin's effort was direct and to the point. At home, he mixed into the water inside a Leyden jar an especially potent purgative, one of the most common medications in the eighteenth-century arsenal. He charged the jar and then electrified himself. If the "cure" had taken, he would have spent the next day within several steps of a chamber pot. But nothing happened. In his own humble way, Franklin reached the conclusion: Electrotherapy didn't work. He didn't broadcast this news.

Although Franklin had not published a word recommending electricity for medical use, the halt and lame began appearing at his door as early as 1748. His friend and mentor, old John Logan, the wealthiest man in the Pennsylvania colony, came to him hoping for a new lease on life after a stroke had partially disabled him. After suffering a stroke, Governor Jonathan Belcher of New Jersey also made a similar desperate appeal for healing.

Franklin administered the spark. More than three decades later in France, he would continue to crank up the Leyden jar to treat the paralyzed and the lame, a poker-faced physician willing to oblige, secretly convinced the treatments had no value.

In a 1757 letter to Sir John Pringle, Franklin explained that patients on first treatment might gain a little movement in their paralyzed limbs and that "these appearances gave great spirits to the patients, and made them hope a perfect cure; but I do not remember that I ever saw any amendment after the fifth day: which the patients perceiving and finding the shocks pretty severe, they became discouraged, went home and in a short time relapsed; so that I never knew any advantage from electricity in palsies that was permanent."

In the late 1740s, electrical science had moved beyond the *virtuosi* and into the streets, the lowest inns, and the fairs, as showmen in England and on the Continent brought electrical displays to the middle and underclasses. The spark was not exclusive to the expert. Now as an alternative to the physician or apothecary, you could visit some market Johnny set up under an oak tree at a fair, cranking furiously on a portable, roughly assembled friction machine, ready for a few guineas to *snap* you back to health. How humiliating for Watson that during the very weeks he failed at beatifying before lords in his laboratory, footmen and kitchen servants could amble two doors past the intersection of Crane Court on Fleet Street, and for a single shilling admission see the showman Benjy Rackstrow fire up halos. The medical claims circulating were even more appalling. The refutations made by the great electrical scientists were blithely ignored.

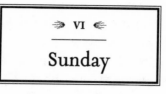

We rub our Tubes with Buck Skin

⇝ BENJAMIN FRANKLIN

I N THE WINTER OF 1746, HE WOULD HAVE WAITED ALL WEEK for this day.

Franklin stepped into the empty room. Throughout the week he would have found himself nearly drowning in the clattering of carts and wheelbarrows, the roar of crowds surging past on wooden heels, the shrieking of street sellers. At times his wife Debbie could not hear him even when they tried to hold a conversation nose to nose. They lived across the street from the Jersey Market in the very center of howling eighteenth-century commerce.

It was Sunday. Bright sun spilled in across the bronze of the pineboard floor. The cups and pots hung peacefully on the mantel. His experimental glassware and wires waited on the table. All around him was the vast silence of a New World Sabbath. Debbie and daughter Sally had already departed to Christ Church up the street. Benjamin was the colony's most well known nonattender. Once as an experiment, he had tried to see how many consecutive Sundays he could attend the Presbyterian church. It lasted five Sundays. Now he stayed home to pursue his studies.

As a mechanic, "leather-apron man," and tradesman, Benjamin Franklin had acquired some skills needed to delve deeply into the nature of electricity. In his Philadelphia, during the early years, he was known as a "Hand." This slang, part reduction of a man to the body part by which he earned a living, part compliment to his manual dexterity, was common enough in the labor-intensive colonies.

He put his hand to electricity.

Just as poets develop unique idioms, these eighteenth-century electrical scientists set about their experiments with distinctive styles. In London, William Watson typically sent his electrical charges through ten or twelve men of rank and fortune holding hands. At Versailles, Abbé Nollet caused long rows of soldiers or religious men to convulse, in the process perhaps commenting upon and satirizing a highly stratified society. In Philadelphia, Franklin made his first experiments using a cannon ball, a glass jar, a thread of silk, and a cork ball the size of a child's marble.

He suspended the cork ball in midair by a thread, its silk acting as an insulator. Next, he found a glass jar with a wide mouth. He nested the iron ball—it was about four inches in diameter—in the mouth of the jar. The glass would serve as his insulator.

He pushed the metal ball next to the cork one.

Now, the electric machine. It was a glass tube about twenty-seven inches long set on a metal axle. The Americans put together a device that resembled the grindstone of a tradesman. No European-style pulleys, no wheels. When Franklin turned it, the glass tube rubbed against buckskin and the friction produced static electricity—if the Sunday morning air was dry enough. Anything might do to channel electricity into his experiment—many demonstrators used a gun barrel—this conductor could be hung from insulating silks or rested on glass, and one end touched the metal rod on which the glass turned and from the other end snaked the wire of copper or iron or lead that would deliver the force to the iron ball.

He gave the electrical machine a few brisk turns.

Immediately, before his broad thumb and finger could release, the cork ball leapt and then hovered some five or six inches from the charged metal.

What caused the cork ball to leap? How did the force charging the iron ball operate invisibly across five inches of space and affect the cork? Was electricity, since it countered the effects of gravity on the cork, as elemental as gravity itself?

Franklin started looking for answers with the directness of a man looking for a house cat. Light, gravity, electricity, how were these elemental powers related? When he brought candlelight within a foot of the setup, the electricity vanished. The ball dropped. Did light have the power to dispel electricity? But when sunlight fell on his device, the cork persisted to float (later he realized that the subtle atmosphere of the burning wick moving through the air, even invisibly, was enough to steal away the electrostatics).

✷

Many of Franklin's experiments began as solitary studies, but he soon passed them on to others. "My house," he remembered in the *Autobiography*, "was continually full, for some time, with people who came to see these new wonders. To divide a little this encumbrance among my friends, I caused a number of similar tubes to be blown at our glass-house, with which they furnished themselves, so that we had at length several performers."

Early on, Franklin had made the discovery that he didn't have to depend on electrical friction machines produced by specialists in Europe. The magnificent machines were expensive—an analogy might be made to an elegant harpsichord crafted by one of the legendary craftsmen in London, a fixture required in any wealthy and fashionable residence, but not necessarily a guarantee the owner had the performance skills to live up to the equipment. Franklin was soon using "rough machines" he put together with his own skills as a doer and in the process using American materials. He also describes keeping "rough minutes" of the Philadelphia discoveries. If you can bang together machines that will do, you can bang together your own theory, too.

In May, 1747, Franklin wrote his first report on what he called "American electricity." It was an extraordinary letter, brisk, jaunty, joyous. It covered more than a year of Franklin's experiments, and proclaimed a place for America in the international linkage of experimenters. This was nothing like the queer and anecdotal input the European *virtuosi* might have expected from a provincial. In the first passages, Franklin introduced ideas "which we looked upon to be new." In the second half, with a casual style and possibly an accompanying wink, he passed along suggested improvements in both parlor tricks and practical method.

Franklin wrote of the "wonderful effect of points both in *drawing* off and *throwing* off the electrical fire." The newcomer theorized that a pointed object such as a needle, for instance, gave the spark and drew off electricity from a charged body at greater distance than did a blunt object. He reported a sharp-pointed dagger *snapping* at eight inches from the charge, whereas a blunt object needed to approach within one inch to produce similar effects. Several years afterward in France, Franklin's claim would be dismissed with the observation that for decades experimenters everywhere had as a matter of course used swords and needles to summon electrical fire. To claim a *doctrine of points* was to dignify as a hypothesis what amounted to nothing more than an operational description. But Franklin defended his insight. Experiments performed with Debbie's darning needle would lead to points on lightning rods— erected domestically on wood frame churches and municipal buildings and abroad on palaces and cathedrals.

"We suppose, as forsaid," offered Franklin in his account, "that electrical fire is a common element." The sweeping assertion could

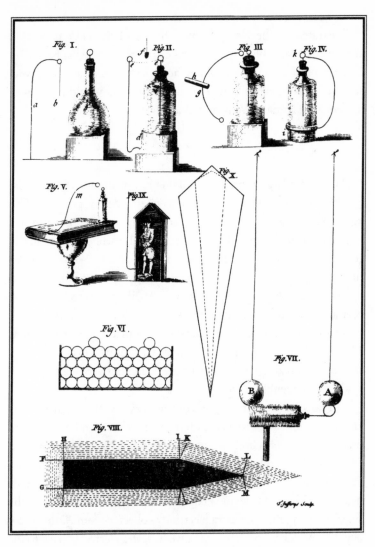

The page of illustrations in Franklin's Experiments and Observations. *A typical item is Fig. II, involving a cork (f) suspended on a silk thread between a wire from the inside of the Leyden jar and another from the outside. The ball is attracted to one wire, charged, then repulsed, attracted to the other wire, commencing to "play incessantly" until the jar is restored to equilibrium.*

be illustrated in the closet-format theater of the cork balls. Although the majority of his report dealt with cork balls, he introduced several experiments done on a large scale, and one was fleshed out with exposition. This demonstration would have great consequence abroad. We need to look at it.

✳

Picture the large room in Franklin's home attended by friends. Franklin described this experiment as one made on "persons." The experimental subjects were, in fact, an unemployed Baptist minister by the name of Ebenezer Kinnersley, a large hulking man whom the generous Franklin helped find work, first as electrical showman and later as instructor in the English-speaking academy Franklin and others established in 1749; Philip Syng, a silversmith revealed in a portrait as a tradesman with a tired face, but memorialized today in museums by the elegant artifacts he manufactured; an attorney, Thomas Hopkinson, a silk-coat man who sported expensive wigs and resided on an estate outside of town; and lastly, Benjamin. They made a very republican group.

In Franklin's experiment, one of them, *A*, say the attorney Hopkinson, stands on a wax cake. He rubs the electric tube, giving up the electricity in his body to the tube. Because he stands upon wax, which is a nonconductor, *A* is not replenished with electricity from the earth. A second person, *B*, say the Baptist Kinnersley, stands nearby on his own cake of wax. The glass tube is applied to *B*, the Baptist, giving him the extra electricity collected from *A*, the attorney. The person who is *B* cannot give his extra electricity back to the earth because he also is insulated on wax. Now Benjamin introduces *C*, say Franklin himself, a person "having only the middle quantity of electricity."

If *C* touches either *A* or *B*, there flashes a spark. *C* receives the spark from *B* who has excess electricity. And *C* gives the spark to *A* whose electricity has been lessened. If next the attorney should reach across the way to touch the Baptist, the shock is felt more strongly because the difference in their electricity is even greater. But once *A* and *B* have touched, the force is equalized. No more sparks. *C* can't fetch up a spark from either person now.

As Franklin notes, "All is reduced to the original equality."

Franklin reduces the sparkling party-displays to this principle: an abundance, or a lack (*wanting* is his eighteenth-century term). "We say," continues Franklin, "*B* . . . is electrised positively; *A*, negatively; or rather, *B* is electrised *plus*, *A*, *minus*. And we daily in our experiments electrise *plus* or *minus*, as we think proper."

During an era in which some Englishmen carried Newton's *Principia* in their pockets and gloried in calculus and Continentals worshiped Descartes and appealed to complicated diagrams of vortex-mechanisms to explain nature, here was simple science from a printshop, requiring only addition and subtraction. Science historian H. O. Sibum has pointed out that when Franklin hit upon his wonderful theory, he applied the debit-credit bookkeeping that he used at B. Franklin Printer to describe electricity. During the same months, in fact, that Franklin established his electrical theory, he was being advised by his mentor James Logan to escape the exhausting variety of duties in his daily business by bringing in a partner to shoulder the weight of miscellanea and details, confining himself then to keeping a sharp eye on the credits and debits in the accounts book.

It was science close to home.

*

To return to Franklin's *A* and *B* standing on wax cakes—when the two touch, they restore with a spark an imbalance in nature; they return the electric force to an equilibrium. There is never more—or less—electricity. It is a vision of electrostatics all around us as if we were submerged within an ocean of electrostatic energy. Within weeks, he would put his findings to brilliant use when he confronted the Leyden jar.

In this early experiment, Benjamin Franklin clearly announced four hypotheses. These include:

1. Electrical fire is a single fluid.
2. The force exists in two dissimilar states, one a lack and the other an overabundance, states defined as *plus* and *minus*.
3. There is conservation of energy.
4. Sparks and charges circulating occur to restore an imbalance of a universal force whose normal state is one of equilibrium.

There's a lovely moment in his report revealing the attitude behind his simplicity of method: "To electrise *plus* or *minus*," he notes, "no more needs be known than this; that the parts of the tube or sphere that are rubbed, do in the instant of the friction attract the electrical fire, and therefore take it from the rubbings." Here's a scientist who refuses to be lured into the page-long sentence of exegetical import, balanced on five subordinate conditional clauses in English and climaxed with a sixth in Latin or Greek (take your choice). Simple English will do the work. Some gentlemen thinkers of the time commonly announced that they were prepared to explain the *cause* of electricity (or gravity or fire). Take these pronouncements as a warning. They announce that a buffoon is about to take center stage.

There's another element in Franklin's report, too. In an age of rank and class distinctions, here was a tradesman informing the polite world that the force that had become the toy of the fashionable was a "common element" and his landmark demonstration ended with "all reduced to the original equality." There was a vein of republicanism in the rhetoric addressing the pursuit of kings.

In the sweep of those skylark days, he had no idea what waited for him in this developing science. He must have known, however, that attention from the Royal Society was merited. He did know where first to send his science.

It was London.

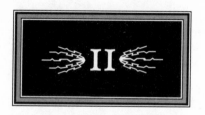

The Virtuoso

Among Gentlemen

Him wot prigs wot isn't hisn,
When he's cotched he goes to prison.

⇝ Epitaph scrawled on a wall
at Newgate prison, London,
eighteenth century

THE ROYAL SOCIETY OF LONDON AND THE ACADÉMIE
Royale des Sciences at Paris ranked foremost among the many
scientific associations that appeared in the Age of Reason. Char-
tered by Charles II in 1662, the Royal Society had a history glitter-
ing with the names of Hooke, Boyle, and Newton. Over the
decades, the Society had evolved into a forum for the scientific experiment performed, a place for *doing,* rather than scrutinizing ancient authority. From the start, the Society also championed English
as the language of science, asking for reports in the native tongue
"without any prefaces, apologies, or rhetorical flourishes."

This plain style suited perfectly the ordinary language that in the
1740s reported electrical science. It was in addition the very style reflected in the Society's physical setting, a startlingly plain London
house at the end of Crane Court with a relatively small, cramped

This, the historic Royal Society home at the end of Crane Court, no longer stands. On appointed days, the beacon above the door was lit signaling a meeting had been scheduled. In 1710 when the Society purchased the building, some members had been dismayed to leave the monumental dignity of Gresham College behind. The Society President, Sir Isaac Newton, argued that the new site "being in the middle of town, and out of noise, might be a proper place." (*Historical and Literary Curiosities* BY CHARLES SMITH AND HENRY BOHN, 1847)

meeting space. The members didn't meet in the palatial splendor of the academies at Paris and St. Petersburg.

Crane Court was a peaceful cul-de-sac that opened onto Fleet Street, the noisiest thoroughfare in London. The residential lane was so narrow that arriving Society members were forced to exit their carriages on Fleet Street and then walk to the clubhouse. Gentlemen accustomed to traveling behind velvet curtains had to descend, however briefly, into bustle, noise, and rudeness: Porters rocketing by on foot, the chairmen shouting clearance for their shilling-a-mile burden, chaise after chaise hurtling past, the streaming of foreign tourists just off the boat, the flooding of rural people displaced by mills, the air babbling with European tongues and mixing with the dialects of Devonshire, Derby, and Lancashire and the bawling of street vendors. The eighteenth-century physicist and master of the *bon mot*, G. C. Lichtenberg, reported that if you named the great capitals of Europe for the first words heard by visitors, London's name would be "Damn it."

When electrical science came of age, it was part of this London's story. The sheer intensity of the streets ranked with the biting energy that scientists explored in their demonstration rooms, the hurry and urgency and democracy of what we can now recognize as the first modern metropolis found its way into the science and its premiere academy.

W. H. Auden wrote of an unarmed revolution in the Age of Reason. It worked this way. "Anyone," explained Auden, "who can learn to acquire the habits and live according to the standards of a gentleman becomes one." The Royal Society offered splendid opportunities, although the opportunities were only granted to a select few. To a considerable extent, the Society was a very exclusive men's club. Perhaps two-thirds of the membership consisted of blue bloods. Most of the remaining third included high-level cabinet members, the decision-makers of the financial system, influential barristers whose legal briefs set precedent for centuries, and great numbers of well-paid physicians earning annual incomes greater than the yearly incomes of some peers.

The tradesmen such as Watson were a mere handful. These men, hands or shirt-sleeve men, kept shops. Their occupations included apothecary, surveyer-engineer, optician, clock-maker, instrument-maker, and hydrographer. But their names loom large in science and technical history—after all, they *did* the science—and they were avid attenders of meetings.

In the summer of 1747, William Watson was riding the crest in London. As the leader of the British electrical scientists, he did not suffer fools gladly, nor frauds. With a brief review published in the Royal Society's *Philosophical Transactions,* he could sink a man's reputation in the international field of electrical experimentation.

Franklin's electricity letter dated May 25, 1747, found its way to Watson. The letter, unfortunately now lost, had been dispatched on the clipper *Greyhound* that cleared Philadelphia on June 1. Franklin had addressed his communication to Peter Collinson, his London contact and a member of the Society. Collinson's first step was to take this fascinating letter to the top, to President Martin Folkes, Esq. Was it Collinson or Franklin or both who decided where to submit? As the pair knew from the graceful dedication in Watson's first electricity book, that tradesman had started up the path to electrical celebrity with submissions to the president. But Folkes didn't respond to Franklin's letter, passing it on to Watson.

Perhaps Watson had the letter on his desk that summer, but he may not have read it until several months later. When he finally did get to Franklin's letter, he would have come upon it fresh from a remarkable experiment that was garnering him international acclaim. That summer, Watson had set out to measure the velocity of electricity. Using a Leyden jar, he had sent electricity across Westminster bridge and then back, completing the circuit through the waters of the Thames. In total, electricity had traveled the length of eight football fields. Continuing his experiments outdoors, he had concluded his summer with a grand circuit at Shooter's Hill outside London, sending electricity for four miles.

"*Magnificentissimis tuis experimentis superasti conatus omnium,*" wrote the great Professor Musschenbroek from the University of Leyden upon learning the news.

Watson, now famous, a celebrity who had devoted a whole summer to performing one grand, orchestrated experiment and then preparing to present his findings to the Society at the end of October, confronted the unknown Franklin via letter, a man whose pages gushed with many experiments and hints, most of them demonstrated by cork bits the size of a child's marble.

Many years before in 1725, young Benjamin Franklin had knocked at the doors of Watson's club with his small asbestos-woven purse. Sir Hans Sloane had bought his curio and sent him on his way without so much as a complimentary visit to a meeting or a handshake from the president.

Now he was back.

※

Traditional histories portray Watson as welcoming Franklin into the forum of the Royal Society. The evidence points to a different story. But would Watson have been less than gracious? A recently uncovered account depicts this other William Watson. The source is Benjamin Wilson, who many years after the incident recounted would establish himself as an eminent electrical scientist, a favorite of George III, and a leading portrait painter and theatrical set designer.

In 1745, Benjamin Wilson had arrived penniless and with few connections on the London scene. He saved his shillings from wages as a court clerk to purchase art supplies and train himself after hours in the trade of portrait artist. The youthful enthusiast also found his way to electrical demonstrations by William Watson. Wilson, original to a fault, soon conceived his own hypotheses and began his own experimenting. "I apprehended that all the electrical phenomena," he wrote, "might easily be explained upon a very simple principle: because many experiments tended to show, that the electrical fluid did not proceed from vitreous or resinous substances only (as the philosophers had all along imagined) but from the *Earth* itself, and all bodies surrounding the apparatus."

Wilson conveyed this discovery to William Watson, President Martin Folkes, and several other eminences at the Society. Watson and Folkes advised him to continue developing the idea and also—for the sake of promoting his portrait art career where better opportunities might open—to move to Dublin. Wilson retrieved his papers (he later noted that the papers had been in Watson's hands for twelve days), moved to Dublin, and not long after he had arrived, Wilson learned that Watson had read a paper before the Society, claiming Wilson's theory as his own.

The astonished Wilson hurried back to London and disrupted a Society meeting in outraged protest. "An altercation immediately ensued upon it," he later remembered. "But being very young, and not having so many friends as Mr. Watson, I had not the advantage in that dispute."

A new contender from the tradesman alleys, and a theft—if Wilson told the truth, not hidden by a cloak of secrecy, but sweepingly performed in public. If the victim rose to protest, he sank in the esteem of the members. The incident appears in the Royal Society Journal Book of 1746 as a mere rippling of its polite surface, a plagiarism dispute from which Watson emerged the unscathed hero; Wilson, the tarnished upstart.

A memoir by Benjamin Wilson opened up after two and a half centuries tells the story of this theft. A transcription of this autobiography mysteriously surfaced more than half a century ago at the archives of the National Portrait Gallery of London. Wilson's account, intended for family eyes only, is a remarkable literary work, nearly as charming as Franklin's autobiography, which was also, incidentally, first intended as a memoir to be passed down as a private family heirloom. Wilson depicts himself as an outsider networking up in Hogarth's London through both electrical science and portrait painting. With disarming self-disclosure, Wilson observes "I had always an ambition of keeping *better company than myself.*"

Wilson's ambitions were the very ones motivating William Watson when he walked up the six entry steps at Crane Court on meeting days, nodded to the doorman in ancient silks, and took his place among the powerful.

✳

Wilson was not alone in questioning Watson's originality. *Gentleman's Magazine,* the eighteenth-century London cheerleader for nearly everybody in electrical science, in his case made an unusual exception. In its June, 1746, issue, the magazine published "A Short View of Mr. Watson's Treatise on Electricity" by a reviewer identified only as "D.D." The review of Watson's first book, *Experiments and Observations,* appeared swiftly on the heels of the book's May publication. "This pamphlet," observed D.D., "contains very few particulars which are not to be met with in our *April Mag.* 1745, and where several surprising effects of electricity are mentioned, which have not been produced by Mr. Watson." The reviewer said that Watson was reporting other men's experiments, and despite some veneer of Georgian politeness in D.D.'s prose, it was a slap in Watson's face. It was also a slap to the Royal Society and a criticism of the prestigious Copley Medal, given for *original* experiments, which six months earlier had been awarded Watson. To add insult to injury, the reviewer also speculated that Watson was deficient in his hardware, achieving lesser effects because his electrical friction machine used a glass tube rather than the emerging and fashionable glass globe.

Predictably, in the July issue of *Gentleman's Magazine* there appeared a rebuttal. The anonymous "P.B." entered the lists to defend Watson. P.B. points to Watson's "most generous manner" in sharing his knowledge with others; P.B. extols Watson's account "drawn up with great judgement, and in the plainest manner," and P.B. attributes to Watson "a great many particulars not to be found in any tract." It is a just and level-minded portrait of Watson. His contribution to electrical science is in the small, shrewd particulars of the experiment done, in the clarity of his reports, and in the dissemination of knowledge. Implicit here is something startling: By omission P.B. agrees with the original reviewer that the large experiments and theories reported in the booklet are *not* Watson's achievement.

In *Experiments and Observations,* Watson played a leading role in introducing the German experiments to a British audience. Brandy was set afire and chains of hand-holders convulsed as Watson presided. As the Society's leading expert in electrical matters, Watson was acting as a sort of international broker of remarkable science, a channel, a referee, but he went beyond that in screening new reports. When he repeated these experiments and wrote his booklet, he did not credit the names of the originators. At the same time, in the next several years when he would expose a report from abroad as bogus or himself find a solution to results that puzzled his international correspondents, he invariably mentioned the gentlemen's names.

The novelist Laurence Sterne has described the process of an eighteenth-century natural philosopher claiming an idea—by making an analogy with a man on a walk spying an apple and picking it up.

When "a man in a state of nature picks up an apple," observes Sterne, "it becomes his own."

*

On the darkening winter afternoon of January 21, 1748, William Watson arrived at Crane Court. He had in hand his report. In it, he would claim Franklin's three men/two wax cake experiment for himself.

President Martin Folkes, Esq., loomed over this meeting. Despite the simplicity of the room, Folkes sat raised on a huge carved-wood throne built for the president that had been Sir Isaac Newton's inspiration. To Folkes's left rested the grand ceremonial mace given by the king in 1662 and the leather and gilt charter book also dating back to the Restoration. Folkes also loomed between Benjamin Franklin and his acceptance as an electrical scientist.

Martin Folkes left a portrait of himself to the Royal Society painted by his friend William Hogarth. It shows a middle-aged man with brown eyes, sensual lips, and a pudgy face. The subject is blithely off-balance within the pictorial space, a five o'clock shadow over his lips, one button of his coat attached, the rest opened, perhaps after some indulgence of appetite. He points a sly finger aside, a command issued by a fleshy commander, no lines under the eyes of the eighteenth-century roaring boy, no regret marking his pink ripe face.

When Watson joined the crowd of gentlemen in the meeting room, he had in addition a second Franklin letter dated July 28 that had followed after the first. More brilliance. Again, most of its experimental vernacular was small scale—iron shot and cork balls—but used to great effect. Yet Watson had swooped down on the gentlemen-linking-hands experiment from the first letter. It resembled the experimental arenas in which Watson pursued his own hypotheses.

Centuries of debate have followed in the wake of Watson's report. Some British science histories even give Watson credit for the single-fluid, *plus* and *minus* electrical theory illustrated in the experiment.

Franklin's claim to this theory is stronger. He made his first and reported his discovery in writing. Watson asserts he *announced* the claim earlier, presumably at a formal meeting of the Society. No document supports him. It is interesting that his two booklets had gone to print with dispatch, but here with a landmark discovery to add to his portfolio, the delay lengthened. In fact, Watson never did publish the landmark announcement, and it is Franklin's words that would later appear in *Philosophical Transactions*.

Why didn't a member of the Society leap to his feet in protest? Why not question Watson's claim? The physicist and eighteenth-century electrical instrument curator Ellen Kuhfeld points out, "When people don't know what they're doing, it's hard to understand what they *think* they're doing." Electricity for all the shocking here-and-now of the snap was a discovery veiled in mystery. One of the advantages of reading science history centuries after scientific truth is agreed upon is that we all become armchair Newtons. But much that is obvious is only so in retrospect. By analogy, look at these eighteenth-century thinkers as a roomful of gentleman blindfolded and feeling their stumbling way about the furniture, until someone pulls off the blindfold and *sees*. Newton beneath the falling apple and Benjamin Franklin with his cork balls had such moments.

At the nod from Folkes, Watson rose to his feet. He plunged ahead briskly, reading aloud in the eighteenth-century style, gripping the sheaf of pages in his left hand and with his right forefinger pressing his spectacles tightly to his nose.

We can encounter the printed version of Watson's report in *Philosophical Transactions*. It is a startling letter. His first paragraph has no content. Watson devotes significant time to telling what this report is *not*. *Not* his famous experiment sending electricity across the Thames. The antithesis of the Royal Society English, it starts out all preface, apology, and rhetorical flourish. In the process of mentioning the Thames experiment, which trumpeted his name across continents, Watson here re-molds his authorship to the community of the distinguished friends in the room who helped him the previous summer, claiming the experiment is not his but theirs. In a sweeping verbal gesture, he flattens himself to the ground. Humility is the note struck, before he sets to work.

There was an ocean separating Watson from his victim. Any outrage and protest was beyond earshot. And what was America? "America," advised Edmund Burke, "serves for little more than to amuse you with stories of savage men and uncouth manners."

The London celebrity quoted two pages of Franklin verbatim in his report. "As this experiment was made," wrote Watson, "and the solution thereof given up on the other side of the Atlantic Ocean before this gentleman could possibly be acquainted with our having observed the same fact here, and as he seems very conversant in this part of natural philosophy, I take the liberty of laying before you his own words." Liberties in the extreme. At first Watson's claim is *we-did-this-too*. The Franklin letter according to Watson is dated June 1. But after Watson finishes the quote two pages later, he rolls on . . . *we* contracts to *I* . . . the claim made for himself now expands. "The solution of this gentleman, in relation to this phenomenon, so exactly corresponds with that which I offered early last spring, that I could not help communicating it." He was claiming priority. He was claiming *plus* and *minus*.

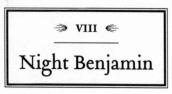

VIII

Night Benjamin

Benjamin Franklin invented the lightning rod, the hoax, and the republic.

⯮ HONORÉ BALZAC

THE YEAR 1746 HAD BORNE FRANKLIN A REMARKABLE HAR-
vest of electrical ideas that the Society at London smothered,
but during the same breakthrough months of his experimenting, he
wrote a nonscientific piece, an anonymous effort, which crossed the
Atlantic and spread rapidly in newspapers, magazines, and books to
become the talk of the civilized world. This piece was spiced with
scandal. In the colonies, although he certainly disclosed his authorship to his son and possibly an intimate friend or two, Franklin otherwise kept silent.

✳

Picture him after-hours about to sit down and pen a hoax.
It would have been after the last bell had rung at a tavern, possi-

bly the Indian King, his drinking companions stumbling home, when Franklin let himself in the house and came into the darkened rooms.

He lit one candle.

He could hear Debbie's heavy breathing in the far room, a stirring as she turned in bed. There was freedom for him in these moments. No interruptions. No customers. No journeymen to direct. At night, matters simplified to a quill, a pen knife, an inkbottle, and a piece of paper.

The blank paper was his opening.

He created an imaginary person from Boston and stamped her with a common name, Polly Baker, and supplied her with quite a history. Polly had just given birth to her fifth illegitimate child. She was already a single mother by at least two different men, possibly more. Her zest for sex was one Franklin could share. But her willingness to stand up and defend her sexual liberty was not something that Franklin as a businessman profiting from government contracts could afford to venture, at least in public.

Polly stood before the Court of Judicature in Connecticut near Boston. The Puritans had found her guilty, her crime was fornication, the damning evidence the baby who had issued from her loins. But Polly asked the judges "to indulge me a few words." At first she humbly offered her request to give a speech, pleading that the fine be remitted. But reasons followed. She defied her enemies (if she had any) to say she had harmed any man, woman, or child. She explained that by her own industry and no welfare, she had previously supported her four offspring, but "would have done it better, if it had not been for the heavy charges and fines I have paid." Once her defense started, it wouldn't stop. "Can it," asked Polly, "be a crime (in the nature of things I mean) to add to the number of the King's subjects, in a new country that really wants people?"

Polly explained that, in effect, she was willing to play the housewife to nearly any man who would ask for her hand. "I readily consented," offered Polly, "to the only proposal of marriage that ever was made me, which was when I was a virgin; but too easily confiding in the person's sincerity that made it, I unhappily lost my own honor, by trusting to his; for he got me with child, and then forsook me: That very person you all know; he is now a magistrate of this country; and I had hopes he would have appeared this day on the bench, and have endeavored to moderate the court in my favor."

Surely the dignified magistrates stirred uneasily at this news. But Polly continued to offer arguments, appealing to theology, to modesty, to morality. Then she suggested that "the great and growing numbers of bachelors in the country" should be compelled to marry or be fined double the penalty for fornication on an annual basis.

Polly—or Benjamin Franklin, take your choice—had a full head of steam by now. She insisted she was only doing her duty, "the duty of the first and great command of Nature, and of Nature's God, *Increase and multiply*, a duty, from the steady performance of which, nothing has been able to deter me."

In the last sentence of her appeal, she observed that in her "humble opinion" she deserved not a public whipping but to have a memorial statue erected in her name.

Franklin preceded the speech with the information that not only did Polly win her appeal, but that the next day, one of the admiring magistrates induced her to marry him.

Although Franklin might have tossed off the piece in one sitting, it's a work developed with extensive character, locale, and plot development (for him) all set in motion in the logic of a bogus court transcription. More often Franklin's narrative efforts develop and finish in a paragraph. In the freedom of the hoax, he expanded to unusual length and touched on issues close to home. He was publicly known, of course, as the father of an illegitimate son, his son William having been born in 1731 to a woman whose identity remains hidden.

Somehow in the months that followed, Polly Baker's speech found its way across the Atlantic and first appeared on April 15, 1747, in Henry Woodfall's *The General Advertiser*, a London paper.

Within days the item appeared in other newspapers, *The St. James's Evening Post, The London Evening-Post,* and on to Kent, Bath, Northampton, and within less than two weeks was hawked on Dublin streets in *Pue's Occurrences.* The wave of sweeping notoriety reached a high point in the *Gentleman's Magazine* April edition (it would have appeared on the street at the very end of the month), which then spread throughout the empire and beyond. Curiously, Polly never surfaced in *The Pennsylvania Gazette,* although her story rapidly found its way among other colonial newspapers. Perhaps Franklin withheld Polly from his own paper, fearing that his neighbors might recognize its style and topic and guess he had written it.

When Franklin admitted authorship decades later, he also indicated that he had written the piece to fill space in his paper when there was an expected shortage of text. But if you look at his paper and the others, you often see mere one-inch column items used as filler. His intent was surely different. Polly was so large she wouldn't have solved space problems; she would have created them. And the speech entire was reprinted so rapidly not because many printers were at once afflicted with a great shortage of space; she was reprinted for her sizzle.

The Polly Baker story was a cause célèbre in Europe—it intrigued the intellectuals, who carried on debates as to whether it were true or not. In France especially, where the salon set harbored utopian visions of common New World folk who naturally acquired moral wisdom and discovered natural truth, Polly's speech seemed very believable—it verified what they already thought, and Franklin's tale grew to be part of the standard intellectual baggage of the smart set in Paris.

There was also a target. *Gentleman's Magazine* had printed Polly's speech in its April issue. In the next month's issue there appeared a letter from "William Smith," explaining that the magistrate who had married Polly Baker was Paul Dudley, the Chief Justice of Massachusetts. The dignified and morally stern Dudley must have been astonished to read in an internationally distributed paper that his wife had slept around with several men and his children were the illegitimate offspring. Dudley was in fact a member of the Council in the Puritan governing body that had given James and Benjamin Franklin and their *New England Courant* such a hard time. It seems very possible this was payback.

A month after Smith's letter a London-based correspondent who had lived in the colonies wrote a letter explaining that Judge Dudley and his wife had no part in such scandalous doings. After some confirming research, a deeply mortified *Gentleman's Magazine* published a red-faced apology to the eminent colonial jurist. No one ever provided an account of William Smith. It has been argued that Franklin couldn't have written the Smith letter because the transatlantic sequence of Franklin receiving the *Gentleman's Magazine* in America and sending a letter back to London required at least a four-month interval.

Yet it seems an incredible coincidence that of all the people on the planet, the man whose reputation was damaged by the William Smith letter turns out to have been someone the Franklin brothers would have numbered among their enemies. William Smith is likely Franklin's imaginative creation, the bawdy mechanism of Polly's tale developing in two stages over two months into an international brouhaha. There is the distinct possibility that Franklin arranged with a London accomplice to deliver Polly's speech to the printshops and a month later to drop Smith's letter on the doorstep of *Gentleman's Magazine*. In fact he had access to an ideal accomplice: William Strahan. Strahan was Franklin's close friend and business associate, had an extensive network of London printing connections, would share in Franklin's hoaxes later in the 1760s, and had supported the philosopher David Hume's schemes, taking a special delight in arranging intrigue and deception. Franklin and Strahan would have made a very effective duo.

How long could Franklin keep a secret? In the case of Polly Baker, forty years. He was an old man in 1778 entertaining some of the leading *philosophes* of France in the elegant mansion at Passy. It was a golden afternoon, and the talk, though spirited, was genial. The men were debating and the famous case of Polly Baker was mentioned to prove a point. Franklin began to shake with laughter and at last confessed to them that the story was the product of his imagination.

✷

Spanning nearly seven decades and continuing into the last year of his life, Franklin's hoaxes were many. Some of the hoaxes were slight, transparent, and humorous, but others were serious, misleading by intent, and had great impact.

Historians often discount the significance of Franklin's hoaxes by arguing that everyone else then was also doing it. But when a London gentleman published a letter in a newspaper, signing off as *Scribblerus* or some Latinism, he hid his identity out of modesty or because he preferred the delights of acknowledging authorship to a small elite—or he intended simply to duck the scorn of his opponents. Franklin was different. The sheer number and pervasiveness and imaginative power of them raise Franklin's hoaxes to another level. The London gentlemen would serve up one generic Georgian prose style whatever their nom de plumes. On the other hand, Franklin invented false characters with seemingly authentic voices, mimicking the Puritan, the Londoner, even the Muslim cleric. Franklin was a master at this literary ventriloquism.

In the nineteenth century, some of Franklin's imaginative outrages were suppressed in archives, guarded by bibliophiles intent on protecting the public morals, and the publicly known deceptions often were given a spin by historians to render them consistent with Franklin as an icon central to America's financial establishment and national identity building. Victorian science histories echoed similar tones, utterly out of context adding a Romantic exterior to this eighteenth-century experimenter.

Midway in the twentieth century two landmark pieces of scholarship appeared that at last explored Franklin's false presentations. Max Hall published a slim book, *Benjamin Franklin & Polly Baker: The History of a Literary Deception,* a brilliant piece of literary detective work, which in tracking down the Polly Baker hoax shed light on the pervasiveness and art of Franklin's hoaxing. Verner Crane's *Benjamin Franklin's Letters to the Press* documented at least ninety-eight pseudonymous items using forty-two different signatures that are attributable to Franklin. The hoaxes have never had the impact on Franklin's reputation they might have had if they had, say, been published as an addendum to the first edition of his *Autobiography.* Instead, their discovery came after nearly a century and a half of mythologizing and solidifying of his cultural identity.

We need to trace the career path of Franklin the hoaxer if we are going to follow him into electrical science. To do so is not to engage in debunking, but to treat the real evidence of this very real man with sympathy and genuine respect. Certainly no other Founder had the odds stacked so highly against him, early and late, as a runaway teenager walking a hundred miles to a city where he had no connections, as an ailing old man representing a rebellion that was arguably foundering, yet arriving in Paris jaunty, confident, and smiling.

Franklin was a master at self-presentation, some of them false presentations, and his repertoire included not only full-blown hoaxes with their manufactured "evidence" and assumed identities, but also lies and simple deceptions, in some instances delightfully charming; in a few, eyebrow raising. We need to look at their variety. Examples include:

- The sixteen-year-old Benjamin pushed essays under the printshop door at night, efforts signed "Silence Dogood," which his brother James published. The sly hoax gave Benjamin his first existence as a published writer.
- After the Puritan Assembly forbad James to publish the *Courant,* James pretended to discharge Benjamin's indentures, publicly hand-

ing the paper over to a seventeen-year-old boy, a deception that made Benjamin the editor.

- Although James possessed a contract of indenture on his brother, Benjamin arrived in Philadelphia presenting himself as a journeyman printer. It landed him a job.

- In 1729, masquerading as "B.B.", Franklin published an influential essay arguing for paper currency. When the bill was passed, he was awarded the government printing contract.

- In the same year, Samuel Keimer foiled Franklin at starting a newspaper by leaping into the market first. Franklin penned letters signed "Busy Body" in a rival paper, which so delighted colonial readers and destroyed Keimer's market share that he was forced to sell his *Gazette* at a fire-sale price to Franklin. This hoax gave Franklin his first newspaper.

- In 1732, he launched his almanac with the Titan Leeds hoax.

- In 1747, he wrote "Plain Truth," the apparent product of a scripturalizing, Bible-thumping Scottish Presbyterian. The essay argued for defensive military preparations against forthcoming attacks by fleets of Spanish and French privateers. The essay had enormous effect in changing the direction of a colony begun as an experiment in Christian pacifism.

- Beginning in 1755, Franklin appeared in English drawing room parties after dinner reading from a phony Bible chapter he himself had written in King James English. Franklin's Hebrew God voiced a curiously eighteenth-century command for religious toleration. Having bamboozled his fashionable hosts, Franklin tucked the elegant leather and gilt volume under his arm, smiled, and, nodding politely to all, exited, never revealing his fiction.

- In 1761, he fabricated "the famous Jesuit Campanella," apparent author of a discourse offering Machiavellian advice on statecraft. Franklin published phony "excerpts" in the *London Chronicle,* hoping to "put us on our guard" against the crafty wiles of Catholic nations such as France and Spain.

- In 1763, English newspapers carried "An Edict by the King of Prussia," a deceptive trade policy announcement planted by Franklin, which, if true, would likely have led to war.

- In the 1770s there appeared a letter by Franklin claiming that dead flies returned to life when submerged in wine. The transparent humor was lost in translation upon a learned Italian scientist at the University of Pisa, who devoted great efforts to the experiment and was puzzled at the poor results.

- During the American Revolution, Franklin arrived in Paris on his diplomatic mission minus his London lace and silks, making his entrance wigless and sporting a fur cap, the picture of humble Quaker innocence.

- In 1782, he printed an elaborate fraudulent report that representatives of King George III had set Indians to taking 1062 scalps of colonial men, women, children, and infants.

- His last public writing, on March 23rd, 1790, was a hoax, the purported thoughts of "Sidi Mehemet Ibrahim," a Muslim whose zest for slavery was intended to shame American slave owners.

※

The hoax was as much Benjamin Franklin's tool as a wooden mallet. It was put to use. If successfully done, it could change reality. Was this the extent of Franklin's reason for the hoaxes? He used a hoax to break into print as an author, to arm a pacifist seaport; he did it to shame an empire suppressing an insurrection, and in the last year of his life, he did it propagandizing against slavery. But other times, and here is where you pause and try to scan his depths, he simply did it.

A London gentleman, hidden behind his literary veil, might fancy that his literary creation was a brick in the intellectual foundation of his times. A Philadelphia "hand," however, might author a piece and see his anonymous literary creation as a brick to heave through someone's window.

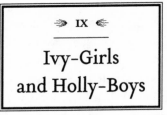

Let a person standing on the ground offer to kiss another electrify'd on the stand.

❧ JOHN NEALE, *Directions for Gentlemen Who Have Electrical Machines,* 1747

THE ELEMENT OF SEXUALITY IN POLLY BAKER'S TALE WAS also part of 1740s electrical science. One of Franklin's biographers, Carl Van Doren, noted that in 1746 Franklin apparently returned to the sexual activity of his earlier years and called it "his salty year." That the year brimmed with sex and electricity experiments was not a coincidence.

For starters, *spark* was a sexual term in 1746. It denoted a young male looking for a sexual partner, a bit of a fop, not a person of substance seeking marriage, but someone seeking a partner in bed, his interest, upon his conquest and orgasm, immediately waning. In Georgian dirty-joke books (a printshop near Drury Lane Theater in London clunked them out), it is sparks who go adventuring.

According to the Oxford English Dictionary, *spark* was also an electrical term by 1742.

The 1740s in London were a time of astonishingly rapid cultural change. It was a time that was blunt, raw, overrefined, and coarse all at once. For instance, the word *piss* was used in fashionable parlors, mysteriously and suddenly turning disreputable around 1750. It was an era when men pulled their breeches down in polite company, continuing conversation as they sat on chamber pots pursuing even the most violent eliminations. The biographer James Boswell has recorded having his way atop a prostitute in the middle of the newly completed Westminster Bridge, curious about what it would feel like to have sex with the Thames running under him. On a bet, Lady Chudleigh, maid-in-waiting to the Prince of Windsor, had stepped before the king at a formal event in virtually naked glory.

Historian J. H. Plumb describes this reckless scene: "There was an edge to life in the eighteenth century," he notes, "which is difficult for us to recapture. In every class there is the same taut neurotic quality—the fantastic gambling and drinking, the riots, brutality and violence, and everywhere and always a constant sense of death."

Where began the curious cultural crossing of the sexual and scientific in a *spark*?

Dialecticians identify *spark* as part of the traditional folk vernacular of Oxfordshire. The term referred to the lover of a servant—as when a maidservant desiring an evening out with her paramour asked her mistress if she might have a *little spark*?

Samuel Johnson never had much sympathy for the dialect English the servant classes brought to London. When he assembled his magnificent project *The Dictionary of the English Language,* he was defining a standard English. It is a curiosity that his beloved rambling halls at old Cave's printshop were the same place where Franklin's *Experiments and Observations* was published. Johnson obviously knows about electrical science, as his definition of *electricity* makes clear. Not only that, he knows about Franklin: "The philosophers," he wrote near mid-century, "are now endeavoring to intercept the strokes of lightning."

But he didn't know about the electrical *spark.*

He includes, however, *spark* in its sexual meaning as standard English, as a moralist inserting it last in his list of definitions. Terse, too, for Johnson: "5. A lover," he wrote. In addition, he inserts *spark-ish* in his dictionary. His definition: "Airy, gay [not in the contemporary sense denoting homosexuality]. A low word. It is commonly applied to men rather than women."

In the tumultuous culture of 1746 electrical frolics, *spark* appeared with several implications. The merry participants didn't just mean embers from the hearth.

The new phenomena given up by the jar may have been compared to the short-lived vagaries of male orgasm. It was, after all, an experimental scientific demonstration famous for some fellow cranking madly, furiously perspiring, and for all the buildup, nothing came. Or after the man went through his feverish paces, a mere little spit erupted, something they termed at times a *convulsion.* After which, a lady might have stared wide-eyed over the top of her fan and asked, "Is that *all?*"

✳

From the earliest months in this sweeping international party-science, the focus had been on fiery women.

Both *Philosophical Transactions* and *Gentleman's Quarterly* featured new and also recycled old reports on women who issued electrical fire. A maidservant made newspaper headlines because when she removed her petticoats in the dark she flamed spectacularly. Naturally, numerous curious gentlemen went to her darkened bedroom to investigate.

At parties, ladies' layered petticoats rubbing contributed to static electrical effects. There was some hilarious outrage to be found in sending electricity into their polite bodies and then flickering it out the hoop of their skirts.

These images of desirable members of the opposite sex going up in flames were powerful archetypes for all social classes. One of the provincial English village instances happened once a year. They did it on Shrove Tuesday. The young men of marriage age descended on a band of young women of similar status and grabbed from them a figure of a girl they had knotted together from ivy. It was an effigy of explicit anatomy. "Uncouth," polite folks would have said. And during the same moments, one of the girls grabbed from the young men an effigy of a male they had fashioned from holly cuttings, "uncouth" too. Each group ran to opposite ends of the village, cheering, laughing, and at last setting fire to the effigies.

In fashionable circles, however, with the advent of the Leyden jar, concern grew that if electricity was fire, at some point it might advance beyond a spark flickering from the skirt hoop and consume her person. They investigated old tales of spontaneous combustion, wondering if electricity had done the work. The Italians told of a well-bred lady sixty-two years of age who retired for the night, seemingly in good health, but next morning when the maid opened the door, she saw:

> Four feet distant from the bed . . . a heap of ashes, two legs out-stretched, stockings on, between which lay the head. The brains, half of the back part of the skull, and the whole chin burnt to ashes, among which were found three fingers blackened.
>
> All the rest was ashes . . .

The conveyor of this news, Dr. Giovanni Bianchi, the famed electrical scientist of Turin, speculated that excessive alcohol in this woman's system contributed to her fiery fate.

Other scientists speculated that electricity might be intimate with the reproductive principle of Nature. In France, Sigaud de Lafond offered as proof the report that eunuchs were unable to transmit an electrical charge. But when Sigaud tried the experiment for the pleasure of the Duc de Chartres, the assembled line of *castrati* holding hands jumped as satisfyingly as Nollet's soldiers.

On Fleet Street in London, the showman Benjy Rackstrow lured the *virtuosi* and the servant class with electrical displays performed for the "honor of the nation," charging one shilling; his repertoire included electrifying the "pizzle [penis] of the whale"—surely for gentlemen only. The bubbling London pamphlet scene produced *Teague-Root Displayed* by "Paddy Strong-Cock, Fellow of Drury Lane." Mocking "W___ W___ F.R.S.," Strong-Cock churned out pages that even today raise eyebrows with their explicit descriptions of male and female genitalia presented in the vocabulary of electrical science.

Across the Channel, the approach to electric sexuality took a more serious and religious bent. Some savants wondered if electricity was the making of the world. In the book of Ezekiel the prophet details a vision of the physical body of the Lord that includes electricity as the Divinity's reproductive fluid. In the Hebrew world, amber with its gleams and tiny sparks was the only known source of electricity. "I beheld," says Ezekiel, "a likeness as the appearance of fire from the appearance of his [God's] loins even downward, fire, and from his loins even upward, as the appearance of brightness as the color of amber."

✳

Franklin didn't go the metaphysical route. He read in London papers that the gentlemen sauntering in pleasure gardens, playing at billiards, and strolling through quadrilles had now stepped nimbly into science. Franklin always loved a party.

Electricity gave this man with no pedigree enhanced social access to what his century called "celebrated beauties." They arrived at his Market Street shop, young women with high cheekbones, aristocratic noses, complexions as stunning as orchid petals, long and silken eyelashes, and quick black eyes, pressing close to see the wonders cranked out of his machine.

Look again at Franklin's famed electric spider experiment. He reported it in his first letter to the Royal Society. "We suspend," he explains, "by a fine silk thread a counterfeit spider, made of a small piece of burnt cork, with legs of linen thread, and a grain or two of lead stuck in to give him more weight." He dangles this spider between two stiff wires, one charged by the Leyden jar. Then he causes the cork to bounce between the wires charging and discharging. His spider appears "perfectly alive." Nothing new by way of science, its principle already demonstrated by the cork balls. Nor was the burnt-cork spider designed for the dashing beaus who routinely dared the Leyden jar with the point of their swords. This effect was intended solely for the delights of flirtation.

Franklin's parties also included Bose's famous kissing game: "We increase the force of the electrical kiss vastly," the American boasted. As these pages were written, every effort was made to locate an authentic description of a Franklin electric party, but without success. Parson Weems is a nineteenth-century biographer of Franklin, unreliable because of his penchant for fictionalizing, yet he does describe a Franklin electric party. Weems claims that Jonathan Dickinson, Franklin's Jersey market neighbor, was one source of his party account. The only merit Weems has to offer is that in his time he did introduce authentic new discoveries of Franklin materials (in addition to his own unannounced creations). His *Life of Benjamin Franklin* appeared first in 1818 and became a popular favorite. A contemporary scholar notes that in his book Weems "created a Franklin who personified the virtues of Christianity, cleanliness, industry, frugality, and scientific inquisitiveness, all in the service of civic responsibility." Curiously, the party insert totally runs counter to such intentions. Weems claims that Franklin used two celebrated beauties for his subjects, "Elizabeth Seaton and Eliza Sitgreaves." The party at moments turns flirtatious, sexually aware, and, by Pennsylvania standards, blasphemous.

Long after the electricity craze died down, some of these Franklin games would reappear. In 1779, the quack James Graham arrived in London and established his Grand Temple of Health and Hymen, where a paying couple could "enjoy the delights of love" as

THE ELECTRIC SPARK, *1790s*

*Louis-Léopold Boilly, a Parisian artist, created images of seduction, spe-
cializing in what the leading Boilly scholar terms "teasing, slightly
naughty scenes which depicted the intrigues and snares of the game of
love." This little-known painting has an allegorical element. It shows
three stages of life, the boy studying scientific treatises, the old men experimenting with an electrical friction machine, and the young, sexually
energized male ready to convulse in union with a fashionable beauty.*

(VIRGINIA MUSEUM OF FINE ARTS, RICHMOND, THE ARTHUR AND MARGARET GLASGOW FUND) they were magnetized and electrified. At some point in the mating ritual, electricity sparkled out words on a sheet of glass, a Franklin trick, and the words were, in fact, Polly Baker's favorite command-ment—"Be Fruitful, Multiply And Replenish The Earth."

As late as 1790, Louis-Léopold Boilly, a Paris artist who special-ized in scenes of seduction, painted "The Electric Spark," now hanging at the Virginia Museum of Fine Arts in Richmond. Boilly depicts a boy reading scientific transactions on one side and, on the other side, two elderly scientists whose electrical friction machine is charging a bronze statue of Cupid placed near mid-image. Only the dog nearby with his animal sympathies responds to the drama as—in the middle—an amorous young couple reach for the electrified Cupid, ready to unite in one convulsion.

Electricity would give Franklin access to women in the 1740s, es-pecially the beauties far beyond his social orb. But he had other aims too.

He wanted recognition for his work.

⇒ X ⇐

Deadly Box

He [Peter Collinson] got them [the Philadelphia Experiments]
read in the Royal Society, where they were not at first thought
worth so much Notice as to be printed in their Transactions.

⇒ B. Franklin, *Autobiography*

W ATSON HAD DEALT WITH FRANKLIN. DURING THE WIN-
ter months of 1748, the results must have seemed splendid.
It was a game he could play forever—courtesies veiling theft, polite
delays announced, and barriers quietly constructed. Of the first four
electrical letters Franklin sent to the Royal Society, Watson would
intercept all of them, shunting Franklin aside in four different but
equally effective ways.

First, Watson squelched the May 25, 1747, letter, reading aloud
only one experiment, the one he claimed for himself.

Second, Watson dealt with the July 28, 1747, letter, a brilliant mis-
sive in which Franklin used his plus/minus theory to account for the
mystery of the Leyden jar. Watson never read aloud so much as
even a phrase in meeting; the letter simply vanished.

The third Franklin letter took a different route. Someone—
perhaps Collinson—stood up with it at the December 14, 1749,

meeting at Crane Court, but the effort to leapfrog standard Royal Society procedure utterly failed; this letter went unread, handed over to Watson for consideration. A week later when Watson returned to the meeting, the letter was read, followed immediately by verbal refutations from Watson, which were recorded at some length in the notes of the Society Journal Book. Franklin's letter sank from sight, and Watson's expanded response—it included refutations, claims of priority, some polite nods of affirmation, and exceptional focusing on Franklin's clowning—was finally passed along to the New World hopeful.

Next, Franklin sent the electrical letter described in the *Autobiography* as the item "laughed at by the connoisseurs." Franklin dispatched his letter via Dr. John Mitchell, an American member of the Society then resident in London—by this date Franklin may have suspected that Collinson was simply the wrong messenger.

*

The fourth letter was different. In his first three letters, Franklin would at times present his findings with the elegance a baroque composer in that era might use to frame a theme and variations. In addition to miscellanea often randomly stacked in the later pages, Franklin's letters at their best presented elegant series of hypotheses and experiments, moving from his single-fluid theory to an account of the Leyden jar to electricity induced on a flat pane of glass, the modern configuration of the capacitor. In the third letter, attempting to explain where the electricity was in the Leyden jar, he designed an incisive sequence of experiments isolating and denying each possibility—an if-not-A-then-B, if-not-B-then-C process unfolding, until he concluded that electricity was *on* the glass.

But the Mitchell letter was pathetic. It was a vast soggy pudding of hypotheses offering suggestions about planetary systems and electrification of the atmosphere, free-swinging guesses Franklin admitted were "suppositions." Unfortunately, the letter was also a

A nineteenth-century French illustration depicting Franklin scorned at the Royal Society in London. It appears in Louis Figuier's remarkable Les Merveilles de la Science *(1868).*

target—the men at Crane Court had a reputation as "the lords of laughter." They were known to roar until their cheeks turned red at utter nonsense submitted by cranks and would-be Newtons. When electricity was the topic, Watson led the famed "laughing fraternity." In a chorus of coughing, hooting, tapping of canes, and shaking of wig-powder in the air, Franklin became their Georgian victim.

Franklin's lack of success in London spanned nearly five years. In the century afterward, the events were glossed as warm, international cooperation, an interpretation that resonates to this day.

Franklin knew differently. In his *Autobiography,* he remembered that he had been "stifled." Worse than he knew—Collinson discreetly fudged his account to Franklin, pluralizing what was welcomed at Crane Court, indicating that letters one and two had been read aloud and in their entirety. The extraordinary length of this rejection could be explained by delays—it might take five or six weeks for an eighteenth-century sailing ship to cross the ocean. But most of the delays occurred in London. By dated letters, we know that Watson promised Collinson a personal response to Franklin but then waited a year and seven months and then replied in an insulting, refuting letter that did not even address Franklin by name in its salutary greeting. Collinson, who had promised Franklin Watson's "further favors," understandably delayed four months before shipping the result.

Watson won. He had all the advantages. Franklin had no society to back him.

The year before he began electrical experiments, Franklin had tried to organize a small group of sympathetic friends into a scientific association, perhaps one resembling the Royal Society. Histories embellish this time as the period when Franklin "established the American Philosophical Society." But how can you establish what in those years never rose above the state of collapse? "The members of our society here are very idle gentlemen. They will take no pains," Franklin had bitterly complained. The pleasures of the coffeehouse satisfied his friends. Franklin had also tried to set up a scientific journal published by this society, similar to the London *Transactions*. He had volunteered to do most of the editorial work, but the project never materialized because no one wrote any articles.

There was an ocean between Franklin and the arena where he struggled for recognition. How could he defend his intellectual claims? Who could imagine he would do any better than Benjamin Wilson had, self-destructing by his protest into an impolite ripple in a very polite science. What advantage did Franklin have?

He had a sly, subversive sense of humor.

✳

Franklin had sent the third letter to London soon after he discovered Watson's initial theft published in *Transactions*. This report is part experimental report, part reaction to robbery. Embedded within are two comic strokes. One, often quoted, is humor that gently but ironically calls up a vision of international cooperation. Franklin announces:

> The hot weather coming on, when electrical experiments are not so agreeable, tis proposed to put an end to them . . . in a party of pleasure on the banks of the Schuykill. . . . A turkey is to be killed for our dinners by the electrical shock, and roasted by the electrical jack, before a fire kindled by the electrified bottle, when the healths of all the famous electricians in England, France and Germany, are to be drank in electrified bumpers, under the discharge of guns from the electrical battery.

The second comic item, however, is an insult. Franklin suggests creating an electrical picture of the king on a glass pane. He explains:

> Hold the picture horizontally by the top, and place a little moveable gilt crown on the King's head. If now the picture be moderately electrified, and another person take hold of the frame with

one hand, so that his fingers touch its inside gilding, and with the
other hand endeavor to take off the crown, he will receive a terrible blow and fail in the attempt. If the picture were highly
charged, the consequences might perhaps be as fatal as that of
high treason. . . . If a ring of persons take a shock among them
the experiment is called the *Conspiracy*.

Today, this humor strikes charming chords. But in 1749, trying to
take the crown off the king's head would get you hung. Just three
summers before, the Duke of Cumberland and his soldiers buried
Scotland's finest lords under Drunmossie moor for just such an intent. The lengthy paragraph that tells how to remove the king's
crown wasn't science. It was an international tweaking of the nose of
William Watson. The message delivered, freighted and angled
specifically to the thief. It said, *You-claimed-my-experiment-was-
yours; go-ahead-and-claim-this-one.* And more was to come.

✳

It appears in Franklin's July 29, 1750, letter. At first glance, the letter seems a businesslike report. It is drafted two days after Franklin
sat down and tried to refute Watson's letter that treated him as
something near a comic nonentity. In the middle of the 1750 letter
appears an unusual suggestion. It is a passage that in three decades
will become an icon crucial in the history of Western civilization
and the survival of the American republic—in addition, within two
years it will kill a man. The experiment requires what the eighteenth
century widely recognized as a *sentry box*, an enclosure resembling
a phone booth intended to protect a sentry on duty from rain and
other inclement weather. Franklin writes:

To determine the question, whether the clouds that contain
lightning are electrified or not, I would propose an experiment to
be tried where it may be done conveniently.

On the top of some high tower or steeple, place a kind of sentry box big enough to contain a man and an electrical stand [an electrically insulated platform]. From the middle of the stand let an iron rod rise, and pass bending out of the door, and then upright 20 or 30 feet, pointed very sharp at the end. If the electrical stand be kept clean and dry, a man standing on it when such clouds are passing low, might be electrified, and afford sparks, the rod drawing fire to him from the cloud. If any danger to the man should be apprehended (though I think there would be none) let him stand on the floor of his box, and now and then bring near to the rod, the loop of a wire, that has one end fastened to the leads; he holding it by a wax-handle. So the sparks, if the rod is electrified, will strike from the rod to the wire and not affect him.

Scores of observers before Franklin had remarked on the analogy between lightning and electricity. During the very year Franklin wrote this, the Bordeaux academy had announced an international essay contest on the subject of whether lightning and electricity were the same. But Franklin suggested an experiment to prove the hypothesis. The experimental subject would invite down the thunderbolt.

Was this a serious suggestion? William Watson took very seriously his responsibilities as a validator who repeated at London electrical demonstrations reported internationally. At times Watson hazarded his own body in the extreme, but he must have taken this proposal lightly, as did all other English scientists, because he never did it.

Nor did Franklin.

To understand this letter and the context of the sentry box proposal, consider the next paragraph after Franklin recommends standing beneath the metal pole during a thunderstorm. Franklin writes:

Before I leave this subject of lightning, I may mention some other similarities between the effects of that and those of electricity. Lightning has often been known to strike people blind.

Here surfaces the deadpan humor of an editor well known to readers of *The Pennsylvania Gazette*. The same laconic frontier humor appears more than a century later in *Huckleberry Finn*. It is distinct from London satire. The object of Franklin's humor is William Watson. After all, if the sentry-box proposal were a serious experiment meant to be done, why didn't Franklin, a highly effective doer, simply do it?

Some have suggested that Franklin postponed the effort because he didn't have a high building. Twenty years afterward, this rationale first appeared in Joseph Priestley's 1769 history based on interviews with Franklin. "The Doctor," wrote Priestley, "after having published his method of verifying his hypothesis concerning the sameness of electricity with the matter lightning, was waiting for the erection of a spire in Philadelphia to carry his views into execution."

The explanation has been that he was awaiting the completion of a steeple on Christ Church, where Debbie and Sallie attended. The congregation had commenced building a steeple to house chiming bells in May of 1751. Franklin himself contributed money and, as an experienced veteran of lottery administration, served on church committees that managed the fund-raising. There were numerous delays and the project was not completed until early in 1755 after the significant expense of nearly £3200.

Hence, during these years Franklin had no opportunity to erect his sentry box.

But he did. In the year 1751, Benjamin Franklin personally supervised on nearly a daily basis the erection of a steeple at the Academy. "We have bought for the Academy," wrote Franklin, "the house that was built for itinerant preaching, which stands on a large lot of ground capable of receiving more buildings. . . . The house is 100 foot long and 70 wide, built of brick; very strong; and sufficiently high for three lofty stories."

What did Franklin mean by "lofty"? Or "sufficiently high"? The Academy building had been completed in 1742 to accommodate the huge crowds wanting to hear the evangelist George Whitefield. After interest in Whitefield died down, the sizable structure, which was larger than the State House, proved to be more real estate than was needed for a Whitefield follower, Gilbert "Hellfire" Tennent, a preacher noted for his "beastly braying." At that time Franklin was the moving force in plans to open an English school for boys eight to sixteen years of age. In 1749, he had been elected president of the school's board of trustees, and his was the effort and negotiating that landed the great building for them, getting it for less than half the price of construction. In the spring of 1751, Franklin was given responsibility for the erection of a steeple that would house the school bell and loft a spire and weather vane above. On April 11, 1751, the belfry was raised.

What was this building? No architectural plans survive, but there is a neat scale drawing at the Historical Society of Pennsylvania possibly done by Franklin's friend and construction associate Isaac Norris after the steeple had been completed.

If the base of the Academy building was 100 feet, according to Franklin, then the steeple they built, based on the scale of the Norris drawing, reached more than 80 feet. If Franklin had used, for instance, the 40-foot pole the French later chose, a 40-foot rod could have been secured atop the steeple, reaching to 120 feet. It would have been three times the height of what the French afterward used to do the actual experiment. It would have far outreached any of the ensuing lightning rod setups recorded in France in 1752.

It may be that in all the civilized Western world there was no electrical scientist with more privileged access to a lofty spire for the performance of lightning experiments than Benjamin Franklin in 1751.

Some have argued that Franklin felt the greater height of the Christ Church steeple, probably 190 feet when completed five years later, was needed to properly perform the experiment. But note that, for all the bragging in his other reports, when Franklin describes early experimental setups he doesn't venture the Bigger-Is-Better path; in fact, he goes the opposite way, boasting that Americans don't need the fancy, multiwheel artifacts to create enough electricity for experiments. His is a mind that typically settles for the small and convenient at hand, Debbie's sewing needle, for instance, rather than a jewel-studded spear.

Not only that, but in June of 1750, he wrote his friend Cadwallader Colden that plans had been made to use this Academy building for science, informing him that "[we] propose to have an observatory on the top." Although Franklin often discussed electrical projects with Colden, he failed to mention any plan to erect a lightning experiment on top of the building.

That Franklin was waiting hopefully for a church to let him experiment on its roof during these years seems questionable. There was a wave of steeple-building in the late 1740s as prosperous Philadelphia turned its attention to decorating its places of worship. The projects were great struggles for the congregations, too—the city didn't have the Old World tradesmen who knew steeple carpentry (within twenty-five years most Pennsylvania steeples were in serious need of repair) and the costs were staggering. Most lavish was the Christ Church project, which twice went broke and came to a standstill. Old Parton, Franklin's nineteenth-century biographer, may have stared through Victorian spectacles at much that Franklin did, but he was closer than we are to the world of these congregations that sacrificed to build these fancy, ornamental erections. "Could there have been found," Parton asks, "anywhere in the world, a vestry that would have lent their steeple to a philosopher bent on drawing down the very lightning from heaven, that he might try conclusions with it?"

The truth was closer at hand. The first letter written to Collinson two days before Franklin proposed the sentry-box experiment was really a response to Watson. The refuted refutes back: "Mr. Watson I believe wrote his observations on my last paper in haste," began Franklin, defending himself.

And then within two days, he proposed the sentry box to Watson.

It was deadly if followed exactly. Over the centuries some extra-historical help was needed to clean this up as science. In his book *Franklin and Newton,* I. Bernard Cohen, a Harvard professor whose work on Franklin's science is indispensable, stepped in to help. Cohen wrote: "Franklin thought there would be little danger. Yet if any 'should be apprehended,' the man standing on the floor might hold in his hand a wax handle affixed to a 'loop of wire' that has been attached to the ground." In a blink, Cohen depicts a Franklin helpfully offering grounding.

But look again at Franklin's passage: "If any danger to the man," wrote Franklin, "should be apprehended (though I think there would be none) let him stand on the floor of his box, and now and then bring near to the rod, the loop of a wire, that has one end fastened to the leads; he holding it by a wax-handle. So the sparks, if the rod is electrified, will strike from the rod to the wire and not affect him."

In 1750, *leads* didn't refer to electrical wires conveying electricity. The electrical meaning didn't exist. According to the OED, the electrical sense of *lead* does not appear until 1881. The term in Franklin's era referred to "sheets or strips of lead used to cover a roof." If an apprehensive experimenter wished, Franklin advised him to attach the wire to the roof cover of the sentry box. Was this grounding? Not at all—the whole point of the sentry box with its dry clean floor beneath is not to drain the electrical energy away into the ground. The roof would protect the box beneath also from any covering of moisture offering an escape path down for the energy to earth.

Vladimir Rakov, international authority on lightning, points out that the *leads* might be the roof of the structure on which the sentry was mounted rather than the roof of the sentry box. His point is well taken. If the wire is attached to the building's roof, its *metal* guttering system would ground the charge in the earth below. But look at the French translators and experimenters who later do this experiment. Both Thomas François Dalibard in his 1752 translation and Barbeau Dubourg in his 1773 translation working with editorial input from Franklin translate the *leads* as "la couverture," the covering or roof. Dalibard and others set their sentry box at ground level, so the only *leads* available were the sentry box roof. There was no electrical grounding.

A Cohen associate, Sir Basil Schonland of England published a lightning science history in 1964 complete with a full-page illustration of the sentry box to which he helpfully inked in a thick wire leading from the wire loop down into terra firma. Functioning as an international tandem, working outside eighteenth-century context, the two professors created grounding where there was none.

But at mid-century in the Age of Reason, Watson understood.

He likely got the message. Behind the polite instructions, which if followed could result in the end of his life, behind the curious directive to stand under a pointed metal pole in a thunderstorm, was another suggestion—

The Devil take you!

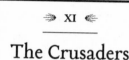

XI

The Crusaders

*The [Royal] Society has reduc'd its principal observations, into
one common-stock; and laid them up in publique Registers, to be
nakedly transmitted to the next Generation of Men.*

⁂ Thomas Sprat

Franklin's London ally, Peter Collinson, must have
struck William Watson as patently harmless.

Collinson played a minor role at the Royal Society. He was a
member of the Quaker minority, a fifty-seven-year-old investor
"below the middle size . . . somewhat corpulent," known among the
genteel people as a collector of rare flowering plants. As a biographer noted, "Collinson was fond of fruit to an extreme, and of flowers. He was seldom without them in his house."

Collinson invested in silks, he kept a countinghouse at Grace-
church Street, he had married a woman with a fortune, and, when
his father-in-law died, he moved into the man's house, the delightful and widely envied estate Mill Hill just outside of London.

Scholar Lisa Jardine has specifically located Collinson "among
the ranks of wealthy London merchants . . . exploiting their privileged access to the trading routes plied by their own merchant ves-

sels." She grants these men their genuine enthusiasm for collecting curiosities and the pursuit of science but also their passion for fortune-building. "These businessmen-collectors," writes Jardine, "were well aware their expensive 'hobby' doubled as an efficient means of locating luxury commodities that could be exploited commercially." One interesting example is Sir Hans Sloane, president of the Royal Society, whose merchant vessels had brought back chocolate to sell as a digestive therapeutic. When Londoners found it unpalatable and his warehouses bulged with unsold product, Sloane came up with a new scheme: Mix the chocolate with milk and advertise it as a drink. Sloane made himself a fortune when hot chocolate proved as fashionable as coffee.

Collinson worked these angles, too. His letters reveal him scheming to amass ginseng—he had discovered a Pennsylvania source—and create a London market for it as a medicinal. He cautioned his associate working on the project, "conceal thy intention from every one." Here operated a businessman far removed from William Penn's famed commandment of openness to first-generation Quaker shopkeepers. In his merchant dealings, Collinson resembled many wealthy second- and third-generation London Quakers—a document at the Royal Society states he "withdrew" from Quaker meeting. Yes, he was Franklin's friend, but he also worked personal and scientific relationships for investment angles.

During the same years Collinson tried to gain recognition for Franklin he labored mightily for Cadwallader Colden, New World investor and later lieutenant governor of New York, whose science was as baffling and addled as Franklin's was clear and brilliant. Colden was the most dismal physical scientist produced in colonial America. This New York dignitary had written a cloudy treatise in which he critiqued Newton and presumed to "explain the cause of gravitation, after all the great men in philosophy failed." Collinson peddled it to some of the great scientists of Europe. The pattern curiously resembled Franklin's reception at the Society: rejection abroad, encouraging and misleading reports returned to the colonies.

When Collinson at last somehow persuaded a London paper to print an excerpt, the editor attached a disclaimer that he couldn't understand any of the murky essay. Finally, the would-be Newton in New York grew suspicious of the flow of hearty encouragements from Collinson. "I perceive that you are unwilling to tell me everything that may discourage me," Colden wrote his ally. In maintaining a network of international connections, the London silk merchant was not above disguising brickbats as bouquets.

✳

Picture this short, heavy man opening Franklin's historic first letters in electrical science surrounded by blooming American flowers. A strange sight, with even stranger sights succeeding. He lost the early rounds at the Society. But stung by the members' mockery of Franklin in November, 1749, Collinson took a fateful step. He decided to publish the electrical letters. He was joined in this effort by fellow Royal Society member Dr. John Fothergill, a London Quaker and colonial investor. According to Fothergill, Franklin "had said more sensible things on the subject [electricity], and let us see more into the nature of this delicate affair than all the other writers put together."

Fothergill was known for helping lower-class authors get into print. It is reported that he sponsored a poor schoolmaster self-taught in Hebrew and Greek who had translated the Bible, providing editorial labor and £1000 to publish this Bible. No one knows whether Collinson or Fothergill negotiated the publishing arrangements for Benjamin Franklin, but all the small clues suggest that Collinson played that role.

In the winter months of 1750, Collinson was a man on a mission. He would have paid a personal visit to the printer Edward Cave to make a deal.

Cave's printshop was located in St. John's Gate, a dark and shabby building that resembled, and in fact had been, a medieval embattle-

St. John's Gate stands today at Clerkenwell, London. This splendid nine-teenth-century photograph depicts the site where the modern magazine was born. (GUILDHALL LIBRARY, LONDON)

ment. Here had been housed the priory of the Knights of St. John, who from this site rode forth three thousand miles to fight for the holy city of Jerusalem. The structure surviving above ground dated from the sixteenth century, a relic from an era when cities were also fortresses. Two squat ancient stone towers with a portal between them now funneled busy commercial traffic. The gatehouse walls—some nearly nine feet thick—were intended to discourage siege and battering ram but also intimidated eighteenth-century real estate developers. Science history would be made at this dank site, just as it already had been made here in journalism.

In February, 1731, Edward Cave had published the first issue of his *Gentleman's Magazine; or Trader's Monthly Intelligencer.* The masthead announced that its editor/publisher was *Sylvanus Urban of Aldermanbury, Gent.* In fact, Sylvanus Urban was the nom de plume of Cave himself. The name implied a periodical that could sweep easily between cosmopolitan London and the sylvan pleasures of a country manor, uniting readers from all of genteel Britain. However, the ink-smeared, shirt-sleeve publisher behind this concept didn't resemble the image; he was "Ned" Cave, the cobbler's son, and no gent.

The tradesman Cave had nursed a vision of this scheme for years. He had tried in vain to interest partners or booksellers to join him, but finally he launched the breakthrough project on his own. *Gentleman's Magazine* contained a miscellany of items. There were political articles, poems, scientific reports, descriptions of far-flung countries and cities, botanical essays on specimens from the New World, arrivals and departures of merchant vessels, and during wartime lists of ships caught by the privateers. Cave had designed this monthly booklet to be small enough to stuff in a broadcoat pocket, and in the introduction to his first issue he announced that it would be a *magazine.*

Although *magazine* in this martial era often referred to a powder magazine, Cave had something else in mind—the eighteenth-century meaning of *magazine* defined in the OED as "a storehouse or repository of goods . . . a warehouse depot." Just as the East India Company brought home to its warehouses a luxurious abundance of silks, gems, pearls, strange healing roots, and other commodities, so the mythical Sylvanus Urban assembled a sort of intellectual warehouse, collecting plunder from all across the empire. There was a colonial aspect to the first magazine.

Cave soon found he had a runaway success. The magazine appeared on tables in the parlors of every polite London home. A score of imitators promptly copied him, and one of them, *London Magazine,* established itself as a worthy rival, but none of them ever surpassed Cave. According to one eighteenth-century account, Cave sold 10,000 copies a month; another source estimated 15,000. His periodical was regularly sent to places as far away as colonial America and St. Petersburg in the east.

Occasionally historians trace the origin of the United States motto *e pluribus unum* to Benjamin Franklin's stay in France, the saying that in fact originated in Virgil's recipe for a salad dressing and that was repeated with political meanings at Versailles. Franklin would use it as a call for unity among the rebel colonies. But he would have discovered it many decades before on the masthead of *Gentleman's Magazine,* a motto in that context resonant with imperialism. The staunch royalist Cave would have blanched had he known the journey and transformation awaiting his motto.

When Collinson paid his visit to the fortress-shop, there was no refinement visible. The place resembled a forge or butcher shop. It was a word-factory. The ill-ventilated warren of rooms, rambling halls, and ill-furnished larger spaces bustled with production, boys dashing down hallways with sheaves of copy in hand, authors rummaging through stacks of paper for missing sheets, and the never-ending *thunk-thunk-thunk* of the press.

Samuel Johnson later told Boswell that when he first came to London and "saw St. John's Gate, he beheld it with reverence," as awed as young science hopefuls had been in making the pilgrimage to the meeting house at Crane Court.

We know the man Collinson confronted from several portraits. Cave was a huge man, huge in every direction, a mountain of a person with large protruding eyes, his fat chin collapsed into jowls. His eyes were dark and gleaming, and his nose was straight—a nose that might belong to another face and a higher social class. He had small delicate lips, the exception to the ruinous downward drift of his face.

According to an employee, "he had few of those qualities that constitute the character of urbanity. Upon the first approach of a stranger, his practice was to continue sitting, a posture in which he was ever to be found, and, for a few minutes, to continue silent." Samuel Johnson, who had worked in Cave's shop, had also observed this unsettling strategy. "He was," said Johnson, "watching the minutest accent of those whom he disgusted by seeming inattention; and his visitant was surprised when he came a second time, by preparation to execute the scheme which he supposed never to have been heard."

Collinson came to a publishing agreement with this tradesman. Every advantage went to Cave. The terms were: Franklin would receive no author's payment for his essay, and he and his two London allies would supply the art at their own expense. The printing would be scheduled at Cave's convenience. Once the booklet was printed, from sales Cave would receive every last farthing.

✳

Experiments and Observations on Electricity, Made at Philadelphia in America, by Mr. Benjamin Franklin, and Communicated in several Letters to Mr. P. Collinson, of London, F.R.S. finally appeared in April, 1751. It included all of Franklin's letters ill-treated at the Society, a note on the Leyden jar, a page of charming illustrations, and some corrections and additions appended. The booklet appeared in five English editions during the eighteenth century. Following the splash made later by lightning science, supplements were published in 1753 and 1754 for gentlemen wishing to attach them to the first edition. A second edition (1754) and a third edition (1760) were printed by Cave's shop. The fourth and fifth editions in 1769 and 1774 issued from Cave's successors. Franklin was in London during production of the last two editions, and he made significant revisions to the texts and added other scientific papers.

Experiments and Observations is often portrayed as having great impact and extensive circulation. "Nothing," Joseph Priestley later recalled, "was ever written upon the subject of electricity which was more generally read, and admired in all parts of Europe than these letters." Franklin's booklet found its way into French, German, and Italian translations.

The effort to get the first edition into print, however, proved a struggle. Collinson and Fothergill may have formed their plan in January, 1750, little more than a month after the laughing reception and only a few days after Watson's *how's-the-turkey-killing* summary. Emotions surely boiled up. A February letter to Franklin from Collinson uncharacteristically flares in a single sentence: "Your American electrical operator," he writes, "seems to put ours [Watson] out of countenance by his novelty and variety." Here is the letter where Collinson announces to Benjamin his intention to collect Franklin's electricity letters and "put them into some printer's hand to be communicated to the public." It was not a step to take lightly. Collinson was going to return to the Society with the booklet in his hand. It was a slap in their smug faces. It was to say to Watson and his friends they were wrong. Franklin's letters were the most brilliant electrical science of the era. They should have found a place in the Society's journal.

A year and three months passed before the booklet at last was printed. Why the delay? In a March 27, 1751, letter Collinson complained of the "dilatoriness" of the printer Cave. In fact, part of the time was consumed in corresponding with Franklin, revising by the author, and assembling illustrations. But much of the time lost is unaccounted. The Yale Franklin papers, paraphrasing Cohen's history narrative, explains, "After the immemorial manner of printers, Cave was dilatory."

But this explanation is inadequate. Dilatory? Cave was publishing a monthly magazine, every issue a booklet itself, illustrated with multiple cuts, triple-indexed at year's end, sent out on streets to bookstands promptly on the first day after the month on the labels, done with the exactitude Britons would bring to their railroad system a century later. Samuel Johnson records firsthand the driving energy of production at St. John's Gate. The reality is that Cave's exclusive focus was on the magazine that had turned out to be his pot of gold. It raises questions concerning Collinson's choice of printer.

Why Cave?

Was it the coverage *Gentleman's Magazine* gave to electrical science? Probably not; periodicals issuing from other London printshops also gave extensive coverage to electrical science (at this point *London Magazine* gave more column space to electricity). Was it that Cave had a special expertise in book publication? Rather the reverse; he had published few books and several had amounted to financial disasters. The cobbler's son looked grimly upon book publication.

To examine the pages of *Gentleman's Magazine* is to discover that Collinson was joining ranks with one side on a preexisting battleground. Yes, Cave was enthusiastic about electricity, loyal to the "sons of Newton" undoubtedly, but the printer had bones to pick with William Watson. In 1746 when Watson in high glory had won the Copley and published widely popular booklets, Cave published the anonymous D.D.'s sneering assessment of Watson's worth. Cave also published John Freke, a physician and Tory mystic who bled ink trying to refute Watson. Benjamin Wilson, whose disputes with Watson were well known, was likewise welcomed into the pages of *Gentleman's Magazine,* in addition to essays by Wilson's close friend John Smeaton, whose reports on Wilson's efforts at long-range electrical conduction implicitly questioned Watson's originality.

What did Cave have against Watson? Edward Cave, aka Sylvanus Urban, the center of so much literary communication, left be-hind precious little in the way of self-revelations. But he did share the interests of Society members in science, improvements, inven-tions. This new-rich tradesman purchased a splendid carriage wor-thy of a man of rank, painting on its door perhaps with a sardonic sneer the emblem of his magazine instead of the typical blue-blooded family crest. Perhaps Cave wanted into the Royal Society but was refused. That had soured other men to the celebrities at Crane Court. But we can be sure of one thing.

The shrewd Peter Collinson found in Cave an ally.

What better marketing aid for Franklin than the most popular magazine of the day? Three issues in 1750 of *Gentleman's Magazine* mentioned the upcoming electrical book. And then the April, 1751, issue announced that Franklin's booklet was finally published and could be bought at St. John's Gate. At the June 6 Society meeting, Watson reviewed the booklet, not mentioning points and clouds and electricity, nor the sentry box, but rather noting that he himself brought up many points there reported, and emphasizing the dan-ger of joining Leyden jars in a battery. In the review later published in *Philosophical Transactions* he devoted significantly large space to insignificant parts of Franklin's letter, especially the Franklin boast of turkey killing by electricity.

Perhaps the publication raised Franklin a bit in the eyes of the *virtuosi*. In the fall, a short Franklin letter was not only read at a mid-November meeting but published later in *Philosophical Trans-actions*. It wasn't a major effort on par with his early letters. This note commented on Captain John Waddel's account of the effects of lightning on ships' compasses, but while dealing with magnetism and electricity, Franklin tossed out a suggestion that rods on ships or buildings might conduct the stroke by wire harmlessly into the sea or ground, an offhand remark that would prove to be of immense import in years to come.

The initial impact of *Experiments and Observations* on informed English opinion was slight. Scholar John Heilbron points out that

Franklin's science "was either ignored, as by Wilson and his group, or minimized, as by Watson, who thought it similar to his own." In France, the Abbé Nollet, who knew more international names in electricity than anyone when the Marly success was first reported in 1752, had never heard of Franklin. The Abbé had not seen his booklet.

Franklin's judgment of the success of the first edition is just: "It was however some time before those papers [*Experiments and Observations*] were much taken notice of in England."

Franklin was a rags-to-riches story in his career, a man who often pulled himself up and played against the odds. He was going to be a rags-to-riches story in his electrical science, too. It is likely that after a season or two copies of his booklet mouldered in dank storage at St. John's Gate—or pages of circulated copies served to curl milady's hair, the fate of books that didn't make a splash.

It was all going to come down to one copy of his booklet: a single copy "happening" to cross the English Channel.

XII

Marly

The discoveries made in the Summer of 1752 will make it memorable in the History of Electricity.

ꝗ Abbé Nollet

I N PARIS, FRANKLIN'S BOOKLET CAME INTO THE HANDS OF Georges-Louis Leclerc, known to all the civilized world as Buffon, a celebrity botanist, Versailles favorite, author of *Histoire naturelle,* and superintendent of the king's garden. In the spring of 1752 Buffon made the momentous decision to try Franklin's sentry-box experiment. The site was a sleepy village north of Paris known as Marly-le-ville. Buffon chose two associates, Thomas Dalibard and a professional showman today remembered only as Delor.

Buffon's associates set up their device in a garden on the outskirts of town. They erected a 40-foot iron pole about an inch in diameter, sharply pointed and gilded at the top. A triangle of three wooden poles supported the rod. The pair used glass wine bottles to insulate the device from the ground. The idea was: Lightning would descend but not drain away in the earth. Thus the experimenters could hold a wine bottle with a brass wire affixed to its mouth, present the wire to collect energy from the heavens, and draw a spark.

At 12:20 P.M. on May 10, 1752, with one *boom* of thunder, history was made. When the bolt dropped, Dalibard and Delor were not at the site. We know the exact time, however, because a cleric known only as Raulet, the village priest, had been inducted into their plan. The priest later wrote Dalibard that he noted the minute on the clock as soon as he heard the clap. "The desire to please you," explained the priest, "drew me out of a chair where I was busy reading," and he took off running through the storm to see what had happened.

✳

The events at Marly instantly captured the imagination first at Versailles and soon after in the other capitals of Europe. Over the centuries, the Marly experiment has been portrayed as central to the foundation of electrical science. The resulting narrations, often short and summary and flowery, ignore any context and also fail to bestow so much as a glance at the relationship between what Franklin proposed and what the French in remarkably detailed and rarely quoted accounts in fact did.

In 1979, John Heilbron published *Electricity in the 17th and 18th Centuries,* including a chapter that took a new look at the background of the historic Marly experiment. A number of questions had for long been unanswered. One was, why did Buffon, a botanist, set up this crucial experiment in electrical science? Why hadn't the Abbé Nollet, for instance, or some other leading French electrical experimenter taken the initiative? And why did the men who performed the experiment vanish so completely from electrical science afterward?

The answers are fascinating. Heilbron presented evidence that the effort at Marly grew out of a feud between two distinguished philosophers, Buffon and his enemy René Antoine Ferchault de Réamur. Each of these men had a clique and each exerted great authority over a train of protégés and underlings. Buffon had felt the sting of injury when one of Réamur's favorites had produced a lavish folio volume attacking Buffon and accusing him of encouraging bad science and bad morals in his publications. "His way of reasoning," sniffed the protégé, "is even more revolting than his hypotheses."

How to strike back at Réamur? Buffon soon picked a target, the Abbé Nollet, one of Réamur's dearest protégés. He then had to determine where to get scientific counsel and assistance, especially as his own party lacked anyone intellectually capable of standing up to Nollet in electrical debate. In his *Autobiography* Franklin wrote of his booklet "happening" to come into Buffon's hands. In fact, Franklin had learned a political principle from his treatment by William Watson. Namely: If you approach an institution with new electrical ideas, you don't go to its leading electrical authority. You go to the most powerful *enemy* of the leading electrical authority. In the French edition, the translator reveals what "happening" means. "He [Franklin] asked Mr. Collinson to send one of the first copies to Mr. Buffon," records Dalibard.

Buffon would prove central to Benjamin Franklin's renown as a scientist. If there had been no Buffon, Franklin's science might have remained buried in obscurity.

Buffon was a magnificent physical specimen. He was a tall, extremely muscular man in his mid-forties with an athleticism described admiringly by Voltaire. Portraits reveal the dark haughty eyes of a man who was accustomed to getting what he wanted, the assurance of a man who had reaped a fortune at court. The French published how-to style manuals in the *haute monde*, which included directions for entering a room. No one aced Buffon coming through a doorway. He arrived with a slow sweeping theatricality, turning slowly, hesitating a mere blink or so, *clicking* the door, and with magisterial slowness, turning back to face his admirers.

Some of the *virtuosi* whispered behind his back, calling him *Count All Proud*, a character of amusing self-importance in a popular drama. But to his admirers, Buffon's fabled assurance was the quality that launched that vast intellectual encyclopedia the *Histoire*—the quality that, in fact, would spark a new direction in electrical science. His salon devotees referred to Buffon as *le Glorieux*, regarding him with the adoration some of the English reserved for Sir Isaac Newton.

But there were dark rumors. He was described as a brutal sexual predator whose tastes ran to extremely young girls. In his essay *De la Nature de l'Homme* he wrote with unsettlingly precise knowledge about the sexual responses of girls in early puberty. When microscopes became the mode, he deposited various sperm deposits under his eyepiece, attempting to prove the existence of a Universal Semen. He noted in a later essay, *Discours sur la Nature de Animaux*, that the most glorious sexual act was that which was purely physical, untainted by feeling or regard. At Versailles, Buffon's views seemed so radical that Madame de Pompadour, herself no stranger to sexual adventures, read the essay, found its author, and slapped him smartly across the nose with her folded fan.

Buffon was an unlikely man to join league with the Quakers from London in establishing the scientific reputation of Benjamin Franklin.

And yet he did.

❋

Buffon organized the little sally at Marly to attack his enemies on two fronts. While Dalibard took care of literary business, translating *Experiments and Observations* into French, Delor set up the proper apparatus to perform Franklin's curious experiments and intrigue King Louis XV. Dalibard wrote two new additions and inserted them in Franklin's book, one of these a brief history of electrical science. With only a slender understanding of electrical theory and no status in the field, he conspicuously insulted Abbé Nollet. Though Nollet's name was not used, Dalibard tossed off references to a "blockhead" performing experiments at his Louvre apartment. The implication was that Dalibard, owing to his great tact and warm humanity, would refrain from mentioning the man's name. The Buffon clique had carved up Nollet very well.

When it came to actual electrical experiments, the results were even more splendid. They performed a number of Franklin's early experiments, presenting them as the "Philadelphia experiments," before King Louis XV and his entourage in February of 1752. His Royal Highness was pleased with Buffon's melodramatic flair and the droll combination of high spirits, games, and philosophical insight. His success at court raised the bar for Buffon and it is almost certain that Buffon left the palace already looking ahead to a second installment, a demonstration no one had done—the sentry-box experiment.

*

What force drove the trio to venture the risky experiment? Royal favor had its weight, but there were other factors.

It would be a mistake to think of this era as one solely in which polite gentlemen pursued a science akin to a hobby, where brilliant generalists found in electricity some of the challenges that today one might encounter in a stiff crossword puzzle. There was a genial element in the science of 1752, but the stakes went far beyond "*I'm right and you're wrong*," especially in France.

Heilbron noted the stern consequences of Buffon's feud. Réamur played a role, for instance, in sending one of Buffon's associates, the encyclopedist Denis Diderot, to the royal dungeon in 1749. Indeed, the vitriolic folio attacking Buffon had emphasized his moral perniciousness. The author suggested that Buffon himself needed penal reform.

Great rewards as well as great punishments hung in the balance. As French investors reaped immense fortunes in their rapidly growing colonial expansion, as ships laden with precious and unfamiliar commodities came to port, the Versailles scientists who specialized in studying these discoveries put themselves in a position for plum appointments, but even more alluringly in a position to make fortunes for themselves in the opening of new mass markets. To remember Buffon as the superintendent of the Jardin du Roi, as a man fond of rhododendrons and camellias, is to miss the point. He was also a government contractor who was awarded significant sums of money for planting thousands of trees along French roads. He tended to roses for the king while landing lucrative contracts to supply lumber for the French navy's warships. Benjamin Franklin himself was a scientist who did well in his own milieu with government contracts. But compared to Buffon, Franklin was small potatoes.

*

The resounding note in the journalism that announced the Marly experiment was admiration for the bravery of the French experimenters. Later Franklin wrote to Dalibard praising him "as being the first of mankind that had the courage to attempt draining lightning from the clouds to be subjected to your experiments." But if you look at what happened on the historic date, the man lauded for bravery was eighteen miles away. Dalibard wasn't there. Nor was his supervisor Buffon.

And Delor?

The member of the duo who supplied the expertise and handiness at *doing* experiments, he too found himself that day with business to attend to in Paris.

The man who remained behind with the experiment was an illiterate old soldier known only as Coiffier, who had spent thirteen years as a dragoon and had some rough carpentry skills.

And he wasn't there either.

The sentry box was empty.

Storm clouds had blown up after noon on the historic date. Coiffier was passing the time at such a distance that he couldn't see the device, but he heard a sharp thunderclap, at which "immediately he flew to the machine." Then Coiffier took the glass with the wire and presented the wire to the iron pole. He saw the jump of a small brilliant spark and heard the crackling. He tried a second time. This time a big spark snapped.

Coiffier stood beneath occasional droplets and spatters of hail, flourishing his wire-bottle as if it was a sword. He must have sighed with relief after the terrifying moment had passed when he wondered whether spark or lightning bolt would greet his brass wire. His voice roared. He shouted out to the peasants staring from door stiles, to the field hands. He had survived.

Old Coiffier shouted again.

A boy was sent running to bring the priest.

The metal pole had not been set on anyone's house, an arrangement that would have given structural stability and extended the reach of its point. Remote from Versailles palace, the steeples of Paris, removed even from the modest peak on the local chapel, this was a scientific demonstration initially as popular as a contagious disease. Coiffier began his task alone. When the Marly residents crowded about afterward—with the exception of Raulet—they wouldn't venture within fifteen feet.

When lightning experiments arrived, the *virtuosi* found it inconvenient. At the very start, Buffon, Dalibard, and Delor stayed at the *salon*. For more than four years, Benjamin Franklin had found the lightning experiment he proposed a puzzling inconvenience. Soon William Watson would join the ranks of scientists explaining why they hadn't done anything.

Coiffier was the first man to pull intentionally a spark from heaven.

The fear did not vanish in the mad dash that followed at Marly. The boy dispatched met the priest Raulet who was, as he later assured his superiors in Paris, running "double speed." Upon seeing their priest sprinting down the street the parishioners imagined that poor Coiffier had died for his part in thunderbolt science. The vil-

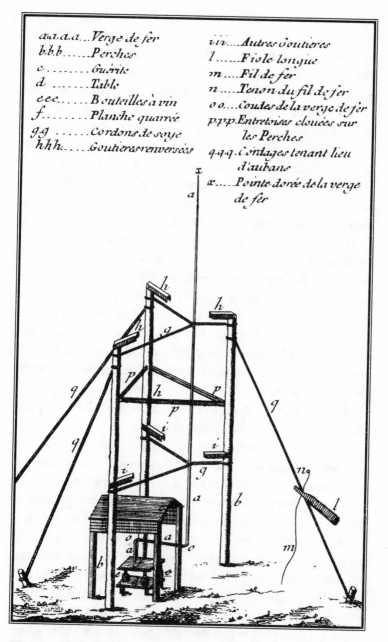

a.a.a.a...Verge de fer
b.b.b......Perches
c.........Guérite
d.......Table
e.e.c......Bouteilles à vin
f.........Planche quarrée
g.g......Cordons de soye
h.h.h......Goutieres renversées

i.i.i....Autres Goutieres
l......Fiole longue
m....Fil de fer
n....Tenon du fil de fer
o.o...Coules de la verge de fer
p.p.p.Entretoises clouées sur
         les Perches
q.q.q.Cordages tenant lieu
         d'aubans
x....Pointe dorée de la verge
         de fer

The apparatus that made history on May 10, 1752 at Marly, France. Dalibard included this how-to-do-it illustration when he published the news.

(BAKKEN LIBRARY AND MUSEUM)

lagers poured into the streets, disregarding the pelting downpour. The air sounded with the spatter of hail on slate roofs and fields, peasant shabots clattering on the road as the flock followed its leader.

When they arrived, Coiffier didn't need last rites or a funeral— he was alive, upright, asking his priest to continue the experiment.

The priest clasped the bottle, extended the wire. Abruptly, a bluish flame hit the extended wire. The smell of sulphur in the air wrinkled noses. The crowd hung back, murmuring with fear. But Raulet repeated the thrust. He did it six times. "Each try that I made," he reported, "lasted the length of an *Our Father* and an *Ave Marie.*"

There was only one thunderclap that day. The storm was moving swiftly overhead, darkening the east, breaking through with sunlight in the west. Brilliant shafts of sunlight fell on them even as the last of the hail peppered down. To this day on the plains of Marly it's the kind of weather combining sunshine and storm that causes the locals to announce that "the devil is marrying his daughter and beating his wife." The eerie light of this strange weather fell on soldier and priest. Raulet wanted to keep discharging the pole, but as the storm blew on, "the fire slowed down little by little."

He tried the wire closer and closer to the pole, but the sparks continued to diminish and finally were gone.

The gentlemen scientists had left explicit orders for their rural assistants. Dalibard instructed Father Raulet and Coiffier to attempt three observations. First, he hoped they might see a luminous glow at the top of the pole—something similar to the gleam appearing at the tip of a needle when brought close to an electrified body in a parlor experiment. Second, he expected them to pull a spark from the pole, if electricity and lightning were identical kinds of energy, the same as the spark pulled, for instance, from an electrified gun barrel. Lastly, Dalibard tossed in a more daunting request. He wanted one of them to take "the sting of these sparks."

Coiffier didn't follow this third direction. He didn't offer up his knuckle.

Nor did the priest Raulet.

But unintentionally, the job was done to Dalibard's satisfaction. In the excitement, in the pummeling of hail, the spattering of fat drops of rain, the priest accidentally took a shock on the arm just above the elbow. "I cannot say," he later remembered, "whether it was from touching the wire or the rod." He ignored the pain in a kind of dissociation as he dashed through the paces of the landmark experiment. But as Raulet and the soldier walked back home afterward, he grew aware of a constant sharp bite on his arm. In the presence of Coiffier as witness, he disrobed his upper garment and revealed a burn neatly circling his arm, as if a wire-whip had lashed him.

Father Raulet also arrived home with a scent. In his report, the priest testified that "the vicar, Mr. De Milly and the school teacher . . . they all complained that they smelled the stink of sulphur." The human body was once again an experimental implement. Events moved quickly. Raulet immediately wrote down his account and dispatched Coiffier with instructions to hurry to their superiors. The early messages swept like battle reports to Paris.

Now lightning science would be pursued in the lanes of the Jardin du Roi and outside shops on the Estrapade and at grand mansions in the Seine River valley outside Paris. The lightning assemblies would include dukes, legendary beauties, and intellectuals. As Raulet handed the letter to Coiffier, its sealing wax still warm, Coiffier was about to drop from sight in electrical history, the experimenter reduced to messenger boy.

Upon arriving in Paris, Coiffier first passed the baton to Delor. As the designer of the construction at Marly, Delor knew what to do next. Delor raised a bar of iron ninety-nine feet high outside his shop on the Estrapade, and late in the afternoon on May 18, a passing thunderstorm supplied him with spectacular results. A day later Buffon and Pierre Bouguer reported similar success at Buffon's chateau in Montbar. In Paris others zealously set up lightning experiments for crowds in public places. Within weeks, the grand sages of Berlin had heard the reports and were also duplicating the lightning experiment.

From the start, the Marly experiment was heralded as proof that lightning and sparks were one and the same. A bit of fuzziness was needed, however, to permit that conclusion.

The point was not exactly proved. None of the witnesses at Marly had seen lightning hit the pole. In fact, in the next month, several French experimenters would discover that the metal pole could flush with electrostatics even when there was no lightning. The pole sometimes electrified under a clear blue sky.

The honor of proving lightning and electricity identical was earned by Louis-Guillaume LeMonnier, a botanist whose temperament didn't fit him for swashbuckling experiments with thunderbolts, a man who preferred the serene pleasures of the garden. A tender fellow, LeMonnier was so shy and humble that when he was introduced to Louis XV, he swooned to the ground. After Nollet published a caustic review of LeMonnier's effort at translating an English scientific treatise, the vulnerable LeMonnier was so crushed he ceased publishing for years.

But he had some great moments in lightning science. One of these came on June 7, 1752, when, as he wrote, a "tempest" gave him the opportunity. He chose to plant his pole in the garden of the Hotel de Noailles. As his account testifies, it was "plainly perceived that at the first flash of lightning that fell on it, the rod was electri-

fied ... [as] according to art. An abundance of persons of indisputable credit were eyewitnesses to the events."

This really *was* the experiment. Lightning dashed down the rod by

The sentry box depicted in Franklin's Experiments and Observations. *Here is the sum of visual help offered would-be lightning experimenters.*

conduction. The charge did not simply gather on the pole by induction. Lightning was at work.

A month later that summer—reported *London Magazine*—another demonstration took place at St. Germain-en-Laye on a terrace overlooking the river. The experimenter was le Noine, the king's physician. As an especially dark cloud passed above, le Noine stepped up on a thick resin cake and proceeded to experiment.

He put his finger in the air.

"One of those who were with him," explained the report, "having touch'd him to make him remark something, he instantly received a most violent shock." A man's forefinger would do as well as a ninety-foot pole, this account suggested. Although electrical science now raised issues for metaphysicians as well as shirt-sleeve experimenters, it could still serve up what the eighteenth century termed a *frolic*.

*

After unleashing Franklin's lightning experiment, the three perpetrators, Dalibard, Delor, and Buffon, dropped out of the picture. The field would be left to competent specialists. Buffon had no further contributions whatsoever to make. *Le Glorieux* found experimental detail boring: "After all," he explained, "a fly ought not to occupy a greater place in the head of a naturalist than it does in nature." The showman Delor disappeared. Despite the joint nature of the project, Dalibard dropped any reference to Delor in the "Avertissement" of the second edition of the French translation of *Experiments and Observations*. Franklin soon discovered that Dalibard was not a sharp instrument. When Dalibard exchanged correspondence, the puzzled Franklin realized that in debate with Nollet, his new disciple was "not yet quite master enough of his subject to do the business effectively." Dalibard offered Franklin other excuses than thickheadedness for his absence from electrical experimentation. He explained that he had no electrical apparatus—perhaps already Buffon had withdrawn his sponsorship. Dalibard also pleaded physical

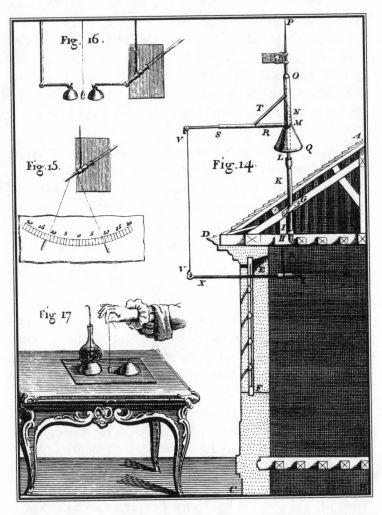

Nollet tested the sentry-box proposal. He devised this elaborate setup (Fig. 14) for dealing with the very real moisture problems a genuine lightning experiment would encounter. (Bakken Library and Museum)

trauma, that after having taken so many shocks, now a single small spark would so numb his hand that he couldn't sign his name for the rest of the day.

Buffon, on the other hand, couldn't have been more happy at how satisfyingly a single electrical experiment advanced his already high-powered career. In the year that followed, he was inducted into the Académie Francaise and an admiring Louis XV made him Comte de Buffon and commissioned the famed sculptor Augustin Pajou to cast him in bronze. Buffon's victim, Abbé Nollet, was less happy.

Nollet returned to a Paris in ecstasy over electrical experiments that he had not first himself conceived or validated. In his view, a foreign scientist had wrested away his place in the sun. "The Abbé Nollet," wrote Buffon, "is dying of chagrin."

Nollet immediately guessed who was the source of the attack on his scientific reputation. "Mr de Buffon is the promoter of the whole business. He does not appear openly himself, because he knows too little about the subject; he has two assistants in his service [Dalibard and Delor] who take care of everything." More exasperating to Nollet was that the lightning experiment, in fact, didn't any more prove the single-fluid theory of electricity than it did his own dual-fluid theory. Indeed, Nollet had already speculated that lightning and electricity were identical and his followers at the Bordeaux Academy in 1749 had announced a contest calling for essays on the subject, bringing the issue to the attention of the entire European scientific community. Nollet immediately wrote letters in self-defense.

But it did no good. An unpublished letter now in the British Library addressed to a member of the Royal Society throws light on the chain of events. It came from Bose, a scientist who knew himself so well how to please a crowd. "Mr. Franklin's terrible concussion is as it were the thunder," announced Bose. Right and wrong and priority were swept aside.

Now Franklin had the thunder.

The deep dread-bolted thunder

❧ KING LEAR

AFTER HIS NAME APPEARED IN NEWSPAPER STORIES ABOUT Marly, Benjamin Franklin would become as essential as Zeus and Thor to the myth of lightning.

Lightning operates in this tale as much a character as Franklin.

Lightning, the only weather phenomenon Jesus Christ is recorded to have mentioned: "I beheld Satan as lightning fall from heaven." The thunderbolt, the power of Zeus's authority—an affliction, but consolation too that mayhem is not random but part of a divine pattern.

Lightning, the flash that struck at Martin Luther's feet on the road to Erfurt, the dazzle and spit that changed his life, leading to the Reformation. And in the grand finale of Homer's *Odyssey*, when Zeus brings an end to the merciless ravages of retributive justice, he flings a shaft of lightning in the vicinity of Odysseus, at last calling the vengeful hero to his senses.

✳

From the start, Franklin's approach to lightning was local and secular. His path differed from that pursued by his rivals across the ocean. He approached lightning through his weekly editing of *The Pennsylvania Gazette.*

Lightning death was common in America. No census records or hospital tallies exist for the period, but if you page through colonial newspapers, it soon turns to a grim business. The lightning deaths seem as prevalent in colonial newspapers as traffic and crime deaths are in today's newspapers.

Most of these eighteenth-century lightning deaths grew out of the fabric of labor culture. Men in the field were overtaken by thunderstorms or outraced the first assault only to take shelter under a lone tree or seek protection, ducking inside an isolated barn in an open field, a cover that when filled with moist, new-mown hay proved especially inviting to the fireworks from above.

Indoors, women workers shared this vulnerability. When the air grew dark, for instance, one young Pennsylvania woman dragged her ironing board to the doorway for better light to do her work by. In those days, ironing boards were metal—the bolt descended, fatally rippling inside under the palm of her hand as she pressed a handkerchief.

Soldiers ran harrowing risks in a thunderstorm. When lightning struck a gunpowder magazine, the impact rivaled twentieth-century bombing damages. In 1763, a storehouse in Jamaica, which stored 12,500 barrels of gunpowder, was hit by lightning. Afterward the survivors could find few human remains but estimated that more than thirty died, and counted more than a hundred injured and maimed. "The explosion was so great," reported a witness, "that not one stone of the magazine or foundation of it is to be seen, but the ground where it was situated is so sunk as to form a large pit, about 10 or 15 feet deep, in which the water is springing up."

Sailors did not fare much better. Under a storm cloud, nothing beckoned more alluringly than the point of a mast.

For years, Franklin the editor was receiving, revising, and writing these reports of lightning death. Paradoxes abounded. He must have puzzled over them, even without science to help. No one could predict with Newtonian mathematics the path of lightning. No one could track its zigzags down. One eighteenth-century author did suggest, likely tongue in cheek, that lightning's shifting path as it descended was the force altering its direction as influenced by sudden prayers below—it looked for the worst offender beneath to reduce to toast.

Lightning deaths were reported by eighteenth-century newspaper writers without their typical abstract vocabulary—especially in one chilling aspect, the evidence of damage. Franklin and his brethren in journalism wrote or, in the hurry of an approaching deadline, lifted many such reports.

The servant girl destroyed at her ironing board, for example, showed "no mark of hurt but a small blue speck under one of her eyes."

The young man "killed by a flash of lightning, which melted his watch, shoe and knee buckles."

The boy trying to outrace the storm home knocked down—"a squirrel he had in his pocket was struck dead with lightning; the child providentially escaped without hurt. The squirrel was taken out of his pocket in the very posture in which it had been sitting, gnawing a grain of corn."

These newspaper accounts from the era remain curious—always the name of the place, the date, the circumstances, perhaps the time of day, the sex of the victim, child or adult, but never the person's name. In a curious way, these police blotter items are more affecting than if the name were given—this is not news, not in the sense that if the name of the injured does not identify friend or relative, the reader remains unscathed, a spectator.

The bolt descended. The lad died.

Everyone had a lad. Franklin often recalled with shining eyes the death of the first child born to Debbie, Franklin Folger Franklin, "our Frankie," who died from smallpox at four years of age. It was bitter irony for Franklin, who was a science enthusiast and a major voice in the colonies favoring smallpox inoculation, that, not wishing to pain this favorite child, he had postponed the inoculation. His anguish lingered.

Lightning was a painful fact but not a transcendent one for Franklin. When he revised his *Experiments and Observations* for the fourth edition, he changed all the spellings of "lightening" to "lightning." The older spelling, "lightening," in Franklin's time also implied the visitation of divine enlightenment.

An altogether different lightning disaster visited England and the Continent. Any number of accounts in the era tell of steeples on great cathedrals hit by lightning that then descended, often down the bellropes, to find a human victim. In Europe, it was widely believed among the pious that if you rang consecrated bells during a thunderstorm, the cathedral and its community would be shielded from lightning stroke. In fact, by the lights of Franklin's later theory, in regard to his doctrine of points, the high tower with the sharpening of its point reaching toward the storm cloud, the attraction of the metal bells, the ropes offering a downward path to the bellringer below, all of this made the whole arrangement a sort of death trap.

Many bellringers went to early graves. But the ancient custom was widely practiced. "It is a dogma of faith," explained Thomas Aquinas, "that the demons can produce wind, storms, and rain of fire from heaven. The atmosphere is a battleground between angels and devils. . . . The aspiring steeples around which cluster the low dwellings of men are to be likened, when the bells in them are ringing, to the hen spreading its protecting wings over its chickens: for the tones of the consecrated metal repel the demons and arrest storms and lightnings."

Of course, when lightning did strike the faithful, the theologians had to offer after-the-fact explanations. Perhaps the church attenders were punished for hidden sins, or possibly the bell had not been properly consecrated.

In the heights, housed by lead roof, hung bells that were often elaborately scribed, boasting *Fulgura frango:* "I break up lightning."

The custom wouldn't die easy even in the decades after Franklin's theories began to spread. In Munich in 1784, an author published a study indicating that in the German states during the years since Franklin announced he had invented the lightning rod in 1752, lightning had taken the lives of 103 bellringers as they pulled at their ropes to ward off disaster.

✳

The month was likely August; the paper, likely *Gentleman's Magazine*, where Franklin learned that he was famous, that the polite world was taking him to its bosom.

Meanwhile, in London at Crane Court, William Watson and his elite circle grimly received the same news from across the Channel. Along the Seine, in the most elegant terraces before the highest people, the French scientists pursued lightning with cavalry-charge ferocity—and offered grand sweeping compliments to Benjamin Franklin with every effort. In 1752, the conditions for thunderstorms blessed Paris.

The British were less fortunate. The Royal Society's Daniel Wray visited France in July. "The weather," he wrote, "has suited extremely the Salmonean projects of those *virtuosi* to rob Jupiter of his thunder and to subject the clouds and storms to their electric laws." In Greek mythology, Salmoneus was the king who drove a chariot dragging bronze kettles behind while he tossed torches in the air, all to create his own version of Zeus's thunder power.

Wray smiled at the competition among the French: "If one made an experiment another instantly laid claim to it with a '*Zounds that's my Thunder.*'" And he knew what these events would mean to the men at Crane Court: "It will go hard with Lord Charles [Cavendish] and Watson."

The French showed no mercy. "You may assure the ladies in your part of the world," one wrote to London, "that we are doing our best here to secure them against thunder and lightning; not forgetting some of your pretty fellows, who, with all their courage, may possibly be no less terrified by thunder than the ladies."

While French scientists performed lightning experiments before King Louis XV, there were only two successful lightning experiments in England. Neither was staged for his Royal Highness. Nor did the English experimenters belong to the clique that met behind the veil at Rawthmell's. Both were relative outsiders, the schoolmaster John Canton of Spitalsfield and Benjamin Wilson, the impertinent young upstart that the Society had closed its doors upon.

William Watson made a valiant effort. Although he and his Crane Court associates had managed to "prepare and set up the necessary apparatus for his [Franklin's] purpose, we were defeated in our expectations, from the uncommon coolness and dampness of the air here, during the whole summer. We had only at London one thunderstorm; *viz.*, on July 20; and then the thunder was accompanied with rain; so that, by wetting the apparatus, the electricity was dissipated. . . . This, I say, in general prevented our verifying Mr. Franklin's hypothesis."

Nor did John Canton's experiment add much luster to British science. The schoolmaster performed it in his garden, poking a three-foot tin tube toward the skies; to protect himself, he wangled it on a glass handle eighteen inches in length. During a storm he collected enough energy to elicit a few relatively mild snaps.

Benjamin Wilson's attempt deserves more notice. He wrote in his unpublished memoir:

I *repeated* the experiment with success, during the first thunderstorm which happened here; whilst I was upon a visit to my friend Mr. Brownsmith near Chelmsford in Essex. We were at the time amusing ourselves with acting one of Shakespeare's plays; I performed the part of Harry the fourth. In the interim the storm came on: I run out in my royal robes, and got a clean, dry, quart bottle; into the neck of which, I put a curtain rod, and fastened, to the upper end of it, a pin or needle, I forget which, and then stood upon the bowling green before the house with the bottom of the bottle in my hand. Immediately, I collected as much of the electric fluid in the iron rod, as afforded sparks of fire, and all my fellow comedians [actors] not only saw the sparks but caused sparks themselves by approaching the rod with their fingers.

Theater is always satisfying in scientific displays, but it eluded the Royal Society that summer. Watson dutifully concluded his December letter to his fellow members: "Trifling as the effects here mention'd are, when compared with those, which we have received from Philadelphia and Berlin, they are the only ones, that the last summer here has produced."

✳

If you look behind the newspaper announcements that year at Franklin's personal letters, you get a plain and very different picture. He doesn't sound like a man vindicated. A letter of September 28, 1752, written to his friend Colden weeks or even days after learning of his celebrityhood, strikes a different tone: "I see by Cave's *Magazine* for May," writes Franklin, "that they have translated my electrical papers into French and printed them in Paris."

Franklin didn't mention to his friend the focus of the news announcement and what was ultimately more important—and disturbing. *Gentleman's Magazine* announced that the French were doing experiments "in pursuance of those by Mr Franklin . . . to find whether tonitrous [lightning] and electrical matter be not analogous."

What were they doing? Even if the sentry box had been proposed as serious science, the question would have taken Franklin's breath away. After all, he had never done the sentry-box experiment. What risks were these strangers assuming?

"I hope," continues Franklin in his letter to Colden, "[that] our Friend Collinson will procure and send me a copy of the translation [used by Buffon et al.]. Such things should be done by men skilled in the subject as well in the language, otherwise great mistakes are easily made, and the clearest matters rendered obscure and unintelligible."

The concern with mistranslation voiced immediately after the news echoes decades later in a fascinating passage of a rarely quoted letter from Franklin's sister, Jane Mecom, his favorite among the many siblings. He must have spoken to her about translation error, although her topic in the March 27, 1780, letter to Benjamin is the reliability of portrait artists depicting him. "But if the artists," writes Jane Mecom, "that have taken your face have varied as much from each other as that affixed to your philosophical papers done in France some years ago from the copy, it will appear as changeable as the moon."

Meanwhile, the events of 1752 moved on. The July issue of *Gentleman's Magazine* arrived with the news that Franklin's experiments had spread to Belgium. At Brussels a Sieur Torre, a local experimenter, had affixed an iron rod to his house for collecting electricity during storms. We know Franklin received this news because he reprinted it in the September 28 edition of his own *Gazette*. Torre's apparatus apparently had not been grounded. Torre had enthused that the rod was of "great use in diminishing the quantity of fire from whence thunder is formed and in preventing the fatal effects of lightning."

Assembled in October to be sold at the great November market, *Poor Richard's Almanack* offers insights into what is on Franklin's mind every autumn, often in ways this genius at covering his own tracks must never have intended. The mottoes invented reflect the man rather obviously. But others borrowed or nicely rephrased, in their choice, also serve to tell us what his concerns are. For instance, the year he debates plans to hand over his business to David Hall, he advises, "He that by the plow would thrive,/himself must either hold or drive." The almanac for 1753, distributed in November of 1752, contained an unusual item. The motto was about science, invented by himself, addressed to himself perhaps, the only natural philosopher among his many subscribers. He wrote:

Philosophy as well as foppery often changes fashion.

＊

Even if Franklin hadn't announced that his lightning science had made him a famous man in Europe, his friends and neighbors would soon enough have learned the news from periodicals from abroad. Questions would be asked locally. No six-month delay to pen an answer. He had to have answers ready.

The French had called their demonstration the Philadelphia Experiment, establishing a logical corollary. When was the Philadelphia Experiment going to be done in Philadelphia? Every distant rumbling on the horizon would have brought home this question to the new celebrity. His friends would have turned to him with questions, expecting new theatrical displays.

There was a huge sky above Franklin late that summer.

Citizen of the World

XIV

The Kite

That which deceives, also enchants.

≫ PLATO

O N OCTOBER 19, 1752, *The Pennsylvania Gazette* PUBLISHED
a brief article. It announced that Benjamin Franklin had
flown an electric kite. The author, Franklin, also sent the item on to
England care of Peter Collinson, who relayed it to the Royal Society, where it was promptly read aloud. After years of neglect, Franklin would find this piece within a bit more than a year in
Philosophical Transactions among other articles exploring the new
experimental arena he had opened up.

The kite is landmark science. It is, of course, a bit of New World
impertinence, a serious experiment carried out with a child's toy.
There is bravado in the account of the American directly con-
fronting nature at its most deadly and bringing home scientific
truth.

No scientific experiment has been half such a favorite among

American artists. Images of Franklin's electric kite proliferated in fine art, ceramics, educational materials, currency, calendars, and didactic works. It is the only scientific experiment ever depicted on U.S. currency. The zest of this imaginative enthusiasm infected men of letters and science historians, too. Histories might keep a hardnosed focus on dates and documents, but couldn't pass up Franklin's kite without a bit of rhapsodizing. The nineteenth century exulted over this event, as one typical account relates:

> But God, as if pleased with such disinterested virtue, determined to reserve to Franklin the honour of confirming his own great theory. His plan to accomplish this, was in that simplicity which characterizes all his inventions. . . . The lightning soon found out his metallic rod, as it soared aloft on the wings of the kite and greeted its polished point with a cordial kiss. With joy he beheld the loose fibers of his string raised by the fond salute of the celestial visitant.

An early twentieth-century author rambled for several pages. A few culled moments give a sense of how it goes:

> Why should he fear ridicule now? . . . And with death he now believed he was to stand face to face . . . as the storm abates . . . on the thankful upturned face of the man gleams the glad sunshine.

The French and Italians shared this special enthusiasm for Franklin the kite-flier. Sabine declared, "Benjamin Franklin succeeded in one of the boldest experiments ever made by man upon the powers of nature—and from that moment he became immortal." Even Immanuel Kant, the sober and meticulous German, couldn't resist nominating Franklin as the "Modern Prometheus."

So many paintings and literary works have gloried in the event, it has been so often depicted in calendars, textbooks, and school posters, that now after transmission across more than two and a half centuries, often with details wrong or invented, the electric kite has become an icon. An icon does not have to be understood to be held onto. But there are two aspects of the event that need explanation.

First, in essence, Franklin's science is as simple as the kite itself.

He flew his kite near storm clouds, using the kite to deliver the twine near clouds and see what came back down the twine from above. He reported the same snaps, the same capacity for charging a Leyden jar. Lightning, of course, did not come down his twine that day. But he drew the not unlikely conclusion that the flicker and snap in the parlor science was the same energy as the flash and boom of lightning, the differences only ones of scale.

Second, for all the enormity of the experiment, its broad transmission, the proliferation of its many imagings, if you look for authentic sources, the icon turns out to be supported by two startlingly slender documents. The first is Franklin's newspaper announcement. The other is secondhand, based on interviews with Franklin that took place fourteen years after and that very possibly received his editorial supervision. This curious late addition enters a few new details into the narrative and erases others.

Here is the first account directly from Franklin as later published in *Philosophical Transactions:*

As frequent mention is made in the public papers from Europe of the success of the Philadelphia experiment for drawing the electric fire from clouds by means of pointed rods of iron erected on high buildings, &c., it may be agreeable to the curious to be informed, that the same experiment has succeeded in Philadelphia, tho' made in a different and more easy manner, which any one may try, as follows:

Make a small cross, of two light strips of cedar; the arms so long, as to reach to the four corners of a large thin silk handkerchief, when extended: tie the corners of the handkerchief to the extremities of the cross; so you have the body of a kite; which being properly accommodated with a tail, loop, and string, will rise in the air like those made of paper; but this, being of silk, is fitter to bear the wet and wind of thunder-gust without tearing.

To the top of the upright stick of the cross is to be fixed a very sharp-pointed wire, rising a foot or more above the wood.

To the end of the twine, next the hand, is to be tied a silk riband; and where the twine and silk join, a key may be fasten'd.

The kite is to be raised, when a thunder-gust appears to be coming on, (which is very frequent in this country) and the person, who holds the string, must stand within a door, or window, or under some cover, so that the silk riband may not be wet; and care must be taken, that the twine does not touch the frame of the door or window.

As soon as any of the thunder-clouds come over the kite, the pointed wire will draw the electric fire from them; and the kite, with all the twine, will be electrified; and the loose filaments of the twine will stand out every way, and be attracted by the approaching finger.

When the rain has wet the kite and twine, so that it can conduct the electric fire freely, you will find it stream out plentifully from the key on the approach of your knuckle.

At this key the phial may be charged; and from electric fire thus obtain'd spirits may be kindled, and all the other electrical experiments be performed, which are usually done by the help of a rubbed glass globe or tube, and thereby the sameness of the electric matter with that of lightning completely demonstrated.

I was pleased to hear of the success of my experiments in France, and that they there begin to erect points upon their buildings. We had before placed them upon our academy and state-house spires.

Despite its narrative flow, this is more generic than many eighteenth-century news items. No witness, no location named, no year, no month, no day, no hour supplied. More importantly, it is also the exact opposite of what would have been expected in the Age of

Reason for an account of a serious, major scientific experiment. The Marly experimenters reported the month, the hour, the minute, the location, and brought in the village priest to sign his signature as a witness. They produced a document whose tone is legalistic and whose details are so abundant and clear and reemphasized with a picture that any scientist could repeat the effort. The English electricians operated in the same mode. When Watson had done his landmark experiments trying to measure the velocity of electricity, he wrote extensive and detailed reports, he repeated his efforts on numerous occasions, reporting time and place, and he brought along as witnesses men who were of near-celebrity status and known for their reliability and honor and also tradesmen famous in their passion for accuracy and precision.

For all the large-scale, public demonstrations from France, the several efforts in England and Scotland, for all the European demonstrations performed before eyewitnesses and buttressed with attesting signatures, for all Franklin's own delight in repeating his other experiments for the benefit of crowds, for all his associates' many public displays of his other original experiments, neither Franklin nor his associates ever performed his most celebrated experiment for anyone.

Fourteen years afterward—in a secondhand account written by his disciple Joseph Priestley—a witness surfaces. The witness brought forward is Benjamin's natural son, William, a nonscientist, known among some of the better families in Philadelphia as a scalawag. Did William witness the event? He never wrote a word or breathed a syllable about it, as far as is known. But it is worth noting that William was also the person on the planet most intimate and involved in Franklin's hoaxes, the correspondent whose father cautioned him, "Keep all this to yourself."

Despite its importance, the kite experiment is the only science in the Franklin canon that was not given the benefit of report as scientific correspondence. Franklin's friends noticed the discrepancy.

From New York, Cadwallader Colden wrote him, "I have . . . seen in the newspapers the account of the electrical kite. I hope a more perfect and particular account will be published in a manner to preserve it better and to give it more credit than it can obtain from a common newspaper." There is no evidence Franklin ever answered him. A survey of the Franklin/Colden correspondence finds Franklin remarkably quick to answer other information requests from Colden.

*

One concern that appeared very early involved the timing of Franklin's report. The account that appears fourteen years afterward mentions June, 1752—not a date, but a month. The first account did not even give a month. At issue is a claim of priority. First, the Franklin account doesn't claim he was first. He doesn't say second either. The experiment has been done in Philadelphia is all he says. The Marly experiment went off on May 10, 1752.

Franklin's June claim surfaces not as a claim of priority, but one of independence. June dates the kite experiment before he would have heard the news from Europe (the ship transit alone required six weeks). It was a me-too experiment, but glorious withal of course, because Franklin conceived what the French did.

But if Franklin's lightning experiment happened in June, perhaps early June, why wait nearly four months to report such an important event? Why did his formerly very public science suddenly go so private? A few twentieth-century scholars have sifted through the evidence and speculate that possibly Franklin didn't fly his electric kite until late in September. There is another scenario. In *The Pennsylvania Gazette* dated September 28, 1752, Franklin published an account of the early lightning experiments performed in Belgium. The report was similar to and probably lifted from the *Gentleman's Magazine* July, 1752, issue. It's possible that after publishing this report, Franklin dreamed up his own kite claim to announce in the *Gazette*.

If you look carefully at the first account, you will notice that nowhere does Franklin say he actually performed the experiment.

The verbs are future conditional tense, mere falsetto pipe notes where you might expect the basso profundo of the active voice for stating such a magnificent triumph. It's a strange verbal key for a master of English prose to assume. He's usually a writer who can flex his muscle. It's the gift that enables him to turn a soggy old proverb into a zinger. Franklin at times uses future conditional tense and passive verbs, but these are passages, nothing like the entire woof and warp of the October announcement and not likely to be used when he was actively seeking credit for a breakthrough. For example, in his letter to George Whatley, an old London friend, describing the invention of bifocal glasses and in his "Description of an Instrument for Taking Down Books from High Shelves" Franklin is unambiguous; he invented both items, he writes at length, he gives specifics, he uses active voice, he offers diagrams, *he says he did it.*

Lastly concerning text—importantly concerning this major announcement so sketchy and elusive of detail, the author later, without signaling his audience, changed it. Hidden behind the verbal surface of the fifth edition of his collected electrical writings, which were transmitted across the centuries and published as the version of choice by the twentieth century's leading Franklin science scholar, is a different kite text, the one Franklin's rivals in the field of experimental science first encountered. There are two changes. Franklin took out his encouragement to readers "which any one may try." A man would die doing this science. More unsettling for the histories, he removed the paragraph that claimed lightning rods were already installed on two important public buildings in Philadelphia. The lightning rod claim never appeared in his own local paper. The removal sparks a doubt: Did it happen? And if this much of the fabric of the kite text is false, the rest too is suspect.

✻

The most convincing evidence against the kite story, however, comes from the experimental detail of the story itself.

One problem has to do with water on the kite line.

In *Experiments and Observations* Watson demonstrated that even a bit of moisture in the air could dissipate the charge on the twine and ruin an experiment. Franklin knew of Watson's findings and, as a doer, had likely experienced similar difficulties.

Weather conditions and gravity would have created this problem by drawing rainwater down the kite line. The kite line is above the insulating silk ribbon. When the rainwater moistens the twine and moves down it, the water will continue freely over the surface of the silk, and although electricity will not conduct easily through silk, it will stream freely over the silk's wet surface and then through the body of the experimenter into the ground, foiling any result.

At Marly, the French faced this difficulty head-on. To prevent the electricity from dissipating by water on the ropes that supported the rod, they attached covers (*gouttières renversees*) over the rope connections. This problem of wet apparatus ruined Watson's attempt that summer. And according to Guillaume Mazeas, French correspondent to the Royal Society, the French experimenters first doubted the Marly results because of their own "want of success [due] to the abundance of rain, that wet the cakes of resin [an insulator], which they used to support the bar of iron."

Franklin gets this wrong. In building to his climax, he writes, "When the rain has wet the kite and twine, so that it can conduct electric fire freely . . ." But you don't need moisture because dry packing twine conducts electricity freely. A host of experimenters from Stephen Gray to Benjamin Wilson to the French experimenters all testified to that. The ideal condition for the kite experiment is beneath thunder clouds before a drop of rain has fallen, obviating any need for devices such as the ones used at Marly to prevent the silk from getting wet. In our era, experiments discharging lightning from clouds by rocket-and-wire techniques indicate that a small amount of moisture can make twine fairly conducting. But Franklin, swept along by imagination, playing up the drama of the storm, souses the science. In the 1760s, his enthusiastic supporter Joseph Priestley also gets carried away and adds to his second version of the story abundant rain.

This experiment was created by Franklin and Priestley fourteen years afterward for readers, not for doers. If you decide to do this experiment, your attention to what is explained (and what is not) suddenly sharpens.

No one in Franklin's time knew that the lightning bolt's temperature was 50,000° Fahrenheit, five times the heat on the surface of the sun, but anyone who had stood near the blast of a thunderbolt or looked at a corpse after lightning-strike would get the idea.

This is a big experiment, big conceptually, big in creating the first international American celebrity, and big if you come along later and try to duplicate it, big in the sense you are taking your life in your hands.

At that point, every word counts.

What is coming down the string? Is it lightning or the "electrical fire" from polite social games? If it's lightning, the hemp is a conductor. If it's the lesser energy of the games, the hemp has collected this energy by induction. In the first account, Franklin is fairly clear on this point. He refers to "electrical fire." But the second account is another matter. Priestley warms to his task. "Dr Franklin," he writes, "astonishing as it must have appeared, contrived actually to bring lightning from the heavens." This is not a mere slip. It is Priestley's grand theme. "This lightning descended by the hempen string," exclaims Priestley. The Currier & Ives image of the kite experiment takes its cue from Priestley's dramatic excess, the enthused artist depicting the kite aloft, a bolt flashing across the darkness of a nearby cloud, perhaps a millisecond from coursing down the kite string. In a sense, the hint comes from Franklin's news item. Near the end of the account, with the power of a long sentence building to this point, Franklin unleashes the claim that "thereby the sameness of the electric matter with that of lightning [are] completely demonstrated." *Completely.* Boy, that one slides by. Prose that has been cautious, matter-of-fact, suddenly goes for it all. It doesn't completely demonstrate, of course. It raises the kind of likelihood that people navigate by in everyday life, not in science. In fact, the experiment demonstrating that lightning and electricity are one and the same didn't happen at Marly either. That honor went to humble little LeMonnier.

Present-day lightning experiments conducted by the International Center for Lightning Research and Testing in Florida, an international consortium, and also ones performed by NASA, demonstrate what would have happened if Franklin had flown a kite that retrieved lightning. It would not have been a matter of any odds at all, but a certainty. When modern experimenters fire rockets trailing wire toward thunderclouds, on contact the lightning always flashes down the wire. What happens to the wire at 50,000°? The same thing that would befall eighteenth-century packing thread. It vaporizes—leaving behind a column of ionized air.

Franklin's experiment strikes a different note. It does not envision fatality; the experiment is to be done in an "easy manner, which any one may try." But did Franklin always think that way? As we know in his letter to Dalibard, he thanks the Frenchman for first attempting the "Philadelphia Experiment," acknowledging that it was a very brave act. Franklin praises Dalibard as "the first of mankind, that had the courage to attempt drawing lightning from the clouds."

*

The second account of Franklin's kite appears in 1767 in Priestley's *History and Present State of Electricity*. Priestley seems to have based his kite narrative on an interview with Franklin, but recent scholarship from the Papers of Benjamin Franklin project at Yale University points to heavier editorial involvement by Franklin. Here is Priestley's version:

> To demonstrate, in the completest manner possible, the sameness
> of the electric fluid with the matter of lightning, Dr. Franklin,

astonishing as it must have appeared, contrived actually to bring lightning from the heavens, by means of an electrical kite, which he raised when a storm of thunder was perceived to be coming on. This kite had a pointed wire fixed upon it, by which it drew the lightning from the clouds. This lightning descended by the hempen string, and was received by a key tied to the extremity of it; that part of the string which was held in his hand being of silk, that the electric virtue might stop when it came to the key. He found, that the string would conduct electricity even when nearly dry, but that when it was wet, it would conduct it quite freely; so that it would stream out plentifully from the key, at the approach of a person's finger.

At this key he charged phials, and from electric fire thus obtained, he kindled spirits, and performed all other electrical experiments which are usually exhibited by an excited globe or tube.

As every circumstance relating to so capital a discovery as this (the greatest, perhaps, that has been made in the whole compass of philosophy, since the time of Sir Isaac Newton) cannot but give pleasure to all my readers, I shall endeavour to gratify them with the communication of a few particulars which I have from the best authority.

The Doctor, after having published his method of verifying his hypothesis concerning the sameness of electricity with the matter lightning, was waiting for the erection of a spire in Philadelphia to carry his views into execution; not imagining that a pointed rod, of a moderate height, could answer the purpose; when it occurred to him, that, by means of a common kite, he could have a readier and better access to the regions of thunder than by any spire whatever. Preparing, therefore, a large silk handkerchief, and two cross sticks, of a proper length, on which to extend it, he took the opportunity of the first approaching thunder storm to take a walk into a field, in which there was a shed convenient for his purpose. But dreading the ridicule which too commonly attends unsuccessful attempts in science, he communicated his intended experiment to no body but his son, who assisted him in raising the kite.

The kite being raised, a considerable time elapsed before there was any appearance of its being electrified. One very promising cloud had passed over it without any effect; when, at length, just as he was beginning to despair of his contrivance, he observed some lose threads of the hempen string to stand erect, and to avoid one another, just as if they had been suspended on a common conductor. Struck with this promising appearance, he immediately presented his knuckle to the key, and (let the reader judge of the exquisite pleasure he must have felt at that moment) the discovery was complete. He perceived a very evident electric spark. Others succeeded, even before the string was wet, so as to put the matter past all dispute, and when the rain had wetted the string, he collected electric fire very copiously. This happened in June 1752, a month after the electricians in France had verified the same theory, but before he had heard of any thing that they had done.

Besides this kite, Dr. Franklin had afterwards an insulated iron rod to draw the lightning into his house, in order to make experiments.

If you compare the end of the first account with the beginning of this, there's a very similar phrase ("to demonstrate, in the completest manner possible, the sameness of the electric fluid with the matter of lightning"). Priestley has started at the bottom of Franklin's earlier page.

The narration in Priestley's account of the electric kite exhibits the enthusiasm he brought to all his writings. But if you look at the content, this exultant new version not only adds things but takes things out. Just as Franklin removed the claim of lightning rods on the State House and academy, so does Priestley. Vanished also is the claim that this is easy science that "any one may try."

And if you look again, the realization dawns that almost everything added is a response to pointed questions surely asked. One exception is a bit of dramatic huffing and puffing, the waiting, the wondering, will-the-cloud-pass-and-nothing-happen? That done, to the questions addressed by Priestley.

First, why were there no witnesses?

There was. Priestley supplies the ever-silent William Franklin.

Second, why was this experiment not done in public? Why was it kept secret?

Priestley explains that Franklin did the experiment in secrecy because he was afraid of being embarrassed if the experiment failed. Be wary of this one. In fact, there was no individual in colonial America less plagued by embarrassment than Benjamin Franklin. He walked about Philadelphia for decades with his bastard son at his heels, to the recorded disgust and horror of some of the genteel people on whom his career depended. In a crisis, Franklin often struck a disarming note of self-blame, a tactic that may have served him better than his enemies, who only knew to attack. His lack of embarrassment proves a sort of moral strength much later as the colonial representative in England when standing before the Privy Council he meekly endures a savage verbal lashing at the hands of Solicitor General Lord Wedderburn concerning a political letter Franklin may have purloined.

Third question. How do you fly the electric kite out a window? This is not quite pushing a camel through the needle's eye, but it ranks up there.

Franklin originally describes an experiment done "within a door, or window, or under some cover." This suggests a house. Priestley supplies a shed. Yet even a shed presents difficulties. A third kite story narrator discounted by scholars in our time, William Stuber, wrote about the experiment and did away with all the logistics and, contrary to all Franklin's advice, simply put Franklin beneath a tree. Things, of course, don't necessarily improve with time. The current edition of the *World Book* encyclopedia includes a picture of Franklin in a lightning storm flying his kite in an open field.

Another question Priestley dispatches is: After proposing the Philadelphia Experiment, why did you delay for three years before you did your own lightning experiment?

Priestley's answer is the oft-repeated fiction that Franklin was awaiting "the erection of a spire in Philadelphia to carry his views into execution." As discussed earlier, Franklin had access to a lofty spire for the performance of lightning experiments from April, 1751, onward, the date the belfry tower was attached to the academy under Franklin's personal supervision.

✳

Priestley aside, we need to look at the eighteenth-century *things* in the tale.

For starters, the key. What kind of key might Franklin have used?

The key a tradesman in Philadelphia in the 1750s kept at hand was a latch key. It is imaginable but not likely that Franklin possessed a key for an armoire or desk. As the *Gazette* often reported, this was not the halcyon era of the always-open door—in part because of shiploads of criminals the mother nation was continually dumping on the colony. This led to waves of burglaries, "breaking open a house," Philadelphians called it. In the last week of October, 1750, Franklin's house had been "broken open."

The latch key was serious business. A Philadelphia latch key was a big chunk of brass, it might weigh a quarter of a pound, heavy enough to damage the fabric in your coat pocket if carried there, a nuisance causing the key to be kept upstairs. When you arrived home, you shouted up above and a family member tossed you the key, with the consideration to bark out a warning first so you didn't get brained.

For this experiment to have worked, the key would have had to float submissively at just the right height. The truth is, it likely dropped like an anchor.

The nineteenth-century Currier & Ives artist bravely confronted this problem. This poor man has provided good fun for generations of Franklin biographers, who note the many errors committed by the unfortunate illustrator, depicting William Franklin as a small boy when he was in fact nineteen, placing the brave father and son under a tree during an electrical storm (contrary to Franklin's advice), illustrating Franklin holding the kite twine above the key. Bad electrical science—the point of Franklin's story is that his contact with the contraption is below the key, "insulated" from twine and key by a few inches of silk. But the blurry image at the heart of this fanciful experiment is bad science too.

The Currier & Ives artist hurrying to meet a calendar company deadline may not have had the time or the archival resources to research this image. But he did get a few details right. He did include

FRANKLIN'S EXPERIMENT, JUNE 1752.
Demonstrating the identity of Lightning and Electricity. from which he invented the Lightning Rod.

The often reprinted image from the nineteenth-century calendar publisher Currier & Ives.

a mid-eighteenth-century colonial house key. He also faced squarely one of the tale's inherent improbabilities.

How do you keep the key off the ground?

The artist was inspired. You hold the string *above* the key. This is bad science, of course, for the man holding the twine instead of the silk ribbon would drain the electricity into the earth as effectively as the chunk of brass itself resting on the ground. But the essence of the illustrator's problem really is this: trying to depict something that may have never happened.

Three years earlier, in 1749 in Scotland, Alexander Wilson had announced using kites in scientific experiments for temperature readings of the atmosphere. He and Franklin shared the challenge of getting enough lift. Wilson's solution was to devise a multi-kite train linked by twine to raise his thermometer in the air. This was much more kite than Franklin claimed.

＊

On to the main item, the kite. When you look at the design of Franklin's kite, there is good news and bad news. The good news is that the kite described was common in colonial America. The bad news is that the two-stick flat kite required a large tail to give it adequate stability. Although the Malaysians had known for centuries about bowing the sticks to do away with heavy tails and to increase lift and reduce drag, the Western world had not yet made that discovery. Not until 1898 when William Eddy of Bayonne, New Jersey, designed a bowed kite would it have been available to Philadelphians. Franklin needed every bit of lift he could devise because he had attached a rigid metal rod on top and a heavy key below. His design also required a heavy tail—made of broadcloth perhaps—which would grow significantly heavier if—as he described—it was wet by a rainstorm. One crucial issue was going to boil down to: How big was his kite? Put simply, how big the lift?

His paragraph starts with the adjective *small*. It is the first note, the *small* cross, and the wood was cedar, not a typical choice today, but an excellent wood because it is light and flexible, probably red cedar, which admiring visitors of the era report as so common in the colony it was even used for fence posts. Franklin chose silk rather than paper for his kite—both provided lightness, but silk was more likely to bear the wind and wetness of a thunder-gust without tearing. The second note in his account is *large*. He indicated "a large thin silk handkerchief." This goes almost without saying—he needs every milligram of lift and the silk had to be long enough to tie knots around the four extremities of the cedar cross. No staples, no twine knots, no catgut loop, and more bad news, the flouncy bows of the four knots further downsize the kite and add to the drag of this already inefficient kite. But what would a large handkerchief have meant to a Philadelphia tradesman in 1752?

There are two possibilities. One was perhaps a ten-inch square; the other, a thirty-inch square. Was it a man's item? Probably not, little is known about men's handkerchiefs from the time, but historians speculate that a small man's pocket handkerchief must have been used in taking snuff. The small woman's handkerchief, however, was the glory of the fashionable in that era, a stylish accessory, lined typically with lace, whose cut and jib and color came from Paris, required and conspicuously consumed by South Front Street matrons and their daughters.

The thirty-by-thirty handkerchief was different. The Quaker women took this large handkerchief, folded it into a triangle, wrapped it around their shoulders, and modestly tied the ends across the bodice. The Mennonite women of the Delaware river valley and also other Pennsylvania Germans wore similar covers and called it a *Bruschttuch*, breast cloth.

Which did Franklin use?

There's a problem. You don't get large and silk both, especially *thin* silk, which rather than covering would allow you to stare at Quaker cleavage. Silk was the expensive fabric of the French ten by ten. And from the earliest days, Quakers had moral reservations about silk: "The visit of a Quaker evangelist," wrote one historian, "was followed by an event called the 'burning of the braveries,' in which people made a bonfire of their ribbons and silks." William Penn himself had tried to dissuade his colonials from expensive dress: "If thou art clean and warm it is sufficient, for more doth rob the poor," he argued. There were, of course, exceptions as the older families grew wealthy, and "Jack-in-the-box" Quakers, who followed their beliefs only on First Day, the Quaker term for Sunday, but tales about them were anecdotal reports. As late as 1788, a visitor at a Philadelphia yearly meeting reported that 90 percent of the Quakers were dressed in plain homespun. Silk was not only a fashion statement but a religious statement.

A large silk handkerchief kite would always be possible, but unlikely in a story filled with other unlikelys. Franklin presents the entire project as the work of a man dealing in the everyday, with what is typically at hand.

Next, the shed. Only one side of a shed will permit this experiment, because the storm blows in from one direction. In that era, some sheds only had one opening, they weren't made for wind or creature access. You're up against some odds, perhaps a calculation based on shed openings, plane orientation of structure sides, wind direction, size of window or door (bigger would help), and distance of the kite flier from opening. A distance back from the window is helpful to stay dry but narrows the angle available to the kite string. Near even to the plane of the window frame gives greater flexibility with wind direction, but if rain falls on the silk it destroys the experiment.

Once again we have entered the thicket of unlikelys, a trip entirely unnecessary if you're a reader, an unavoidable necessity for the doer. But on.

The best arrangement would seem to be a shed with no sides, merely a supporting timber at each corner. In a thunderstorm, nineteenth-century artists depicting the kite tale dove for just that design. Legions of Victorian and early twentieth-century artists depicted Franklin under its cover. There was, however, a vernacular agricultural architecture for the Delaware valley mid-eighteenth century. The four-sides-open structure is not a Quaker shed, but a Dutch hay barrack. Possibly a short walk away from Franklin's home, but historically much more possible on the east side of the river in New Jersey.

The seeming advantages of even an open New Jersey shed fall away when the experiment is done. The shed liberates the kite flier from horizontal instabilities on his line. But the true difficulties are mostly vertical. You pull the line in to go high; you let the line out for distance. The whole point of Franklin's experiment is height— he's reaching for the clouds. The necessity for height requires the line to be flown perilously close to the frame of window, door, or open shed alike, mere inches in turbulent weather from the experiment fouled.

More operational difficulties facing the kite flier are the ones faced nowadays by jet pilots landing in bad weather. When a storm arrives, there are fierce downdrafts along its front, called wind shears. When the air of the downdraft hits the earth, it immediately bounces up like a ball. It would make for rough kite flying. Later in the eighteenth century, an obscure little man named Tiberius Cavallo did perform an extended series of electric kite experiments at a house in Islington, London, meticulously recording his results over many months (never in lightning weather), and he at times did fly a kite from his window, but he also records experiments foiled by moisture and the wind dashing his kite line against the window frame.

✳

Finally, a major inconsistency of Franklin's kite narrative is that it is simply not characteristic of the way his mind worked. The glory of his Leyden jar experiments is that they are a sequence of experiments, one deftly pointing to the next, a theme and variations with something like the art and high spirit of a Mozart piano sonata.

No high spirits attended the kite prose. Mostly matter-of-factness.

And if you do believe it happened, it was a done-once deal.

If Franklin had flown his kite on even a second day, he might have found what LeMonnier and Mazeas in France soon discovered by repeating experiments in 1752—that even with no storm clouds, with blue sky in dry weather, the atmosphere can supply an electrical charge. The ecstatic Mazeas wrote that "Nature might have designed the air to be [electricity's] great reservoir." Later, Tiberius Cavallo worked through many experimental variations. In a particularly intriguing one, he put the insulating silk ribbon between the twine and the kite—insulating the twine from the kite—and discovered that he received as much electricity as when he had his line directly attached to the kite. He guessed that the kite didn't serve to collect electricity so much as to pull the twine near enough to do the collecting itself. In effect, they had not been flying the Electric Kite. They had been flying Electric Twine. The results recalled Benjamin Wilson's work in the 1740s, his sometimes overlooked experiments collecting great charges along a length of insulated twine mere feet above ground level.

Franklin had several Philadelphia associates in electrical matters, but only one flew a kite. He was Ebenezer Kinnersley and he waited nine years to do so in 1761 in "clear, dry weather." Some time afterward, Joseph Priestley collected the apparatus to do the kite experiment but in the end did not, according to his brother, from fear of getting killed.

Perhaps Franklin's kite experiment of 1752 began and ended in a writing bout at the candle-lit table in his large room. His newspaper reveals there were many thunderstorms late that summer in the Delaware River basin. The heavens rumbled all too often. When Franklin faced opposition or a crisis, he often reached for pen and ink and imagination.

This editorial request appeared a year afterward in the June 21, 1753, issue of *The Pennsylvania Gazette:*

Those of our readers in this and neighboring provinces, who may have an opportunity of observing, during the present summer,

An illustration from Abbé Jacquet de Malzet's book of 1775. It depicts something very close to Franklin's experiment complete with a pre–Eddy kite. The flier is depicted with his kite line angled correctly for reaching as high as possible. Note that if a roof covered this as Franklin specified—to keep the silk dry but also never to touch the twine—the roof height adequate to the task would rival a contemporary airplane hangar. This illustrator sacrifices Franklin's directions to good sense and simply does away with the shed.

any of the effects of lightning on houses, ships, trees, and c are requested to take particular notice of its course, and deviation from
a straight line, in the walls or other matter affected by it, its different operations or effects on wood, stone, bricks, glass, metals
animal bodies, and c and every other circumstance that may tend
to discover the nature, and complete history of that terrible me-
teor. Such observations being put in writing and communicated
to BENJAMIN FRANKLIN in PHIL, will be very thankfully
accepted and acknowledged.

It was not the request of a man who has investigated lightning. It
was the request of a man who has not yet tried the experiments.

*A physical experiment which makes a bang is always worth more
than a quiet one.*

 G. C. LICHTENBERG

BY A TWIST OF FATE, BENJAMIN FRANKLIN'S FORTUNES
would link with those of an experimenter at the Imperial
Academy of Sciences in St. Petersburg, Russia. The man was Georg
Vil'gel'm Rikhman, a professor who taught physics and struggled to
support a young family in the apartment neighborhoods on Vasilev-
skii Island.

These links of destiny also included her Imperial Majesty Empress Elizaveta, a ruler with a sensual dumpling of a face, a tall
woman fabled in her own era as a beauty, but now to our eyes appearing as someone who might need a Rubens to appreciate her.
This sensual and arrogant woman had an obsession with fashion
and never wore the same dress twice. In 1746 she likely read the
same reports that propelled Franklin into electrical experiments and
announced that she wanted to see "sparkles in the dark." Her whim
proved to be a career breakthrough for Rikhman.

The only known portrait of Georg Rikhman shows a small man with an aristocratic face and sensitive eyes. He was happily married to Elizabeth Anna Gintz, a young woman originally from the region of his homeland in present-day Estonia. The couple were German by culture and outsiders in the Russian capital, émigrés, foreign to the people in the marketplaces and also to Georg's Russian bosses. Until the royal command for parlor sparks, the director of the academy had sometimes mercilessly harassed Rikhman, the threat of dismissal in the air. That all changed in 1746 and to support Rikhman's work, orders went to the finest electrical instrument makers in the Netherlands to supply the best available equipment and a purchasing agent in London scoured the book stalls for the latest electrical publications.

Rikhman's city was a striking contrast with Franklin's. St. Petersburg boasted great squares and public buildings gleaming with white- and green-trimmed elegance. At the Neva River site, Rikhman's science academy resembled a palace. By contrast, Franklin and his experimental associates met in the plain house of the Widow Breintnall.

Behind the magnificent wealth at St. Petersburg, however, Rikhman knew another reality. As a result of Imperial neglect, the science academy was teetering on the verge of collapse. Bills went unpaid. Operating funds were so low the doors of the grand library had been locked for a time. And the climate was severe. The site chosen by Peter the Great was used originally to locate convicts in punishment. It was dismal with bleak winters and unhealthy conditions arising from numerous swamps. So many laborers died building Peter's self-named city in the marshes—perhaps as many as 40,000 lost their lives—that locals called it "the city built on bones."

Unlike the Russian capital, Philadelphia was blessed with an agreeable climate and natural abundance. It was a city of thriving commerce—its Delaware River access made it a shipping center. Immigrants were also drawn by the tolerant Quaker culture. At St. Petersburg, very little was tolerated. "The government," observed one astonished English visitor, "is absolute in the last degree, not bound by any law or custom, but depending on the breath of the prince." To populate his city, Peter had forced his dismayed nobles and traders to pull up stakes and move.

But these two cities also had a few similarities.

Each city was planned and called into existence during the Enlightenment where before no city had existed. "Here it has been ordained for us by nature," announced Tsar Peter, "that we shall break a window through to Europe." William Penn had neatly laid down his plans for Philadelphia with quill and straight edge. "I wanted," Penn explained, "to afford an asylum for the good and the best of every nation . . . I desired to show men as free and happy as they could be." Two cities, each of them established as an individual's idea, each of them an Age of Reason experiment, each of them on the dangerous frontier of lightning science.

*

On the morning of the 26th of July, 1753, Georg Rikhman walked the five blocks from his apartment to the academy. The day was bright with summer. For Rikhman, this was a season filled with hope and anticipation, for he was putting the finishing touches to a major publication. On September 6, he was scheduled to address the academy concerning his discoveries. Soon after, the presses would issue his findings, entitled *De Indice Electricitatis Phaenomenis Dissertatio.*

Rikhman and his collaborator Mikhail Vasilevich Lomonosov were inspired by Franklin's sentry box to set up what they called *thunder-machines* in their homes to pursue Philadelphian science. Rikhman alone among the European scientists seems to have known—or been willing to publicly acknowledge—the extent of Franklin's joking in his reports. Fluent in English, Rikhman had read Franklin's *Experiments and Observations* in the first London edition. Rikhman responded with jests. He wrote of "Franclinus, naturalis electricitatis inventor," satirizing his celebrity, and explaining that Rikhman himself had discovered electrical charges to be "perpetually" in the air (no mention of the prior French reports—he obviously hadn't read them yet).

In addition, Rikhman appreciated the danger inherent in these experiments. "Even in these times," he wrote, "the physicist has the opportunity to display his fortitude." In May, 1753, he had brought atmospheric electricity of remarkable strength into his family's apartment. His wife, mother-in-law, and servants were terrified. The household continued in a state of nervous anxiety about his thunder investigations even as the indefatigable professor turned a deaf ear to them, moving deeper into the subject.

If events that July had continued as he had planned, Georg and Anna Rikhman might have soon left St. Petersburg behind. In the spring of 1752, unforeseen blessings had been announced in a letter from Georg's homeland, news that a relative had died and left him an estate. "My cousin has passed away and left a small inheritance in Kimenegorod province," explained Rikhman to his supervisors at the Academy, requesting leave. He was granted twenty-eight days to go and look into the matter. He made his visit, talked to the executor, investigated, but when he returned home, the news caught up with him that the estate had been awarded to someone else. If you weren't on the premises, it seemed, your legal prospects dimmed. Rikhman returned to Liflandia, setting out in May of that year to try again. This time his persuasions or mere presence did the work. On June 1, it was confirmed that he would be owner of the estate.

For Georg and Anna it was a dream come true, a large home, enough money, well-tended fields with a bounty of crops, a climate that would be better for their health, no more would they be outsiders, there would be neighbors who spoke their native tongue, no more would their fortunes depend on whim and politicking from above. As soon as the provincial legal wheels turned, perhaps in a matter of months, the estate would be theirs.

Anna must have felt especially blessed. She had just given birth to their third child in April of that year; they named him Frederick. He was four months old. In addition they had a daughter who had reached the toddler stage. And the eldest was six-year-old Wilhelm, named for his father. The cramped apartment was also home to Anna's mother and perhaps four servants, who were serfs—by our definition, slaves. The slaves were not signs of wealth and ease, but likely wards of charity given by Count Andrei Ivanovich Osterman to Rikhman for keeping when Osterman was banished to Siberia. This was the human and very humble entourage that depended upon Georg for a living.

Did he tell the Academy that he soon planned to leave? There is no certain answer. Politics was fiercely played at the Academy, so it's likely that Rikhman pretended his inheritance was minor and waited until the time was ripe.

That summer day, he attended a meeting in the lavishly appointed library. The topic at hand was impending arrangements for his book. Lomonosov, his collaborator in these electrical experiments, was there. The alliance of Lomonosov and Rikhman puzzled members of the Society, for they made such an unlikely pair. Lomonosov was a huge bear of a man, a brawling physical presence who could vanquish three assailants in an alley fight and was known to have done so; he was emotional, alcoholic, given to violent mood swings. On the other hand, Professor Rikhman was a small, pale intellectual, precise and elegant. Lomonosov was a multidimensional force in Russian culture, establishing a standard Russian language (with greater impact than Johnson had on English), creating from scratch a native metric for Russian verse, and doing pioneer work in the fledgling science of chemistry; Rikhman in the last four years had become an electrical specialist. Lomonosov had been born a state peasant and by intellect and strength risen to his professorship at the Academy. Rikhman had been born an aristocrat and as the result of the early death of his father, plummeted from those heights. For all of these differences, they became fast friends.

As the day's meeting worked through its agenda, beneath the

noises of throat-clearings and page rustlings, Rikhman heard something. The time was several minutes before noon. The day was clear and placid. But far away his ear caught the sullen rumbling of thunder.

"... It thundered at a pretty distance," said the report in a newspaper later.

The thunderstorm season begins in St. Petersburg in May. Generally, the storms are light ones; they aren't the furious, lashing weather events that descend on the central American plains, for instance. This day, the locals would have called it "blind rain," an idiom surviving in Russia even now that describes the rain pouring and the sun shining at the same time.

By coincidence, it was the sort of rain-and-sun event that occurred at Marly on that other landmark date in lightning science.

Rikhman took a deep, slow breath.

He pushed himself away from the damask-covered table.

He rose and excused himself with a polite flourish. Lomonosov too loomed to his feet, thrusting aside a chair. That very morning, the two friends had bantered and debated about the true color of sparks from the heavens. What color were sparks originating from the atmosphere? They would now have the opportunity to go to their machines and see. I. A. Sokolov, the scientific illustrator and engraver assigned to Rikhman's book, had also attended the meeting. He left the library with them. The color of a spark was no issue for him to depict, but Rikhman urged him to take this opportunity to see the thunder-machine in action.

As they exited the doors of the Academy, far on the north horizon they could see dark storm clouds. Sunlight fell on the elegant boulevard. The air blew colder now, the dust swirled on the street. The men would have started running, shouting, laughing, hurrying to outrace the arrival of the thunderstorm. Both scientists had introduced lightning science into the midst of domestic life. The forces at the St. Petersburg Academy of Sciences did not want their palace used as an apparatus in a lightning experiment.

Lomonosov did not have as far to go. He was already seated next to his thunder-machine drawing sparks, while Rikhman and Sokolov scrambled on, holding their wigs down with one hand as they ran to the house on Fifth Line.

According to an article Lomonosov published later, the sparks he was drawing that day hissed weakly, measuring merely fifteen notches on an electrical measuring stick invented by Rikhman. Lomonosov had heard thunder indeed, but it was only a "faint rumbling," nothing suggesting the savageness to come.

Rikhman arrived at his home accompanied by the artist, trotted up the flight of stairs, entered the outer door on the north side, in his excitement only taking a moment to hastily remove his wig and put it on a wooden peg in the entry hall. Sokolov, following, grew terrified at this dash to meet electricity, asking if perhaps it was dangerous. Of course not, answered the scientist. He then pointed out to Sokolov his electrical measuring device across the room: Its marker had scarcely moved.

Those who are involved as a way of life with potentially deadly experiments will tell you that fatal events happen not at the anticipated moments of crisis but at the other moments, when you least expect it.

Rikhman did not in the least expect what was going to happen next.

He marched briskly across the room, leaning his forehead near the thunder-machine setup. Two versions describe the next millisecond, some asserting bolt lightning and others a rare phenomenon known as ball lightning.

Rikhman didn't have that much time to react. Whether bolt or ball, it transpired quickly.

It hit him. As he bent down to examine the marker, it hit him square in the forehead.

When Georg Rikhman died, his life-systems shut down in less than 400-billionths of a second. The heat briefly visiting him was $50,000°$ Fahrenheit. The lightning may have surged with 15 million volts. In a millisecond, this level of electrical discharge made an entrance, used his body as a conductor, and exited.

According to contemporary researchers into pathophysiology of lightning trauma, the lightning would have splashed over the surface of his head, seeking out the cranial holes, entering through the eyes, the nostrils, mouth, and ears, traveling along the web of blood vessels and nerve paths and cerebral spinal fluid channels. Early on, Abbé Nollet had hypothesized that electricity moved along blood and nerve paths in the human body.

The staggering electrical charge backs up in the head because it can't descend all at once through the narrow pathway that channels cerebral spinal fluid. By induction, an opposite charge builds up at the victim's feet. The buildup is so severe that a "flashover" results—in the millisecond a sheet of electricity flows down the body to the earth, discharges, and restores equilibrium between the victim's head and his feet at ground level. Rikhman's death was likely a Leyden jar effect, his own body serving as the jar.

✻

Anna Rikhman had been in the rear of the house. The whole apartment concussed with the bolt, there was a bang and clatter of wood tossed about the home, a crash of glass. Anna ran immediately to the front room. When she got to the door, the room was dim and rapidly filling up with smoke. It was thickest several feet above the floor. It appeared to her as if Georg was still on his feet, as if she still had a husband.

The lightning had flung Georg back and dropped him on a chest, its impact held him there. The engraver Sokolov had already taken to his heels and fled the house. As he told it, he, too, saw what Anna saw—Sokolov had been knocked down and stunned by the blast, but coming to his senses, he thought the professor was on his feet, hence alive, that there must be a fire in the house, and he ran into the street to call for help.

But when she reached Georg, Anna saw the result. "There were not the least appearances of life," as reported the papers. Anna then bent to her husband, she tried all the remedies she knew, according to the French newspaper accounts, she tried salts, liquors, everything she could think of. It must just be a *lethargy,* she thought, that favorite catch-all diagnosis of the polite world. It was a *lethargy.* He must wake up. He must. She had sent a servant for Lomonosov, for the other savants of the Academy who could solve all problems.

Later, people walking in the streets outside the Rikhman apartment would testify to looking up at a very peculiar and rather small dark cloud blown out of the northeast that seemed "to float very low in the air."

Several witnesses reported observing the flash hit the iron pole Rikhman had set atop the apartment building. Some of the Rikhman family's neighbors said they saw "a vapor, in different rays, dart along the whole extent of the street; and that wherever it touched the ground, it emitted everywhere sparks." Several walkers in the street found themselves knocked off their feet and were as stunned and senseless at first as Sokolov had been. "It was such a thunder-clap, as had hardly been remembered at St. Petersburg," said the local newspaper.

Lomonosov arrived within minutes. When he entered the door, his breath caught in his throat. He saw his friend dead, the corpse flat now on the floor. The toddler, the three-month-old, and the six-year-old were roaring at the tops of their lungs, joining Anna and her mother shrieking in terrible grief.

"I may indeed say the whole island was immediately in an uproar," reported a journalist. "There was never a report of a misfortune so speedily spread abroad in this city, as this was." Within minutes a throng of people were in the street. The police officials appeared and cordoned off the apartment and put guardsmen with muskets on the Fifth Line to keep back the excited crowd.

Inside, Lomonosov was stunned.

Within a few hours after the death of his friend, he sat down and wrote these words to Count Ivan Ivanovich Shuvalov, their sponsor at court:

> I consider it a miracle that I am writing your Grace now, because the dead cannot write. I do not know yet or am at least doubtful whether I am alive or dead. What I am saying is that Professor Rikhman has been killed by lightning under the very same circumstances in which I found myself at the time.
>
> At one o'clock in the afternoon of July 26, a thundercloud rose from the North. The thunder was extraordinarily strong, but there was not a drop of rain. I was looking at the thunder machine we had set up but could not detect the slightest sign of electrical force. When the dinner was being served, I expected strong electrical sparks from the wire, and for this reason my wife and the others stepped up and, just as myself, frequently touched the wire and the iron switch suspended from it, because I had wanted reliable witnesses for the color of the electrical fire, concerning which the late Professor Rikhman and I had just been arguing. Suddenly there was a terrible thunder clap just when my hand was touching the iron, and sparks were crackling. They all ran away from me, and my wife asked me to move away also. But curiosity kept me there for another two or three minutes until I was told that the soup was getting cold and until the electrical force had almost vanished.

Lomonosov had sat down at the meal only a few moments when the door pushed open. It was Rikhman's servant. According to Lomonosov, the serf was

> . . . panting and weeping with tears and horror. He could hardly utter the words, '*professors gromom zashiblo*' [the professor has been struck down by lightning]. In utter terror, my strength almost failing me, I ran to him and saw Rikhman lying on ground, dead. His poor widow and his poor mother, too, were as pale as

he. The realization that death had just passed me by, his pale body, the understanding and friendship that had united us, the wailing of his wife and children: all of this assaulted my feelings to an extent that made it impossible for me to answer any of the questions directed at me by a multitude of people who had come running. I could only look at the face of the person with whom I had been conferring just an hour ago, discussing the planned public meeting. The first shock had jumped from the wire, suspended by means of a string, to his head, leaving a cherry-red mark on his forehead. Then the electricity had jumped into the floorboards from his feet. His foot and toes were blue, his shoe torn but not burned. We attempted to get his circulation going again, because he was still warm, but his head was injured and there was no hope. Thus through his lamentable experience he has furnished evidence proving that the electrical force of lightning can be diverted, however, to an iron rod that has to stand in an empty space which lightning can strike as often as it desires.

The last sentence is one of the run-that-by-me-again moments in this bizarre history. Abruptly, Lomonosov reveals that he doesn't have the slightest understanding of the deadly issues involved. As he tells it, all of St. Petersburg was pressing him for explanations, and the conclusion he's drawn is that an ungrounded lightning device might divert electricity. He's not done. Another surprising remark drops:

Otherwise Herr Rikhman died a beautiful death in fulfillment of his professional duties. He will never be forgotten. In any case, I am of the opinion that this accident should not be used to impede the advancement of science, and I humbly ask you to continue furthering the sciences.

The correspondent who began this letter almost too profoundly stunned to keep moving his quill across the page has moved quickly through his stages of grief to make now a curiously contemporary institutional request: Please-don't-yank-our-funding.

A Dr. C. G. Kratzenstein arrived ten minutes later with a surgeon, who opened a vein in the professor's arm. Only a drop of blood came out. He tried another vein. Nothing. The doctor and the surgeon together resorted to chafing, violently rubbing the professor's legs and arms, but the pulse didn't come back. When they had turned the corpse over for rubbing, a little blood spilled out of one corner of his mouth. Kratzenstein dropped to his knees and commenced "blowing" into the victim's mouth; this eighteenth-century variety of mouth-to-mouth resuscitation did no good.

There was a red spot the size of a ruble on his upper forehead, slightly to the left. The blood seemed to have been pushed through it, but the skin was still intact. The shoe on his left foot had been burst open, ripped in two places. They found a blue circle on his foot also the size of a ruble. "It is concluded," reported one source, "that the electrical force of thunder having forced into the head, made its way out again at the foot." At the time eight red and blue spots were counted on the left side of his body from his hips to his neck. Later, when the corpse was disrobed, many other bluish spots were observed, especially on his back.

The corpse was removed to the Academy for examination.

The news of the accident was a sensation in Europe. Although the professor had been unknown except to a few German experimenters, suddenly the name Rikhman was on the lips of every natural philosopher. The newspapers from London to Philadelphia, the magazines, *Philosophical Transactions*, periodicals high and low all publicized the death and devoted extensive space to its reporting.

What went on at St. Petersburg to cause this death? was the stunned question asked in every capital.

The answers in the reports were curious. The day after the accident at the request of the Academy, Kratzenstein and an assistant performed an autopsy. The usual haze of eighteenth-century generalization and abstract nouns lifted at the shock of this death. There

Histories have attributed this depiction of Rikhman's death to Sokolov, the scientific illustrator who was present at the accident. But Sokolov never depicted the scene. This illustration, incorrect in many details, was reprinted countless times for several generations. In this way, the picture resembled the Franklin kite illustrations, remarkable for the degree of incorrectness but potent with iconic force.

(Bakken Library and Museum)

was a hunger for specifics. Newspapers and scientific outlets carried reports much longer than their typical items. Perhaps there was no autopsy in all of the eighteenth century reported at such great length.

The reports were done in tender detail, and utterly beside the point, of course.

This minute examination of Georg's body could not explain what happened. Kratzenstein found that beneath the red dot on the forehead and the blue on the foot there was no damage to muscle or bone, and that the mark did not even show on the fat just beneath the skin. The brain suffered no damage that he could see. The heart looked normal, but had no blood in it. The frontal part of the lungs were as they should have been. The intestines had not suffered any damage, but the pancreas was "hurt and full of blood." And on. And on.

Much attention was directed also to the architecture of the Rikhman apartment. When the lightning hit, the front door jamb had been torn off and the door lifted and thrown out on the porch. At the other end of the apartment, a splinter of the kitchen door was torn out and tossed into the rear stairwell, almost as if the lightning were some person seeking to exit by doors. Questions were raised if the windows had been open—these had been shut, however, for the slightest hint of a breath of wind would disturb the professor's measuring device. None of the architectural questions resulted in answers that explained his death.

The scientists at the Academy had wanted to look at the exploded remains of Rikhman's experimental apparatus to see what had happened. That was impossible. The widow and her servants tore down the whole apparatus immediately after the accident. If all we had were Lomonosov's diagrams, the matter would be suspect, but there are sketches in Rikhman's own hand that reveal what he had been doing. It was an elegant arrangement that brought down all this violence. In the middle, a Leyden jar set on a glass plate atop a table—it was insulated. On one side a chain brought in electrical energy that had been collected from the sky by a rod on the roof. A conductor led from the chain to the outside of the jar. Also attached to the incoming chain was a measuring device that used a thread and marker. On the other side of the jar an electrical friction tube conveyed its charge to a conductor that led to the hook in the mouth of the Leyden jar and would charge the inside of the jar; it also had a measuring device to reveal how "much" was cranked out by the machine.

What was going on? He was measuring the differential between electricity from the parlor and electricity from the sky.

It was the "quantifying spirit" of the century at work. Rikhman might have explained that he was trying to compare the magnitude of sky electricity with earth electricity. At the time the concepts of volt and amp were not yet available. But it was science, probing at phenomena that then existed beyond the known. The Leyden

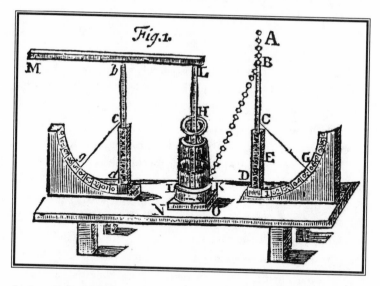

In the middle of Rikhman's setup, his elegant death-machine, rests the Leyden jar. On the right, a chain brings in electrostatics from the sky, charging the outside of the jar. On the left, the stick (M) is a conductor going to an electrical friction machine not here depicted. On each side a thread (C-G) measures the charge, "how much" it is repelled by the electrified pole (B-D).

jar was central to the clever setup. Franklin had already demonstrated the equivalency of the charge on the outside and inside of the jar.

The Rikhman device offered wonderful variations. If you touched one side on its wire, the thread collapsed, but the other thread continued to diverge. If you removed your finger, the mystery of the jar's induction reasserted itself, and the thread rose. There were many variations open—an Enlightenment gentleman, if he were insulated enough by his shoes or his socks or the floor covering, could take away "the thunder of Jove" and dance around the room and give it back to the system, thus causing the threads to move higher. There's no documentation that Rikhman had done so yet, but if *negative* instead of *positive* electricity descended from the sky that was greater in "magnitude" than that produced by the friction machine, the polarities of the Leyden jar would reverse.

✳

The funeral at St. Petersburg was on July 29. Although the coroner had wondered that the lightning had "left few visible traces in the body which it penetrated," he did note one. The body decomposed with astonishing speed. After only two days, "the body was so far corrupted, that it was with difficulty they got it in a coffin."

Throngs of people lined the streets for the procession. It was one of the largest funeral crowds St. Petersburg had ever seen. Although most of the city looked upon the dead professor with great sympathy, many also viewed the poor victim as one who had offended God. The Russian Orthodox Church, unlike the Roman Catholic Church, did not look with approval on electrical studies. "From this terrible event," wrote one Orthodox observer, "we can see this is a secret of God and we should not disturb it." The burial procession concluded at Sampson Cemetery, where Georg Rikhman was returned to the earth.

✳

Many ironies attended this famous accident.

When Franklin had entered the field of electrical studies, it was the Leyden jar that had just become central to any further advances. And at the center of the smoking ruins in St. Petersburg, there was a Leyden jar. It was very much a Leyden jar lightning experiment.

After Rikhman's death, Count Ivan Grigorevich Chernyshev, another eminence in the Empress Elizaveta's court, wrote to Count Shuvalov: "Can you imagine what danger you were undergoing every time you were near this damned machine and how we were all running to it and playing with it like a mere toy? And all of this would have gone on had it not been for the accident with poor Rikhman." Ivan Shuvalov was Elizaveta's pillow partner and minister of state, the second most powerful person in the Russian Empire. Just as Watson's home in London had been visited by princes and dukes who wanted to see electricity, Rikhman's humble apartment had apparently welcomed the powerful members of the court. It's even possible that Elizaveta had hazarded her royal self next to the professor's thunder-machine.

The Dr. Kratzenstein who entered the scene ten minutes after the lightning fell and tried to revive Georg, the man who also performed the autopsy the next day, turns out to be a familiar figure. He was the Kratzenstein at the University of Halle who wrote the first book on medical electricity. The man who claimed to perform the first electrical cure also performed the autopsy on the first fatality in the science. He seems to have been a minor member on the Academy staff. It is especially ironic that the German physician and experimenter who knew so much more about electricity than did Lomonosov ranked so far beneath him at the Academy.

Afterward Lomonosov with some posturing offered as scientifically important such bizarre details as these: the window in the next room was open, and that Rikhman had in his pocket 70 rubles, which did not melt. In another article, Lomonosov swore Rikhman had never read any of Franklin's reports, an inaccuracy belied by the professor's already published articles that mention Franklin by name. Perhaps the reason the enthusiastic, free-swinging Lomonosov didn't seem to understand his friend's science was because he didn't read his publications.

It has been little noted who was one of those hit outside Rikhman's apartment. Franklin had proposed the sentry-box experiment that started this fatal sequence of events. There was an actual sentry box with guard on duty on Rikhman's street that day. When the lightning hit, the sentry was "cast some paces from his sentry box."

But for the widow Anna there was no contemplating irony. St. Petersburg was a city even more brutal than London, a city where the unfortunate could easily perish. Once Georg died, Anna apparently had no claims upon the estate in Liflandia that the couple was on the verge of inheriting. She had no available means of income.

The Academy had paid to her Georg's salary for the months of May, June, and July minus taxes and deductions. They gave her no benefits. In fact, they deducted the several days in July after his death. They even deducted an amount for the afternoon on the fatal day when he did not return to work.

Give Lomonosov credit for what followed. Disregarding what might have been politically expedient, he flung himself into a campaign to get a pension for Anna and her children. He fired off one letter to the Vice Chancellor. He pointed to previous cases where Academy professors had died and their widows were given a year's salary to bide them over.

On August 5th, the desperate widow sent this letter to Her Highness Elizaveta:

My deceased husband spent 18 years serving Your Honour at the Academy of Sciences. But it was God's will that during an electrical experiment he would be killed by thunder, and after his death, I am left with three children, the eldest 6 years old and the youngest three months old, and the daughter one year and a half. So with children I absolutely don't have any income while I have many debts.

She requested a yearly income to support them based on her husband's salary, pensions for the children, and 100 rubles to pay for his funeral.

In September, Anna received the 100 rubles. That was all.

Lomonosov continued his protests, his letter writing, and in some way not clear it at last must have had effect. Perhaps he worked through Shuvalov, who regarded him highly. In November, 1753, there was an order for Anna to receive one year's income. The pension for her children was refused.

*

In the June, 1754, edition of *Gentleman's Magazine* there appeared an announcement that the academy at St. Petersburg was sponsoring a contest for essays on electrical science. The magazine devoted nearly a full page to it. The item read:

Prize proposed by the Imperial Academy of Sciences at St Petersburgh

Notwithstanding the many pieces that have been written to explain the phenomena of electricity, some of which have been honour'd with premiums, a variety of fresh discoveries may probably throw a new light upon the subject.

To this end the imperial academy of sciences at Petersburgh, have proposed their usual reward of one hundred ducats to any one, who, before the 1st day of June 1755, shall *assign the true cause of electricity, and give the best theory thereof.* . . .

No mention of Rikhman, no mention of the lightning accident, no mention that near at hand they had Rikhman's unpublished papers that might have come nearer front-line science than any of the tired academic pieces that contest proposals often dredged up. Who had written the announcement? Was it some bureaucrat? Or Lomonosov? It could have been either in the unhappy choice of language about finding the *true* cause of electricity, a conceptualism that took them back to medieval scholasticism, the phrase that inevitably preceded scientific boobism, a lurching backward into the past.

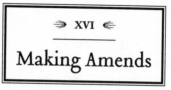

They [the Royal Society] soon made me more than Amends for the Slight with which they had before treated me.

              ❧ BENJAMIN FRANKLIN

A
FTER GEORG RIKHMAN DIED, PUBLICLY HONORS SHOWERED
down on Franklin and privately questions plagued him.
There must have been a secret pang inside whenever he opened a
packet of newspapers from abroad. Would he discover more awards
and memberships or that another man had died doing his lightning
experiment?

The honors were splendid. The King of France offered his personal compliments to Franklin, lightning scientist. In the colonies,
Harvard, Yale, and William and Mary awarded him honorary Master of Arts degrees. The University of St. Andrews in Scotland con-
ferred upon him an honorary doctorate in 1759, a citation repeated
three years later at Oxford. Franklin loved this title so much that
immediately he assumed it among his friends, possibly with a droll
wink, but the usage spread in America and abroad until *Dr Franklin*
became serious standard usage, lasting nearly a century and a half

with the inevitability that *Babe* assumed in the realm of American baseball for the legendary George Herman Ruth. The scientific academies also flocked to give Franklin honors, making him a foreign member. And there were prizes, beginning early on in 1753 with the famous Copley Medal.

The Council of the Royal Society decided the Copley's winner. In 1745, Watson himself had smiled and pocketed the prize, a solid gold coin about half again as big as a silver dollar. The inspiration to make the award a stamped precious metal had come from the Society's president, its shrewd, gentlemanly humor revealing Martin Folkes at his best. If a recipient could afford to bathe in honor and recognition, he could display the coin in a curio cabinet, but if he or his descendants fell on hard times, why they could melt it down.

In 1753, strange events attended the awarding of the Copley. Something went awry at the November 15 meeting. The gentlemen couldn't agree and needed an unprecedented second meeting. Apparently Franklin was an embarrassment to the establishment at Crane Court. He knew as much. In the *Autobiography*, he relates, "Dr Wright, an English physician then at Paris, wrote to a friend who was of the Royal Society an account of the high esteem my experiments were in among the learned abroad, and of their wonder that my writings had been so little noticed in England."

Peter Collinson, who was elected to the Council in 1753 but had rarely attended, came to every meeting concerning the Copley. He must have been a regular bulldog. Franklin was finally chosen, and

FACING PAGE: *This oil portrait by Mason Chamberlin was a favorite of Franklin's. Chamberlin painted the portrait in 1762 and many engravers rushed to repeat it. Franklin ordered one hundred copies from a London printshop. Note the electrical bells on the left while outside the window occurs some melodrama, a bolt descending on an unprotected house. The image also makes a social statement—he wears an expensive wig, silks, and fancy cuffs as he sits on a plush armchair. Here is the Philadelphia hand now risen to status as a gentleman.* (BAKKEN LIBRARY AND MUSEUM)

the prize was announced at the grand annual banquet on St. Andrews Day, November 30, 1753, but another irregularity surfaced. The secretary's notes reveal that William Watson, the most faithful attender of all the Council members, chose not to be present that day.

At the award ceremony, the speech was given by the debonair George Parker, the second Earl of Macclesfield, the president of the Royal Society after replacing Martin Folkes, then disabled by a stroke. The oration was one of the oddest presentation speeches in the history of physics. The speech didn't focus on Benjamin Franklin, but extolled British electrical scientists and their "honor." At the end, Macclesfield, adorned by a lengthy wig, voiced the hope that Franklin or someone building on his discoveries might next invent a way to prevent lightning devastation. The hope revealed that Macclesfield had not read Benjamin Franklin.

The comic gears of the Copley tale continued to grind as *Gentleman's Magazine* announced the 1753 award in two brief sentences, mistakenly identifying the man whose Philadelphia experiments were printed in the same building as a printer from the Maryland colony. Even more oddly, Collinson waited three years before he sent the prize on to its owner. Franklin vividly remembered in his *Autobiography* the coin's presentation. The award was brought to the colonies by the newly arrived governor, Sir William Denny, a London sophisticate handpicked by the Proprietor Thomas Penn. Denny took Franklin aside from a welcome banquet into a private room and then withdrew the coin from his pocket. As Franklin stared into his cynical face, the issue instantly clarified. Denny and Penn wanted his vote, they wanted his influence. The gentleman who had paid for most of the electrical equipment and books given Franklin's Library Company—Peter Collinson functioning merely as purchasing agent—was Thomas Penn, Franklin's most bitter political enemy. Collinson was also Penn's intimate friend and investment associate. A debt needed paying. Was it required that the local scientific celebrity become a turncoat to his neighbors?

Franklin turned Denny down and pocketed the coin.

✳

The debt created by his electrical-science celebrity was of a different nature.

After word of Marly reached Franklin in the fall of 1752, no reports followed of lightning experiment deaths, and surely he slept easier with each passing month. He had gotten away with it. A note of jaunty triumph appears in an April, 1753, letter to his friend Jared Eliot revealing that he has received commendation from the King of France. "*The Tatler*," wrote Franklin, "tells us of a girl who was observed to grow suddenly proud, and none could guess the reason, til it came to be known she had got on a pair of new silk garters. Lest you should be puzzled to guess the cause when you observe anything of the kind in me, I think I will not hide my new garters under my petticoats, but take the freedom to show them to you, in a paragraph in our friend Collinson's last letter." The man who deserves to crow openly as if he were a monarch in realms of science presents himself as a servant girl wearing upper-class underwear. The metaphor brings up class distinctions and also imaginatively strikes other notes—humor, slyness, a sense of something hidden.

The delight, of course, soured. The cost of his celebrity turned out to be heavy. There was a fourteen-month span between Franklin in Philadelphia learning that his sentry-box experiment had been done abroad and the report arriving of Rikhman's death. As soon as Abbé Nollet heard that Italian sentry-box experiments had unleashed powerful discharges, he issued an international warning. The Italians reported men knocked to the earth as if clubbed. Nollet urged experimenters to back away from these perilous activities. Later Franklinist histories would depict this as the response of a jealous man. But as the senior authority in the electrical field, Nollet took a very responsible course in his concern that someone would die. He was proven right at St. Petersburg. What if Franklin had joined the chorus of warning? What if he had admitted that at Marly he had inspired men who apparently didn't know much electrical science and were confused in translation? Would his overnight celebrity have as quickly wilted? Would the true brilliance of his theorizing have lost the public relations luster given by the tandem demonstrations, the Marly experiment and his kite effort?

Franklin was silent.

On November 12, 1753, his friend James Bowdoin sent a letter. "I have seen a short account in the public news," wrote Bowdoin, "of a gentleman at Petersburg being killed by lightning while he was making some experiments to guard against the effects of it: if you have or shall have a more particular account I shall be obliged if you'd communicate it." All of Europe had been echoing with the same question.

Franklin didn't reply.

In the 1960s, the editors of the Papers of Benjamin Franklin project at Yale made an interesting discovery. In the March 5, 1754, issue of *The Pennsylvania Gazette,* there is in translation an extract of a report from Russia about Rikhman's death. It is with a few differences an account that in translations made the rounds of major European newspapers, containing many details from the coroner's report. The significant difference is a fraudulent paragraph that Franklin apparently added to the end. He wrote:

The new doctrine of lightning is, however, confirmed by this unhappy accident; and many lives may hereafter be saved by the practice it teaches. Mr Rikhman being about to make experiments on the matter of lightning, had supported his rod and wires by (non-conductors) which cut off their communication with the earth; and himself standing too near where the wire terminated, helped his body to complete that communication. It is plain the wire conducted the lightning to him thro' the whole length of the gallery; And had his apparatus been intended for the security of his house, and the wire (as in that case it ought to be) continued without interruption from the roof to the earth, it seems more than probable that the lightning would have followed the wire, and that neither the house nor any of the family would have been hurt by that unfortunate stroke.

Several messages are conveyed here. An especially important one is: The man died because he didn't know what he was doing. Rikhman, of course, was brilliant and knowledgeable, a man who with full awareness braved the risks in this new experimental field. Did Franklin really permit himself to believe that Rikhman destroyed himself through ignorance?

＊

The news of Rikhman's death that November must have resonated for Franklin with another dismal event in his past, a hoax in which he had been involved in 1738, an accident, the victim a young man who died because of his ignorance. A mentally defective Philadelphian named Daniel Rees had been deluded by Franklin and his friends with the hope of secret initiation rites for becoming a member of Franklin's Free Mason association. The jokers had taken Rees to a dark room in the basement of a Market Street tavern and administered a mock initiation. Ribald humor followed in the dark, including the unfortunate fellow knowingly or unknowingly kissing someone's hairy anus. The text for the phony oaths and invocations went home that night in Franklin's pocket, and the next day, friends and associates crowded his printshop to see the pages and laugh at Rees.

Another night, the humorists decided Rees needed more initiation. Franklin refused to attend. During the second mock ceremony, a mock toast, an old Philadelphia tavern tradition called a *snapdragon* involving drinking down a flaming bumper of spirits, something went wrong. The flaming drink splashed on Rees, who was burnt to death. Early in the investigation, the magistrate considered charges not only against those present the second night but against Franklin too. The police intended to charge Benjamin as the man who authored the fraudulent Masonic oaths that had lured Rees on. When his friends testified that they had been responsible for the literary part of the hoaxes and that Franklin's role was merely to carry the papers about and display them, he was off the hook. If convicted, Franklin would have been burned on the hand.

Yet there remains some mystery about the Rees incident. Franklin of course has a formidable track record in authoring humorous hoaxes. For his family, who knew more of him in many ways than anyone else, the first bits of news in the Boston papers elicited from them a what-have-you-gotten-yourself-into letter.

Franklin had no direct physical involvement in the death of Rees. He was possibly the gentlest of the Founders. But in his 1738 written response disclaiming involvement, there appears a moral uneasiness that he had kept silent when he might have raised his voice to stop the crude hazing. So many witnesses of Franklin in different stages of his life, friend and enemies alike, note the combination of a generous human warmth conveyed simultaneously with a certain aloofness.

As a regular reader of *Gentleman's Magazine*, Franklin would have in earlier issues read of conditions in St. Petersburg. He would have understood the extreme poverty and peril awaiting Anna and her three children in the Imperial city.

There is no evidence that Franklin made an effort to help the Rikhman family at this point of crisis. But some conjectures may be worth the effort. Mysteriously, despite their poverty, in the decades following both young Wilhelm and Frederick received an education at the Academy. Who paid their tuition?

We can look at Franklin's character over nearly eight decades. We can get some rough estimate of what he might have done in crises. One of his most remarkable qualities is something he wrote of as "correcting errata." It is his own homespun moral code announced in print-trade vocabulary. At the age of twenty-six, he took Miss Read as his wife because, as he hints in the *Autobiography*, he had compromised her. And he raised and cared for William, when others with his wealth might have as easily farmed the illegitimate child out to labor in a settlement. If you look at his immediate family of three, two are family members who are errata corrected.

It would at least have been in character for him to try to correct the Russian erratum. The Russian scholar Eufrosina Dvoichko-Markoff points out that a letter from Ezra Stiles of Yale to Franklin indicates there was correspondence between Lomonosov and Franklin. As this was written, none had been turned up, but it's an interesting possibility. Lomonosov had virtually no scientific communication with the West, and as we saw with Rikhman, he didn't have much with his partner near at hand. There would be no common electrical science ground for the two, but there was the tragedy of Rikhman. Did Franklin contact Lomonosov and ask to help? Who paid for the Academy schooling for the orphaned boys?

A tantalizing possibility is that Franklin might have been fixing errata.

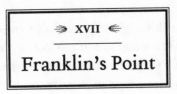

There are some great lords whom one should only approach with
extreme precaution: lightning is such a one.

⇒ VOLTAIRE

THE LIGHTNING ROD SOARS ABOVE THIS DECADE IN FRANK-
lin's career.

In 1752, he had sent the briefest of notes to the Royal Society announcing that in Philadelphia he had flown his electric kite and that
he had also attached lightning rods to two public buildings.

The October 19 edition of *The Pennsylvania Gazette* announcing
the electric kite also mentioned that *Poor Richard's Almanack* was in
press. In it, Franklin offered his neighbors these instructions:

HOW TO SECURE HOUSES, & C. FROM LIGHTNING

It has pleased God in his goodness to mankind, at length to discover to them the means of securing their habitations and other
buildings from mischief by thunder and lightning. The method is
this: Provide a small iron rod (it may be made of the rod-iron
used by the nailers) but of such a length, that one end being three

or four feet in the moist ground, the other may be six or eight feet above the highest part of the building. To the upper end of the rod fasten about a foot of brass wire, the size of a common knitting-needle, sharpened to a fine point; the rod may be secured to the house by a few small staples. If the house or barn be long, there may be a rod and point at each end, and a middling wire along the ridge from one to the other. A house thus furnished will not be damaged by lightning, it being attracted by the points, and passing thro the metal into the ground without hurting any thing. Vessels also, having a sharp pointed rod fixed on the top of their masts, with a wire from the foot of the rod reaching down, round one of the shrouds, to the water, will not be hurt by lightning.

The essence of Franklin's invention was this: If you set up a metal pole sharpened to a point above a dwelling, the electricity from the clouds would travel harmlessly down its length and into the ground. The metal lines that later in the eighteenth century appeared on the sides of cathedrals in Paris, Berlin, and Rome can be traced back to this news item published for Pennsylvania ploughmen—and even further back to Debbie Franklin's sewing needle that served in 1746 to knit leather covers onto books. Using her needle, Benjamin came upon the idea of the lightning rod by way of his insight that its metal point drew off electrical energy. He valued this early discovery. He opened his first electrical letter with it. He defended it more warmly, with greater elaboration than he ever gave the rod itself. In later editions of his *Experiments and Observations*, Franklin generously acknowledged that his friend the attorney Hopkinson had conceived the corollary that points also throw off electrical energy.

*

Two and a half centuries worth of histories have written of the rapid and widespread adoption of the device. Even today, for instance, a recent article on Franklin's lightning discoveries that is splendidly researched, upon arriving at the invention, tosses out, "Soon lightning rods sprang up everywhere from colonial America to the great cities of Europe." But the primary documents don't support such assertions.

In 1762, a surprised Franklin would scan the hazy London skyline. "Here it [the lightning rod] is very little regarded," he wrote Ebenezer Kinnersley on February 20, "so little, that though it is now seven or eight years since it was made public, I have not heard of a single house as yet attempted to be secured by it."

On July 2, 1768, a lightning bolt descended on a hall at Harvard College, setting the building afire. Although Harvard had extolled Franklin's discoveries and awarded him an honorary degree, fifteen years later there were no lightning rods on the Harvard campus. In France, the king sent Franklin commendations in 1752, but no lightning rods rose over his Highness's real estate until thirty years afterward when lightning conductors were finally put on the palace of the Louvre. Gottingen, Germany, boasted electrical experimenters, but the first lightning rod wasn't installed there until 1780.

The tale of this invention, like that of a number of other inventions, is a document of hesitations, late adoptions, feuds, and, on occasions, unnerving lapses. Franklin himself wasn't that clear at first about what he had invented. At the start, he imagined that the lightning rod might drain away electricity from the clouds and prevent lightning strike. In 1752, Thomas Dalibard had claimed that a hundred lightning rods guarding Paris would disarm the thunderclouds of their bolts (Franklin silently dropped this claim from the version of Dalibard's letter he printed in the 1769 edition of *Experiments and Observations*). John Lining, physician and later indigo speculator at Charleston, shared this confusion, relating that one electric kite drained enough electricity to cause a dark storm to pass his city without one bolt descending. The lightning device was a prophylactic. To the old hands in the experimental field, however, this seemed all wrong. Nollet argued that the electrostatic energy in the atmosphere was much greater than a hundred poles over Paris could dispatch. In England, Benjamin Wilson offered that a lightning rod draining the electricity from the sky ranked up there with the likelihood of an air-pump emptying the sky of all its air. Finally Franklin would arrive at the position that the rod could silently drain away electricity *or* conduct actual bolts into the earth.

Undeniably Franklin's rod averted disasters when given a chance. In 1769 St. Paul's Cathedral in London attached a lighting rod. St. Mark's bell tower at Venice, which had often been damaged by lightning over the centuries, was at last protected in April, 1775, and never suffered another stroke. But across the decades, there also appeared reports of incidents where the lightning rods simply didn't work. Doctrinaire Franklinists insisted that improper installation or maintenance must be the problem. By the turn of the century, Franklin's admirer Benjamin Vaughan was arguing that the mishaps occurred because the lightning rod "has now generally lapsed from the hands of the philosophers into those of common workmen."

Early on, a response to the growing number of lightning rod failures was to install thicker conducting wire. Franklin had begun suggesting wire "as thick as a goose quill," but by 1762 he was urging half-inch wire for safety. Among many unsettling events was one reported from Bavaria, where atop a hill set a church crowned by a 156-foot steeple. Professor von Yelin, a German lightning rod specialist known for his meticulous work, had attached a lightning rod, installing brass wiring more than an inch in diameter. On April 30, 1822, a "heavy flash" of lightning dropped, shaking the valley, melting the wire, and hurling the clock and part of its brick wall down, scattering them on the ground. Thirty years later on a December afternoon at Paris, lightning struck the rod-protected Louvre, resulting in damage (no loss of life or art treasure, however), and public outcry caused the Académie to form a committee to rethink lightning rod protection. The lapses, the failures, as well as the successes of the lightning rod continue through the nineteenth century and down to our own day. Unlike his strident biographers who claim a sweeping worldview triumph for the technology, Franklin himself saw it as a hit-and-miss process. In 1762, he wrote Kinnersley, "We find that we are, in this [lightning rod installation] as in others, to expect improvement from experience chiefly."

When did Franklin erect his own lightning rod? Was it attached to his home? He waited nearly a year to claim that back in September, 1752, he had "erected an iron rod to draw the lightning down into my house, in order to make some experiments on it, with two bells to give notice when the rod should be electrified. A contrivance obvious to every electrician." Was this the first lightning rod? A remembrance written in 1772 explains that he attached a rod nine feet above his roof and snaked a wire down through the stairwell leading to his room. The wire from the heavens was adjusted six inches from another insulated wire journeying on downstairs and into his well. Each wire had a bell on its end. Between the bells, he suspended a tiny brass ball on a silk line. When a storm charged the incoming line, the brass ball flew back and forth between the bells in a cycle of attractions and repulsions, merrily ringing (in essence, the iron shot and cork ball experiment *redux*). By the brass ball's ferrying back and forth the electrical charge, the device was grounded.

In his letter, Franklin said it was a "contrivance obvious to every electrician."

This is a blow-off remark, shrugging aside the necessity to explain grounding, which he himself hadn't been clear on for several years. Electric bells were obvious. The grounded rod was the real issue and a contrivance not then obvious to some of the best minds in Europe.

*

There will always remain mysteries about the first lightning rod. It was announced in tandem with the electric kite. Spawned by a wave of international experimentation, its publication was local—the kite in the *Gazette*, the rod in the almanac. For book publication, Franklin would suppress early claims concerning both. On close reading, neither the newspaper nor the almanac says that he himself has done what he describes. He was evasive when questioned about the electric kite, and he also gave the silent treatment for more than seventeen years to appeals for advice on safely installing the rod. We need to look again at the paragraph that first contained news of installations. He wrote:

> I was pleased to hear of the success of my experiments in France, and that they there had begun to erect points on their buildings. We had before placed them upon our academy and state-house spires.

Although he has announced the kite as me-too science, this final passage is different. He voices warmth and gratitude for the French with a sweeping graciousness and then the word *before* drops like a stone. This is a priority claim. He did it first. And he goes a bit farther. He lays claim to immediate, broad public acceptance in Pennsylvania.

Franklin's claim was read aloud to the Royal Society and printed in *Philosophical Transactions*. But he didn't include this paragraph in his *Gazette*. He omitted the lightning-rod paragraph from the kite announcement reprinted in all versions of *Experiments and Observations*. Why did he suppress such glorious news?

It is possible there simply were no lightning rods on Pennsylvania buildings in 1752. If you search the records of the Pennsylvania Academy and the Assembly at the State House (the building we now call Independence Hall), there is no evidence that Franklin attached lightning rods to either building in the 1750s. The Academy daybooks and ledgers record transactions in the minutest detail down to eight shillings, administered personally by Franklin himself, for "brushes to sweep the schools." The minutes of the Pennsylvania Assembly of this era authorize even small expenditures, for instance, the payment of one pound and two shillings "to Plunket

Fleeson, for a bottom for the speaker's chair," but never are lightning rods mentioned.

The drawing of the Academy building from the 1750s at the Historical Society of Pennsylvania does not show a lightning rod. Yet in 1754, Ezra Stiles in his diary mentioned "rods and wires which defend the Academy house from lightning" and also a rod on the house of instructor Ebenezer Kinnersley. Months afterward, Kinnersley advertised an electrical show "in the chambers of the academy" and promised a table-top device to demonstrate the new principle of the lightning rod, without any mention that on the outer wall there was attached the real thing.

The mysteries are more obscure surrounding the State House. No rod can be seen in the dramatic perspective sketch of the State House that C. W. Peale made in 1778. As these pages were researched, the earliest work of art found that showed a lightning rod on the State House was a copper plate engraving "View of Several Public Buildings in Philadelphia" from the *Columbian Magazine* of 1790. The rod is shown attached to the chimney and the depicting line is so tiny it might be a flyspeck or the slip of the engraver's knife. But "Election Day 1815," an oil by John Lewis Krimmel hanging today in the Winterthur Museum in Delaware, indisputably shows a lightning rod at the same spot, in fact the place it today occupies on the building.

Note that in 1752 Franklin had specified his lightning rod was on the steeple. The essence of his theory required it—as he saw it, the deadly bolt would have been attracted to the 170-foot point of the steeple, not the 61-foot chimney stack below where someone later cautiously attached a lightning rod. It's a curious contradiction. To this day, the national shrine that elevates his rod, snubs his theory.

The more you look, the dimmer grow the first two rods claimed in 1752. According to the curators at Independence National Historical Park, none of the stray iron rod artifacts discovered or dug out in Independence Hall over the years is made of eighteenth-century materials, only early nineteenth-century materials at best. The chimney stack does survive from the eighteenth century, but the current lightning protector consists of a cable attached in 1921.

The Franklin Institute keeps on display a scrap from a hexagonal lightning rod that some claim was Franklin's first. According to Ed Battison, a specialist in the history of colonial ironwork, hexagonal iron bars may have been nonexistent in colonial Philadelphia. Battison explains that the iron would have been prepared in flat sheets and rolled or beaten out and then stripped into narrow bands, resulting in a bar that was square—in fact, the shape of the authentic eighteenth-century Maryland State House rod, which dates back to at least July of 1788. "There was very little reason to make hexagonal bars in the eighteenth century," asserts Battison, noting that the development of the hex-nut in the nineteenth century coincided with the production of the iron bars from which they were cut.

Private residences in Philadelphia at some point were armed with lightning rods. The family that gave the lightning rod to the Franklin Institute claimed it bedecked the Market Street home of Franklin's friend and neighbor John Wister. "It was in this house," wrote a nineteenth-century Wister descendent, "that Dr. Franklin made his first attempt to 'snatch the lightning from heaven' and guide it harmlessly to earth."

The late Mike Wister of Philadelphia remembered in an interview a story handed down by the Wisters across 250 years. On a stormy night in the 1750s, the electrical bells rang with a terrible clatter from Franklin's adjacent house and woke and frightened the Wister children. Anna Wister, raised to great self-assurance as the daughter of a leading Quaker assemblyman, pulled on her cloak and went and banged on her neighbor's door and complained. Franklin immediately silenced his bells.

✳

A sense of fear and risk attended the introduction of the lightning rod. It was brilliant work, the only invention from eighteenth-century electrical experimenting to survive virtually unaltered and in use. But to attach a grounded rod to a house, at the time, was also an experiment.

Look again at the sentry box proposed back in 1749. It is really a house, phone-booth-sized, sheltering a human occupant. If you add a grounding wire, you have arrived at the lightning rod.

Fear of stepping into the sentry box during a thunderstorm may have led Franklin to invent the lightning rod.

Franklin's evasive silence about the sentry box, the kite, and the rod nurtured their spread. The Franklinists were inspired by their iconic simplicity and leaped into debates and refutations, supplying the details and operative hints and odd protective subtheories, while Franklin simply genially nodded from the heights of his growing celebrity.

But to his opponents and even to some of the undecided, the lightning rod installation called to mind the setup that killed Georg Rikhman. In fact, as the thunder rumbled overhead, when Franklin, at Anna Wister's demand, reached into the six-inch space between the wires and stopped the grounding action of the bells, he had taken—for a few moments—the place occupied by the man in the death-machine at St. Petersburg.

CLUB—An assembly of good fellows, meeting under certain conditions.
          ❧ SAMUEL JOHNSON, *Dictionary of the English Language,* 1755

T HE DECADES THAT FOLLOWED HELD VERY FEW PHYSICAL
risks for Franklin. In 1757 he was appointed by the Pennsylvania Assembly as its lobbyist in London. When he left Philadelphia, he had no idea that he would spend more than sixteen of his next twenty years comfortably abroad.

Franklin immersed himself in the rapidly expanding London metropolis. Years before, he had strolled its streets as a common worker, an outsider, but now as a scientific celebrity, he clattered up to tall Georgian houses in his own carriage, invited inside to frolics, dinners, and men's clubs, especially the Royal Society.

He at last came face to face with Peter Collinson, the heroic little tub of a man who had championed his cause. Now Dr. Fothergill, the physician with the elaborate wig, was a presence, not merely a signature on a page. And he finally met William Watson, who had months before elevated himself to the higher calling of physician.

These would not be scientific years for Watson or Franklin. Neither man would make any further significant advances in electricity. They enjoyed their status as elder statesmen at the Society, serving as advisers, reviewers, a pair of patriarchs serenely guiding ministers of state and younger scientists. Watson became an effective advocate for lightning rod use. The traditional histories depict Franklin and Watson in this era as friends, but to do that is to mistake the polite locutions of the eighteenth-century club for Victorian sincerities. The fires of the 1740s still burned, but beneath the surface. At a December 17, 1761, Society meeting, Watson was delivering a summary of Nollet's latest findings on electricity. Watson, seeming to approve of single- and double-fluid theory at once, when he came to the issue of *plus* and *minus,* couldn't restrain himself. It popped out. "So early as in February 1745, I communicated to the Royal Society an experiment and some deductions therefrom, which laid the foundation of this doctrine," snapped Watson. A sentence later, he reassumed his tone of lofty arbiter.

Franklin never fired back a salvo.

※

It was a time of waiting, too. Would the news bring word of triumph or death and mishap involving Franklin's discoveries? Good news arrived from Philadelphia. Nine years after Franklin published his how-to instructions, the efficacy of the lightning rod was demonstrated. A number of reliable witnesses had at the same instant heard a fierce crack and seen the bolt descend on the lightning rod attached to the house of the merchant William West on Water Street. Afterward, West and Ebenezer Kinnersley had climbed the roof to inspect the rod, its melted point proof the bolt had struck and then been conducted harmlessly into the ground. Franklin wrote back to Kinnersley of his "great pleasure" at the news.

Another concern—how many gentlemen would loft a kite into a

Lightning striking the rod-protected residence of William West in 1761 in Philadelphia. His house was unscathed, but parts of the lightning rod melted. This was the first demonstration of the effectiveness of Franklin's lightning rod. Here a nineteenth-century French artist depicts the important event, gets West's name wrong, and embellishes the drama.

thunderstorm for the sake of natural philosophy? Thousands had rushed to duplicate the Leyden jar in the months after the news broke. Mercifully, only a few experimenters flew electric kites and often these lightning-chasers were unknown provincials. The earliest was Jacque de Romas, a bureaucrat from southwest France, a little man who chased in the shadow of Franklin's renown claiming it should be his own. Romas said he independently conceived the idea of the kite in 1752 and flew his first in 1753. Although the local silk-coat gentlemen sniffed down their noses at the lowly contender (one member of l'Académie Bordeaux warned Romas he should be "happy competing with Franklin for the honor of inventing the electric kite, without hurting anyone's feelings"), Romas's claim would have great impact later. Other kite-fliers included John Lining in the Carolinas, Loammi Baldwin of Massachusetts, and Father Beccaria of Turin, Italy, who started in obscurity but built an international reputation with his experimenting. Accounts of electrical kite flying came from Petrus Musschenbroek, G. C. Lichtenberg, and, quite late in the century, dapper Tiberius Cavallo of Islington.

Publicly Franklin enjoyed life in London, and *Dr Franklin* spread beyond his circle of friends and became the persona known everywhere. *Franklinist* sprouted up in dictionaries, a term for young academicians across Europe beginning new careers and hoping to unseat the crusty old establishment content with Nollet's theories.

But off the record, the celebrity kept a wary distance from the events that created his celebrity. Impassioned pleas for information on how to safely install lightning rods went unanswered. Although he wrote letters to Kinnersley in the 1760s dealing in part with lightning rod installation, the mystery remains that Franklin waited seventeen years to publish an essay fully addressing the topic. The essay surfaced in the fourth edition of his booklet in 1769. The Yale Franklin project editors note that this essay "reported nothing essentially new" and seemed written for "persons who knew virtually nothing about the subject." Another minor essay on the topic addressed to David Hume waited until 1771 for publication in Edinburgh.

Other pleas for lightning information also went unheeded. In the Royal Society archive is an unpublished letter written by Father Beccaria that reveals the priest veering in passages between comedy and pathos, a would-be disciple desperately seeking for news and response from the great master Franklin, who does not answer back. The Italian priest willing to brave the thunderbolts from storm clouds hurtling down the southern Alps may have seemed to Franklin his worst nightmare, another Rikhman in the making. A terse 1762 response from Franklin reveals his coolness. Beccaria had begged for news of electrical experiments in London.

"I have not lately pursued it. Nor do I know of anyone here that is at present much engaged in it," Franklin wrote.

*

Ensconced in London, Franklin could point to a long string of honors, foreign memberships in academies, and honorary degrees as evidence of his acceptance, his status as a "citizen of the world." But the American colleges that honored him were primarily institutions for training Puritan ministers. In Britain, the universities that awarded him degrees had no status in electrical science and made no contributions in the field. His foreign memberships included a number of second-tier academies.

In the arena of front-line electrical science, there were three preeminent academies. These were the Royal Society, the Académie Royale des Sciences at Paris, and the Academy of Science at Berlin.

Only one of them awarded Franklin membership during that period.

In 1772, when Franklin had turned sixty-six years of age, two years after Nollet died, the Académie in Paris at last honored him with long overdue foreign membership. According to its archives, the academy at Berlin never made him an honorary member.

For a time, the canny Franklin even entertained some doubts about his English support. In a letter written to William Franklin, Benjamin recounts poking about Crane Court to look up how the Council had voted on his membership in 1757. Collinson had already informed him the vote was unanimous. Why not believe him? By this date, Franklin likely realized his good friend often gilded the truth. He was keeping tally—who were his friends and who were not—and on that day discovered that yes, he had all the votes, even Watson's.

He was accepted by the Society. But there was a second struggle for recognition and it came about on the Continent.

*

The skepticism first arrived from the Netherlands in a private letter. Old Petrus Musschenbroek, the grand elder statesman of the electricity craze, sent a curious letter on April 15, 1759, to Franklin. Apparently it was a response to some kind of indirect request from Philadelphia for a list of the foremost publications about electrical science. The Dutchman's answer was curious in two ways. First, Musschenbroek's list did not include a single work by any of Franklin's supporters, notably omitting Father Beccaria and Jean-Baptiste LeRoy, Franklin's most formidable advocate at Paris. Abbé Nollet rated three books on the list—no other electrician claimed as much, although Watson appeared with three items, two books and one published article. The second curiosity was some brisk advice from Musschenbroek. Since Franklin had flown his electric kite once, he needed to repeat it many times noting year, month, day, time, and location and atmospheric conditions if he was going to add to scientific knowledge.

The colonial air, offered the old Dutchman with a humorous edge, seemed full of electricity (*electricitatis plenissimus*), why not do it?

Franklin's public treatment from abroad was worse. Leonhard

Euler, the dean of German mathematicians and physicists, wrote *Letters of Euler to a German Princess on Different Subjects in Physics and Philosophy*. It was widely translated and printed in the eighteenth and the first half of the nineteenth centuries and arguably had greater popular impact than Franklin and Priestley's later efforts. Euler devoted two letters (chapters in fact) to lightning science. He did not mention Franklin's name. He referred to the priest Procop Diviš, who flew electric kites, and brought up the names of Rikhman, J. N. Lieberkuhn, and C. F. Ludolff, a signal unfairness to be sure. Euler's classic text appeared in French published in 1768 at St. Petersburg, but parts were written as early as 1761, and it is possible Franklin came across segments in circulation during summer traveling through Germany with Sir John Pringle in 1766, if not earlier.

Yet the severest blow was delivered across the Channel. In 1764 the Académie Royale des Sciences had officially weighed in on Franklin's electric kite claim (they had never published his 1752 text). The provincial electric kite flier, Romas, who was spurned at Bordeaux, pressed his claims all the way to Paris. The petitioner Romas made two points: one, he flew it first, and two, based on a reading of Franklin's text, perhaps Franklin had never flown a kite at all. To adjudicate, the Académie set up a commission that included Franklin's nemesis, Nollet, and on February 4, 1764, it reported:

> Having regard to all these proofs, we believe that M. De Romas had not borrowed from any one the idea of applying the kite to electrical experiments, and that one must regard him as the first author of this invention, until M. Franklin or some other makes known by sufficient proofs that he thought of it before him.

No one at the Royal Society in London came to the American member's defense. The Paris academy politely offered Franklin the opportunity to respond. But why set himself up for an inevitable flogging when Abbé Nollet was the judge?

They were trying to take away his reputation.

Indeed, Franklin remained a celebrity during his London years, but by the mid-1760s, his intellectual position as a scientist was eroding; he was enduring skepticism not only from crackpots and envious provincials, but from the most respectable scientists in his field.

Franklin would start his own campaign. He would set himself not to performing further electrical experiments, but—nearly two decades afterward—to writing the history of the electrical science that had passed. There is no precedent for this among other eighteenth-century scientists.

For nearly a decade, intermediaries had battled for him in experimental science; Collinson, Buffon, and Dalibard had waged these campaigns, setting in motion events at great distances and out of his control. But there was to be a second installment to his fame.

He was going to take the initiative.

Household God

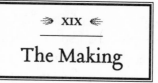

Such a career [Franklin's] bespeaks a country in which all things are making and to be made.

⮞ WOODROW WILSON

I T ENERGIZED HIM. AND CENTRAL TO THE CAMPAIGN IN which Benjamin Franklin remade himself would be the stranger who stepped close in a smoke-filled club in January, 1766. Many Georgian hopefuls pressed themselves upon Franklin in the whirl of his socializing, presenting letters of introduction. This one presented nothing.

The man was thirtyish, with tiny gray eyes, a schoolmasterly manner, and a face that bottomed out in the big stubborn chin of a ploughman. His coat was frayed, possibly secondhand. He spoke his name in a stuttering, utterly unengaging voice—the Reverend Joseph Priestley. At first, the unknown fellow appeared to be desiring a favor, but it wasn't exactly that.

The man was offering to write the history of Franklin's discoveries in electrical science. Several months later, when manuscript chapters from Priestley began arriving at his Craven Street lodgings, Franklin saw where this was leading. Priestley had begun work upon his classic-to-be *History and Present State of Electricity*. Setting to the task without any background in electrical science, Priestley wrote the account in a blaze of passion. He relied considerably on books and information supplied by Franklin, Watson, John Canton, Reverend Richard Price of the Royal Society, and a Reverend Holt of Warrington. As Priestley worked, he grew so interested in electricity that he began to replicate the experiments to better understand, and then he began to perform his own original experiments. A man with a prodigious ego, Priestley inserted what he imagined to be original contributions in the history, occupying a fifth of its pages. The history would take its place among this prolific author's many works as, he explained in his memoirs, "the most hasty of them all." The book, rushed into print in 1767, became a grand success.

Were there comprehensive, full-length histories of science before Priestley? Not really—there had been sketches, Haller's article in *Gentleman's Magazine,* Dalibard's preface to the French version of Franklin's *Experiments and Observations,* devoted to ignoring and insulting Nollet. Thomas Sprat and Thomas Birch had written books about the Royal Society—focusing on the club more than the science it encouraged.

Priestley's fling at writing history would motivate Franklin to help the clergyman in the job market. Although Priestley's zest and enthusiasm infuse his writings, the clergyman was not a very effective person-to-person communicator. When Priestley introduced himself to Franklin, he had already been through several parishes, whose congregations dwindled alarmingly under his guidance. His attempt at schoolmastering also collapsed. "The academy," he recalled, "did not flourish." His stuttering didn't help. But in the humble residential streets of Leeds, it was his religious tenets that distanced him from his neighbors. Priestley disputed the divinity of Jesus and the divine inspiration of the Bible and the existence of the soul. His true love was intellectual debate with Oxford theologians.

In 1772, Franklin's efforts—with some help from Richard Price—produced a large patronage plum for Priestly. He was hired to be librarian for Lord Shelburne, a man of immense wealth and power, in time known as the Marquis of Lansdowne and later the prime minister of Great Britain. Priestley's salary went from the hundred guineas per annum that his family struggled on to two hundred and fifty pounds and a house to live in, with arrangements for the income to continue if Shelburne predeceased him. His duties? They were minimal, "little employment as such," observed Priestley, describing a bit of book and manuscript cataloguing and indexing. Mostly he was hired as an intellectually stimulating companion to attend Shelburne's parties and dinners and accompany him in foreign travel. In the world of stunningly wealthy Georgians, attendants such as Priestley were not so unusual. A poem from the era records:

When Dukes or noble Lords a Chaplain hire,
They first of his Capacities enquire.
If stoutly qualified to drink and smoke,
If not too nice to bear an impious Joke,
If tame enough to be the common Jest,
That is a Chaplain to his Lordship's Taste.

Priestley was delighted with the job offer. Other plums preceded this one.

As Priestley turned out chapters, Franklin put his shoulder to getting the clergyman elected to the Royal Society. Among those whose signature joined Franklin's in nomination were the other editorial consultants to the project: Canton, Price, and Wilson. Priestley didn't possess either the wealth or title that characterized the majority of members nor the skills and scientific track records of the significant minority. But such qualms had not been an impediment

In the fourth edition, Franklin also altered what had appeared in earlier editions. I. Bernard Cohen states differently: "In some cases the actual text was revised. These revisions are never fundamental, but entirely literary." In fact, the revisions were of major importance—the claim of lightning rod installation not inserted, the reassurance that anyone may do the kite broomed, the attacks on Watson muted, and a large footnote paragraph added to explain—or dodge, take your pick—how Franklin could have repeated Watson's distance circuit that had required the Thames River and Westminster Bridge when in 1749 the Schuylkill River had no bridge. In the letter that set the Society laughing at his expense, Franklin had supported one hypothesis on the evidence of an "old sea captain" *singular*, a citation broadened in the fourth to "sea captains."

The realities of the 1740s were in part hidden behind what Franklin chose to tell in 1769. The revisions of the fourth edition appear also in the last eighteenth-century English edition, the fifth published in 1774. The fifth was then reissued by the scholar Cohen for twentieth-century readers. Franklin's revised book and Priestley's history form a tandem that did not take adventuresome steps into new electrical experimenting, but actively reworked what had happened in the past. Cohen, in effect, became a sort of twentieth-century ally.

Late in the 1760s Franklin had breathed new life into his international reputation. It was a reputation that would intensify into myth and fire the American Revolution.

The electric kite and lightning rod became the twin icons of this mythology. Their sparseness of detail sustained them: Their simplicity did not inform experimenters who would do and test—it asked for belief.

Franklin had presented his sentry-box experiment with an illustration no bigger than the end of his thumb—with no details supplied. On the contrary, Dalibard had cautiously depicted with *a* through *h* referents the French sentry box with a full-page illustration. Franklin's kite appeared in misty phrasings. Romas and Beccaria, however, illustrated in detail their kite-flying setups that were elaborately contrived Rube Goldberg devices designed to deal with problems of moisture, wind, and severe electric shock. In doing so, they lost the mythic sweep of the American simply lofting his kite into the storm.

As a Philadelphia businessman, Franklin had a gift for creating simple, powerfully affecting images. The Philadelphia printer developed painted signs that hung over eighteenth-century shop doors. In his newspaper, he yoked simple images and mottoes to advertise—he has been called the first American adman. It was Franklin the newspaper editor urging military unity in 1754 who created the first American political cartoon, an image of a snake cut in segments with the caption "Join or Die." Another Franklin delight was devising emblems for the flags carried by Pennsylvania volunteer militia units. The skills he had learned as a businessman sharpened the presentation of his famous scientific feats and encouraged their evolution into myth.

Myth fit Franklin very well—even in his own lifetime. His silence was part of its effect. Scores of journal keepers have recorded that in person Benjamin was curiously reticent, a halting and somewhat unimpressive speaker. But there was a boundary between being merely well known and full-tilt famous. Once he crossed that boundary, he didn't have to say much.

If he mentioned that Nollet was distracting him from further great experimental discoveries, others leaped in to defend him in debate. His silence was more effective than belabored de facto explanations. And occasionally others supplied or augmented his own delightful wit. It worked this way: For instance in December of 1750, Franklin had tried to kill a turkey with electricity. In the struggle, he accidentally touched the conductor, took the shock, and fell unconscious. This much is fact. Franklin reported it in a letter written December 25. But over the centuries a *bon mot* has been added to the tale. It issued, as later told, immediately from his lips as he awoke to the presence of his concerned friends standing near. "I was

trying to kill a turkey," he said, "and I almost killed a *goose*." A
Franklin scholar has traced the apocryphal remark back to a late
eighteenth-century jestbook. Once Franklin rose to mythic stature,
admirers replayed his anecdotes, spicing them with punch lines.

Scientists were outrageously seduced also and scrambled to repeat the great master Franklin's deadpan humor as serious science.
At Paris, Pierre Cabanis sat in an adoring circle at Franklin's feet lis-
tening to his account of a rare North American bird that, upon
death, sprouted two vegetable stalks from its wing joints. Cabanis,
a serious naturalist, tried to gather more information about the bird
for several years, until at last he realized he had been duped.

Politicians were sensitive to Franklin's power. By 1790, John
Adams waxed testy at the strength of Franklin's myth. Perhaps a bit
jealous, he wrote a friend that America's memory of the Revolution
would reduce to "Dr. Franklin's electrical rod smote the earth, and
out sprung General Washington. That Franklin electrised him with
his rod—and thenceforward these two conducted all the policy, ne-
gotiation, legislation, and war."

After Franklin's death and throughout the nineteenth century,
the image of the Founding Father who conquered electricity would
be used in assimilating a broad American cultural identity. Franklin
societies, printers' societies, workmen's clubs, broadsides, children's
books, serious biographies and histories, advertisements, pamphlets,
schoolbooks, didactic booklets, periodicals, calendars, commemora-
tive medals, pottery, paper and coin currency, all celebrated Franklin.
In the nineteenth century, states or locally designated charter banks
issued their own legal tender in the form of bills, tokens, stamps,
and even railway tickets depicting the familiar droll face. During the
monetary crisis of the Civil War, President Lincoln authorized the
use of a one-cent Franklin stamp as currency.

These commemorations celebrated the Founder of the Republic,
but a number also depicted the kite experiment. Waves of new immigrants encountered these tokens, stamps, and small bills in daily
life long before they learned the language. These mediums of ex-

change had weight, they offered promise, too. One promise was that a common man could start in poverty and rise to fortune. Another was that a shirt-sleeve man could plumb Nature's secrets as successfully as the educated and refined.

In this egalitarian message, the myth was not far from the reality. Franklin became an appealing symbol. Like Lincoln, he was suitably homely, for democratic purposes. Here was science from and for the common man. Here in the province of lightning was the unschooled teaching a lesson to the schooled.

*

In 1772, Franklin sailed back to America after a ten-year absence, expecting to return to London within the year, likely unaware yet of the full usefulness of his myth and certainly not realizing that anything like the War of Independence was on the horizon, nor that he, a Royalist devoted to empire, would become a revolutionary. In England, his old rival Watson would ascend to career heights in 1786 when George III dubbed him Sir William. Watson would arrive as an ornament of state. But out at sea on the heaving billows, charging with the power of his myth as lightning scientist, Franklin was on a different path. He was to become an instrument of state.

Franklin in Paris, *circa 1778, an engraving based on the life-sitting by Joseph-Siffrein Duplessis. More French artists than Americans painted the Founder in his lifetime. This portrait is one of complexity and psychological penetration. It also displays a New World primitive—no wig, no powder, and very plain dress. The Duplessis image is the sketch that likely launched a thousand portraits. Today, one version of it graces United States paper currency.* (Library Company of Philadelphia)

Bolt of Fate

Franklin had lain aside the wig which formerly in England hid the nudity of his forehead and the useless adornment which would have left him at the level of the other English. . . . Such a person was made to excite the curiosity of Paris.

➥ HILLIARD D'AUBERTEUIL

I T WAS REMARKABLE THAT HE WAS HERE AT ALL.

The sailors hurried to help him ashore. He walked with difficulty. The gout and the weeks at sea had taken their toll.

Picture him entering France. He was balding, the hair remaining gray and scraggly, quite heavyset or fat to use the plain language he used, and most of all, seventy years old. With his typical fatalism, he hadn't planned to live so long. Debbie was dead two years now, her bones resting in Christ Church graveyard in Philadelphia.

He didn't measure up to any standard of the heroic. Not young, not tall, not muscular, no aristocratic features. You can see the type he *was not* carved in eighteenth-century marble and in nineteenth-century marble and later in twentieth-century celluloid from Hollywood. No one who saw Benjamin Franklin entering France would have seen a hero embodied.

The man who was sent to rescue the American rebel cause had every reason not to.

Most gentlemen his age would have sat this one out by the hearthside. He had his investments to keep track of, he had a wish to add to his *Autobiography*. Wisdom cautioned him to stay neutral. If he joined either side in the American Revolution, when the war was done there was the chance he would lose everything. We know how much he was a man of precautions. We know he had the fear of sudden reversal of fortune of the newly rich.

But he chose to come.

The year was 1776, the date December 3. The place, the tiny village of Auray, a mere speck on the map. If Franklin had been apprehended by the British navy, he would have been hanged in London. Insurrection *was* prosecuted. The British had spies everywhere. The eighteenth-century British espionage system was the envy of Europe. They knew Franklin was coming. Twice on the crossing, his ship *Reprisal* had eluded British pursuit.

In fact, many Britons viewed him as a man in disgrace when he exited England in 1775. Franklin had been involved in the theft of a Crown document and its use to stir up resentment in the Massachusetts colony. The story made newspaper headlines in London. In a public display remarkable for its polite savagery, he had been lured to an event in an assembly-room known as the Cockpit and verbally abused and mocked by Lord Wedderborne, as the fashionables shouted and laughed at him. Afterward, some said that Franklin left England to avoid legal prosecution for his deed. The climate of British public opinion now defined him by his hoaxes and sexual drives; they called him *Devious Dr Franklin, Hoary Old Sinner,* and *Old Treachery of Craven Street*. If Franklin had been caught in transit that December, the majority of the British public would have been delighted to see him on the end of a rope at Tyburn.

He had risked death to step in this mud.

✳

Franklin had been put ashore because he was sick. The *Reprisal* had anchored off Brittany, waiting for favorable winds to take them to the port Nantes. Instead, Auray, an estuary village, nowhere, the stench of dead fish and low tide in the air, gulls screeching until his ears hurt. They deposited him on the marshy sands with his two grandsons—Benjamin Franklin Bache, his daughter Sally's seven-year-old boy; and seventeen-year-old William Temple Franklin, William's illegitimate son. The group stayed several days in an inn whose days of glory had visited in the fifteenth century, waiting for Franklin to regain his strength. Traveling on, they reached another inn. Franklin learned that an author he deeply admired was staying upstairs, the celebrated Edward Gibbon, author of *The Decline and Fall of the Roman Empire.* Franklin requested an audience. Gibbon, it is reported, sent word downstairs that he had no wish to meet with an insurrectionist.

It was not a propitious start.

But by the time they finally reached Paris, Franklin's strength would have somewhat returned and his arrival became one of those marvelous public crazes whose intensity and causes are difficult later to appreciate. The Parisians thrilled at his entry, crowds thronged his carriage, *huzzah*s thundering in the air, and every quality person at Versailles was intent to bow and curtsy before him.

Here was a culture in some central way ready to love this man.

Distance lent enchantment, of course. The political issues were complicated, but they could be simplified with immense impact. Benjamin Franklin lightning scientist had arrived on a mission to humble the English king. The crowds blocking his carriage cheered for *L'Electronique Ambassadeur.* To the delight of the ancien régime, the famous financier A.R.J. Turgot gave the perception a memorable twist in Latin: *Erepuit coelo fulmen sceptrumque tyrannis* ("he took the lightning from the heavens and the scepter from the tyrant").

When Franklin arrived in the streets of Paris in 1776, few of those in the crowds had heard of Poor Richard. In 1773, his *Way of*

Wealth, a humorous compilation of his almanac proverbs tied to the adventures of fictional Richard, had been translated and appeared in *Oeuvres de M. Franklin* and gone unnoticed. But Antoine Quétant published a second translation in 1777 that was an immediate best-seller. The new title, *Le Science du Bonhomme Richard,* reveals the sea change, in translation the bumpkin Richard who in English is the object of satire is transformed in French into the *good man,* a rural philosopher with precepts for daily living whose wisdom is moral science. Among middle and lower French people, there arose the confusion that Benjamin was Poor Richard. There might be time someday to clear these things up.

At Versailles, his gout would have given him pain as he labored up the grand sweep of the marble stairs. He made his entrance into the majestic Hall of Mirrors at night. As the chandeliers blazed, the elegant arched windows on the one wall and looking glasses covering nearly all else turned the splendid hall into a world of multiplying images, a shimmering confusion of real people and reflected ones, a splintering of selves. There was nothing like this in the colonies. But in the hall, after some whispers, everyone looked around to find out the newcomer, there were cheers, shouts, applause. He had arrived.

From out of the crowd of powdered heads and lace, the faces unrecognized, there appeared a man. He was bluff-faced, almost red-cheeked. He was the eminent Duc de Croy, a man of past military glories who dreamed of future polar expeditions. He introduced himself, excited, staring into Franklin's eyes.

"Only the person who discovered electricity could electrify two worlds," the Duc said to him.

✳

During the year preceding Franklin's arrival, the American commissioner Arthur Lee had obtained a verbal assurance of French aid to the rebel cause. Later when the acclaim for success showered on the magnetic Franklin, Lee argued that he deserved the accolades for his own prior efforts. The other commissioner, Silas Deane, who in the immediate wake of Lee's work began to negotiate the financial reality of the agreement, felt that he had played the decisive role.

How did the newcomer fit into this scenario?

It was a very intense, complex diplomatic mission that Franklin stepped into, an effort riddled with divisions, an Iliad of feuds, alliances, misalliances, spies, adventurers, and intriguers. The verbal promise from the king might, as the days passed, fade from his royal mind. Would France declare itself an ally, would France give the rebels a naval presence? There is every evidence that in the three months after Franklin's arrival, it was up for grabs.

The fact that the Continental Congress sent this elderly man who was so ill he could barely get off the boat reveals how desperate they actually were. Britain's naval forces controlled the sailing approaches to France. It was standard procedure for the American rebels sending messages across the Atlantic to send four in hopes that one would arrive. During Franklin's stay in France, the British navy was so effective in interceptions that a year passed with no communiqués from America. His Majesty's navy controlled the sea-lanes, and on American soil, the British seemed equally effective. New York City had fallen to them, and in the spring, British regulars would march in and take over Philadelphia, sending the Congress fleeing in disarray to the wooded Pennsylvania hill country. The Americans had suffered disastrous defeats on the battlefield. The rebel army was on the verge of collapse, its coffers nearly empty, unable to supply ammunition, supplies, blankets to enable troops to survive who had been pushed out into the countryside. Soldiers deserted in the face of privation or simply didn't come back at the end of enlistment terms. It was reasonable, it wasn't presumption, on the part of the British to think this war was nearly over.

During the week Franklin arrived in Paris, General Washington's forces marched in desperate retreat across New Jersey with General Howe's superior forces on his heels, ready to corner Washington and finish the insurrection once and for all. In the nick of time, Washington reached the Delaware River, crossed over, and was able to dispatch patrols to commandeer all boats and skiffs upstream on his side so the British could not immediately pursue.

As Howe stood on the river bank, staring across the frigid waters, he turned over his options. Why bother to pursue them now? He knew from espionage of their lack of supplies and clothing. He could wait them out, settle in the captured cities to pass the winter in comfort and win this without firing a shot. By spring, there probably wouldn't be a Continental Army left to fight.

This news followed Franklin to France. Only later did news arrive of the denouement in New Jersey. Washington had taken half his troops and marched ten miles north where the commandeered boats were held. In the middle of the night, the evening of Christmas day, Washington and his soldiers crossed the Delaware in the darkness as a winter storm blew down the valley. The weather was severe, raging winds and blizzard-like snow. The worst time, of course, to march and seek a fight. The least expected, too.

At Trenton, New Jersey, the German mercenaries employed by the British were comfortably sleeping off a night of Christmas feasting and celebration. The men awoke to the sound of American artillery strafing the streets. As they stumbled out of their barracks, they found themselves completely surrounded by snow- and ice-covered rebels training their muskets upon them. The German officers surrendered immediately.

At last, the Americans had scored a significant victory. Nearly a thousand mercenary soldiers were taken prisoner and the Americans acquired guns, cannon, ammunition, and blankets that their own treasury couldn't have afforded. The American casualties didn't include any soldiers killed by enemy fire, but did number two frozen to death, a testimony to the bitter, ill-clothed march in the dark.

The extreme nature of Washington's gamble testifies: This was a last-ditch effort as much on the battlefield as at the diplomatic tables in Paris.

On Franklin's arrival, his task was to *not* present a hint of their dire straits. Somehow, he did what he did very well most of his life, outwardly remaining the cool operator, smiling, relaxed and humorous.

When English Ambassador Lord Stormont spread the report in the Paris salons that the Americans had been beaten and lost four thousand men, they asked Franklin if it was true. Franklin smiled and answered, "Truth is one thing and Stormont another." The comeback delighted all of Paris society.

It must have been even more daunting when they came to Franklin with the news that the largest colonial city and capital of the rebellion, Philadelphia, had fallen and his own home had been occupied (and abused) by a British officer. All eyes would have watched his face for the least hint of a tremor.

General Howe had taken Philadelphia?

"Ah," he replied, "it is not he who has taken Philadelphia, but instead Philadelphia has taken him."

❋

It was a bumpy road before Franklin. Even after the agreements were finally signed and made public, the French were very sensitive to maintaining their international prestige. As the news of defeats filtered across the Atlantic, the French might tie their purse-strings and distance themselves, announcing, "This is *their* flop, not *our* flop."

But Franklin was expert at gaining support. The French historian B. H. R. Capefigue described him in action: "He showed himself little, like all men who choose to exercise a mysterious influence. But he made people talk about him a great deal. When he left his residence at Passy, it was to go to the Academy of Sciences, of which he was an assiduous correspondent. There, in the midst of a programme on electricity or a series of physical experiments, he dropped some words about his dear country—solemn and sad—

which would waken the sympathies of those men of science and literature who were the leaders of the 18th century."

＊

The other major factor working against the Americans upon Franklin's arrival was King Louis XVI.

The king had given verbal assurances of aid, but he postponed. The promise hung fire. And the longer he delayed, as the American cause sputtered and stumbled, it seemed less and less likely aid would follow, and the king's tardiness began to seem to amount to wisdom. In fact, His Highness voiced serious hesitations about setting an example by encouraging commoners to revolt against the crown. In light of what followed, the dim hesitant king may have possessed more insight than the staff of French intellectuals urging him on.

Louis XVI was a mild young man, a bit of a bumbler, even then with a sort of pear-shaped center of gravity so that when walking about his mansion he was described as resembling "a peasant waddling behind a plough." There was always something awkward and essentially boy-like about him even as he widened with age; he preferred hunting in the royal woods to politicking in the Hall of Mirrors.

In 1770, as a prince he had been married to the lovely Marie Antoinette, Archduchess of the House of Austria, a union that had been arranged as a political alliance of the utmost importance. The great dictate for the young man was to swell his queen's belly with royal seed. The lineage must go on, but there was a medical problem, and Louis would dither and postpone for seven years, creating unhappiness in the marriage and an international political crisis. In the portraits, Louis has the dreamy eyes of a man with no urgency.

If it took Louis seven years to consummate his marriage to Marie Antoinette, how long would the American Revolution have to wait?

*

Franklin's reception would influence what the king decided. On his first two trips, Franklin had been politely greeted at Paris, never transcending status as a minor news item. He knew more about his myth now—and he also had a mission. He stepped on the shores of France the third time in service of *Liberté*. The *philosophes* and beautiful people had been reading Rousseau and the misty idea of liberty exulted them. As the king noted uneasily, the lower classes also stirred at the drama of the North American throwing off the shackles of absolute monarchy.

Perhaps it was the rejuvenescence of his reputation. When Franklin arrived on his first visit to Paris with Sir John Pringle in 1767, his midcentury science had been old news. His works were out of print. His friend Barbeau Dubourg contributed a new *Oeuvres de M. Franklin* in 1773, which by including the fourth edition of his electrical science and adding many works such as *The Way to Wealth* and *Observations concerning the Increase of Mankind* made Franklin more available between book covers in Paris than anywhere else in the world. In addition, his old nemesis the Abbé Nollet had passed away in 1770; the decades of academic feuding also died away with no polarity to sustain them. The real frontiers of electrical science had moved on and the brilliant work was being done in Italy. Franklin had become a kind of grand old man in his field more worthy of homage than debate.

Another important factor in Franklin's stunning third welcome at Paris were the spinmasters busy at court. The dramatist Pierre-Augustin Beaumarchais, a best-selling author and adventurer and adviser to the king, set himself to marketing the American Revolution to the French. Beaumarchais had a special genius for the task; as author of the successful *Le Barbier de Seville* and *Le Mariage de Figaro* he was able to gauge and catch the public fancy, and as royal adviser, he wrote brilliantly persuasive memos intended for His Majesty's eyes only. His motives were not totally altruistic. He hoped to corner for himself the position of agent for the French aid administration, taking his percentage and surely a little extra. In fact, Franklin's translator Dubourg had similar motives; he set his sights on what seemed a very lucrative position. None of this would have shocked Franklin. In his scientific correspondence many years before, he formed alliances with a number of *virtuosi* seeking advantages in colonial investments. Another Franklin "friend" and Revolution enthusiast was Donatien le Ray de Chaumont, who gave Franklin rent-deferred, perhaps rent-free quarters in the delightful mansion on his own estate at Passy. The other American commissioners, especially John Adams who arrived in 1778 and was honest to a fault, had moral reservations about such doings. Chaumont was, in fact, a speculator who also hoped to corner French contracts for supplying the rebel forces. Franklin knew how to swim with the sharks.

Although the French delight in Benjamin was abetted by these three spinmasters, it depended also on confusions. And the confusions were many.

When Franklin entered salon society, he seemed to step almost naturally into a mythic idea of the *philosophes* concerning an innocent primitive man evolved in the New World, a man brimming with moral insights born of common life. To dress the part got you halfway there. It is not clear when Franklin hit upon the idea of entering Paris society in humble dress. The occasion of course demanded lace cuffs and powdered wig. But he stepped before the ancien régime in a fur cap from the American wilderness, a marten fur cap, wearing a plain dark coat, no silks, no ornaments, not even silver buckles on his square shoes, and carrying instead of a ceremonial sword a crab-apple cane. He created a sensation.

When did he conceive this image? There is every evidence it was a last minute inspiration, an improvisation. The first item in Benjamin's account book after expenses of landing is "101 livres, 5 francs for wigs."

It's possible the idea came to Franklin in his very first days ashore as the carriage jolted on the backroads of Brittany, as the bedraggled traveler was greeted by peasants who had heard news of the arrival of the American who conquered lightning and was asking French help to put the English king in his place. Franklin had suffered a scalp affliction, and perhaps going hatless at times or wearing the soft floppy marten hat instead of a tight wig helped him feel better. But at some point in the responses along the road he realized: The peasants were mistaking him for a New World primitive. It was an early installment of the Continental version of his myth. In 1767 and 1769 he had visited Paris on vacation jaunts and caused no furor. As St. Beauve observed, "This Franklin of 1767, thus curled, powdered, and dressed like a Frenchman, differed totally from the purely American Franklin who reappeared in 1776." He discovered that this myth was bigger than his reality in the nick of time for the Revolutionary cause. He could step into it, he could use it.

His American colleagues—they may have been not unreasonably a little jealous—who knew he had silk coats and fancy wigs in his wardrobe, who knew he had imbibed little from mystical meditations in the North American forests but much from sophisticated London—they were provoked at his casual hypocrisy. Serious, prim, they themselves in his shoes would have tried to explain away these confusions.

"Never contradict any body," Franklin had advised Jefferson.

And Franklin didn't.

He played this to the hilt.

When the French saw him in his drab plain coat and assumed he was a Quaker, he didn't disabuse the notion. If you had wanted to seduce a Parisian belle in that era, to arrive from America and claim you were a Quaker would get you halfway there. A Paris police blotter from the time refers to a young woman who sought criminal charges against a man who took advantage of her by fraudulently claiming to be a Quaker. Voltaire had started the intellectual fad for Quakers. Although he had never been to America, he romanticized the Pennsylvania Quakers in his *Philosophical Letters*. In Quakers, he saw all the virtues lacking in French salon intellectuals, he envisioned they arose in a New World of temperance, morality, and equality. Franklin didn't advise his hosts otherwise.

When the French maidens saw Franklin wearing bifocals, tittering they reassured one another that his natural virtue of *economie* had caused him to wear cracked spectacles instead of replacing them; he merely smiled back at them. Who was he to *explain?*

Nearly every home had to have a Franklin picture over the mantel, even if it was only an inexpensive print. More than two hundred portraits were made of Franklin in Paris. He complained about the sittings. "I have at the request of friends sat so much and so often to painters and statuaries that I am perfectly sick of it," he wrote. But he never stopped complying. Franklin wrote his daughter about the vogue:

> The clay medallion of me you say you gave to Mr Hopkinson was the first of the kind made in France. A variety of others have been made since of different sizes; some to be set in the lids of snuff boxes, and some so small as to be worn in rings; and the numbers sold are incredible. These, with the pictures, busts and prints, (of which copies upon copies are spread everywhere,) have made your father's face as well known as that of the moon, so that he durst not do anything that would oblige him to run away, as his phiz would discover him wherever he should venture to show it. It is said by learned etymologists, that the name *doll,* for the images children play with, is derived from the word IDOL. From the number of dolls now made of him, he may be truly said, *in that sense,* to be *I-doll-ized* in this country.

Franklin's interest went beyond the joys of being admired. When he ordered a portrait replica, he was known to art-direct changes in these emblems that conveyed him to an admiring world. Chaumont's factory in the Loire churned out medallions bearing his face by the thousands, and Franklin kept a stock of them, distributing the keepsake to visitors at Passy.

Franklin was the hero of 1777 in Paris, and cheap prints, trinkets, and curios bearing his image were hawked by vendors in the streets. Every mantel required the admired face of the seemingly innocent philosopher. This terra cotta medallion was churned out by the thousands from a factory owned by Paris investor Donatien Le Ray de Chaumont. The artist was Jean Baptiste Nini, who worked from a drawing by Thomas Walpole. In a later edition, Chaumont added the inscription, Erepuit coelo fulmen sceptrumque tyrannis, *"He snatched lightning from the heavens and the scepter from the tyrant."*

(Franklin Collection, Yale University Library)

His American associate John Adams was stunned at the goings-on. "He has a passion for reputation and fame," wrote Adams, "as strong as you can imagine, and his time and thoughts are chiefly employed to obtain it, and set tongues and pens, male and female, to celebrating him. Painters, statuaries, sculptors, china potters, and all are set to work for this end." Many portraits of Franklin are etched in acid in the letters of John Adams and also in descriptions by his wife Abigail. Franklin is depicted enjoying the merry social whirl. He played chess, he pursued beautiful middle-aged women, he seemed shamelessly at ease.

As Franklin idled away his afternoons playing chess with Madame Brillon and trading flirtations, his American colleagues grumbled that he did not join ranks with them in the overwhelming line-item burdens of the diplomacy.

But Franklin held the view that chess was invaluable that year. "The game of chess is not merely an idle amusement," he remarked in a charming essay, "The Morals of Chess," which he authored and printed on a small press he had installed at Passy. The game of chess sharpened his edge for the real work at hand.

As he noted, "The game becomes thereby more the image of human life, and particularly of war."

He would find himself submerged in the thousand details of their situation in negotiating war-aid from France, the intricacies of the feuding commissioners, the drudgery of the endless accounts, the unstoppable flow of frauds and double billings, the affairs connected to settling privateer prizes, soldiers importuning for appointments, opportunists and merchants on the make. But the afternoons by the lovely woman at the chess board gave Franklin a perspective.

He was trying to get ready for the crucial moments yet to come. Age and the effects of ill health took their toll, but he tried to focus on what was important. He had his myth to work. He ignored his fellow associates' resentments.

He could see farther than the pawns on the board.

This is the civilest nation upon Earth.

➤ BENJAMIN FRANKLIN ON FRANCE

C HESS HAD TAUGHT HIM, SAID FRANKLIN, "NOT TO BE TOO much discouraged by any present success of his adversary, nor to despair of final good fortune on every little check he receives." A startling remark. Check, of course, is only one move from checkmate. He was playing a game in a tight corner. The British not unreasonably sensed victory near at hand.

He spent afternoons sometimes receiving visitors in his pleasant suburban house at Passy, administering electrotherapy to paralytics, utterly disregarding his own advice to the contrary in the fourth edition recently published in French translation. These days may have especially recalled the early excitement of the electrical science craze in the way the young women delighted in him. Mme. Campan of Marie Antoinette's retinue described an event with 300 young women, the beauties lining up for kisses, trilling in excitement *Papa*, *mon cherie, Papa Franklin,* pushing him with lush frontal kisses that knocked his spectacles off. And Abigail Adams describes with her sharp eye, Madame Helvétius entering a dinner party, sitting next to Franklin, and draping her arm with shocking casual intimacy across his shoulders. Mrs. Adams was stunned. She had never observed such goings-on in Boston.

But *this* man. Franklin. Ah, Franklin.

Women might have had more power over what the French thought of Franklin than historians have imagined. Women often reigned in authority over the discussions at salons. A belle at Versailles might sum up a male encounter—"he positively *won* me." A polite world of wins and losses, impressions made, angles played. The question was how far Franklin could use an aspect of himself that was essentially a myth; would he *win* over some of the most savvy and merciless political observers in the world? They were not naive. Although the Marquis de Condorcet cast his lot with the Franklin enthusiasts, he noticed that there was a "shrewd man" behind the primitive man; the French intellectual was able to appreciate both, in a way perhaps not totally foreign to today when some pop star of great sophistication and wealth can sing a phrase derived out of folk-poverty, and buzz with both worlds at once.

Hundreds of descriptions were penned about Franklin during his stay. Franklin-watching became a pastime.

It came down to this.

The ultimate take on Benjamin would be made by King Louis XVI. The brilliant intellectuals surrounding him offered scores of reasons for and against aid to the Americans, so that after the first year's recitals, these were reduced to mere litanies of debating points. Yet something else would be crucial at the start of 1777: opinion in the salons of the ancien régime.

The real battleground in Paris was how these wily court politicians viewed Franklin. They could not help being stirred by the remarkable frenzy as images of the visitor multiplied. "One sees copies [of Franklin] at every street corner," observed Felix Nogaret, noting

To the Genius of Franklin, *1778*

*This etching by Marguerite Gerard is based upon a sketch attributed to Frag-
onard. The artist manages to balance the rococo extravagance of Olympian
cloud drama with the sharp realism of the tired face of an elderly tradesman
from Pennsylvania.* (Philadelphia Museum of Art)

the American was "well and faithfully rendered in medallions, in bracelets, on bonbon boxes, in medals and on every mantelpiece worshiped no less than a household god." There was an intense enthusiasm for him that for some bordered on the physical and for some *was* physical. "My wife," wrote one man to Franklin, "has long pestered me to obtain your consent to be painted in miniature. She wishes to have you hung *en medaillon* at her throat."

Many of the French accounts note there was a seductiveness to Franklin. Elkanah Watson, an American entrepreneur and observer at Versailles, recorded Franklin's impact on Marie Antoinette, who at first seemed coolly indifferent:

> His venerable figure, the ease of his manners, formed in an intercourse of fifty years with the world, his benevolent countenance, and his fame as a philosopher, all tended to excite love and to command influence and respect. He had attained, by the exercise of these qualities, a powerful interest in the feelings of the beautiful Queen of France. She, at that time, held a strong political influence. The exercise of that influence, adroitly directed by Franklin, tended to produce the acknowledgment of our Independence, and the subsequent efficient measures pursued by France in its support.

In the Louvre art gallery hung "the portrait of Franklin near those of the King and Queen, placed there as a mark of distinguished respect, in conformity with royal directions." The pious Marie, youthful daughter of the Holy Roman Empire, would never have descended to impropriety with this diplomat. But the familial threesome intimately proximate on the wall testifies that Franklin had with her, as with nearly all of France, at some astonishing level, had his way.

✳

When King Louis XVI at last assented, the grand day to sign and make public the treaty was March 13, 1778. The Americans, Silas Deane, Arthur Lee, and the others, had been primed by the court chamberlain on necessary etiquette, formalities of dress and coiffeur required to enter His Majesty's presence.

What happened next reveals that Franklin's growing use of his myth was as improvised, by-the-seat-of-his-pants, and last-ditch as the rebel war effort at home. There had been a very expensive formal wig made for him. He had put it on. He stared at himself in the glass and then he put it back on the peg on the wall. The wig-maker was outraged. Ignoring the man's shouts, Franklin hurried away to his carriage.

When they arrived at Versailles, at first the crowd outside buzzed with astonishment, but then they cheered. There was a second close call. The chamberlain was shocked at Franklin's dress. *Monsieur may not enter without his wig.* Comte de Vergennes, the French foreign minister, interceded and got him admitted through the door.

King Louis XVI studied Franklin for a moment as he stepped before him. The room overflowed with men in capes and plumed hats and ribbons and medals on their coats. They all stared at this strange plain person. "I should have taken him for a big farmer," remembered Mme. Vigée-Le Brun, who witnessed the ceremony. Even the Americans looked uneasily out of the corners of their eyes at him.

At last, Louis smiled.

"Firmly assure Congress of my friendship," he announced to the American delegation.

There was one other precipitous moment, when the paper was unfolded on the table for signing. Conrad Gerard of the French Foreign Office signed first. Then it was Franklin's turn as the senior member of the delegation. For a blink, he was almost carried away. You can see it on the treaty. A huge *B* unfurled and out spiraled an expanding and dramatically leaning *F*. His pen glided through the next letters in overly narrow disciplined ranks for greater melodramatic contrast. He was blundering. He was well on his way to laying down Benjamin ultra-fancy on the page. But he reigned in, he caught himself in time, and when he finished, turned a modest flourish, nothing like the dramatic triple swirling loop under, say, the signature on his letter to the Royal Society.

He knew already from his use of hoaxes that a pen could have the push of a bayonet. He handed the quill to the next man.

During the nine years Franklin served as representative of the Americans in Paris there were many crises, many ups and downs. Scores of factors would play a role in maintaining French support of the American Revolution. Millions more in livres would be required. But during the first year of his residence, when a world of palace observers viewed and tested this droll man who had arrived wigless, while Louis XVI as usual dithered, it was Franklin's lightning science that defined him to the public. Not one observer, not one lovely twenty-two-year-old Queen, but the whole polite civilized world scrutinized him minutely.

Because of the kite, as Franklin played it, he had learned how to use his myth as a weapon. Later a scholar would say, "At the French court and in French society his greatest asset had been his prestige as a natural philosopher, and it became America's asset."

It might have been a kite, the story of a kite, the hoax that won the American Revolution.

EPILOGUE

*As having their own Way, is one of the greatest Comforts of Life,
to old People, I think their Friends should endeavor to accommodate them in that.*

                          ❧ BENJAMIN FRANKLIN

AFTER THE PEACE TREATY WITH THE BRITISH WAS SIGNED on September 3, 1783, Benjamin Franklin's career was not done. Congress demanded that he remain in diplomatic harness, securing loans from the French to aid the struggling new republic. Franklin, however, wanted to end his years in Philadelphia and wrote his sister, "Tis time I should go home, and go to bed." He finally returned in 1785. Despite the infirmities of aging, he played a major role in the Constitutional Convention, busied himself with investments, developed expensive real estate on North Market Street, continued writing his autobiography, and actively campaigned against slavery and the slave trade. When he died on April 17, 1790, he was eighty-four years old.

Four days later, on April 21, Benjamin was laid in the earth next to Deborah in Christ Church burial ground. Their bones rest in peace near the southeast corner of Fifth and Arch Streets. To this day, the site remains a tourist attraction—but curiously, the location just beyond the bustle of the Independence Hall mecca draws many more schoolchildren than adults.

On a recent midday in Philadelphia, the grave itself wasn't easy to see over the stream of middle-school viewers. It was autumn, the skittering of the leaves across the pavement merged with boys shouting, girls tittering and shrieking, and adults barking commands and keeping order. At the cemetery, where a small part of the eighteenth-century wall guarding the old churchyard had been removed, there was an opening not much larger than a door with black iron rods barring entrance. Often, the jolly throngs bunched up, hesitated. There wasn't much to do but peek through the grating. And then? The children shot *what's-next* glances at teachers and chaperones. The folklore that follows doesn't seem to rise up from childhood, but to have been delivered down from adulthood above: the ritual tossing of a penny inside for good luck. It is funny, this daily shower of coins on the grave of a man who, if he rose and spoke, would tell them to hold onto their coins.

The better time to see Franklin's grave is late in the afternoon. The buses of schoolchildren have fled to the suburbs, the pneumatic sighs of bus doors opening and closing now gone. Arch Street empties early. Much of this city has a pleasing and very human scale, the genial parks and squares, the Assembly Hall where your footstep can echo in the very room where the elderly Franklin tilted back his gray head and sometimes snored during interminable Constitutional debates.

You look through dark iron bars at one flat rectangular stone covering the space occupied by the couple in the earth. The inscription reads simply "Benjamin and Deborah Franklin 1790."

If William Franklin, raised to London silk-coat style, had overseen the burial, a splendid monument might rise here. But the administrator was Sarah Franklin Bache, the daughter once reprimanded and chastened by her father for requesting so much as one

French silk handkerchief. Three decades later in the last will, be-
queathing her his diamond-set portrait of Louis XVI, he warned
her "not to form any of those diamonds into ornaments either for
herself or daughters, and thereby introduce or countenance the expensive, vain, and useless fashion of wearing jewels in this country."
Concerning his tomb, the daughter followed the instructions in her
father's will.

Another monument to Benjamin Franklin appears later in the
day, as the yellowing last lights die into darkness, and the dimming
canyons formed by the city's buildings glow and bloom with light,
the night-glittering of a whole civilization whose efficiencies and
very intelligence have now become electrical.

Electricity is with us—in ways Franklin didn't imagine. We have
tamed and ruled over this universal force and turned it ordinary.
The electricity of the 1740s was wild, a wonder, a pleasantness. With
our dominion over this force, we have also inherited a pervasive fear
of it. During the earliest and most elemental stages of their development, we train children to be afraid of the three-pronged outlet
in the wallboard. To a degree, we are all Rikhman's children. But at
the start, at least, in Franklin's time electricity was something lightly
taken, a party stratagem, one of the pleasant intimacies connected
with one's own body.

*It's an astonishingly suggestive emblem, the electric kite experiment,
like a dream in the way it blurs details and changes elements in the traditional repertoire of eighteenth-century electrical science. Gone are the
groups of gentlemen and beauties, the chain of hand-holders, vanished are
the military objects, absent the complicated wheel-beset furniture crafted
in mahogany, and its parlor. The salons and palaces and academies have
been exchanged for a green expanse near Philadelphia. There is a lone individual, a field, a big sky, a string mounting up to the heavens, and a
key. The key lets you in.*

Notes

Abbreviations Used

ABF   *The Autobiography of Benjamin Franklin*, Leo LeMay and Paul Zall, eds.

ESEC *Electricity in the Seventeenth and Eighteenth Centuries*, John Heilbron

FW   *Benjamin Franklin Writings*, Leo LeMay, ed.

GM   *Gentleman's Magazine*

HAWD "An historical account of the wonderful discoveries . . . concerning Electricity," Albrecht Haller

PBF   *The Papers of Benjamin Franklin*, Leonard W. Labaree, Ellen Cohn et al., eds.

PG   *The Pennsylvania Gazette*

PT   *Philosophical Transactions*

WBF   *The Writings of Benjamin Franklin*, Albert H. Smyth, ed.

Prologue

xv   *"If there is no other"*: PBF, 3:171.

xvi   *"It is all the vogue"*: HAWD, 194.

xvi   *"historical amnesia"*: David Hackett Fischer, *Paul Revere's Ride*, xiii.

xvii   *"Early to bed and early to rise, makes a man healthy wealthy and wise."*: PBF, 2:9.

xviii *"stifled"*: ABF, 1453.

xix   *"The natural philosophers"*: Horace Walpole, *The Last Journals of Horace Walpole*, 10:22.

xix   *"the kite that won"*: Isaac Asimov, *The Kite That Won the Revolution*, 13.

xx   *"crucial importance"*: Ronald Clark, *Benjamin Franklin: A Biography*, 3.

Chapter 1: Almanack-Writer

The main source of material for these Franklin years is the *Autobiography*. See *The Infortunate* by Willam Moraley (edited by Klepp and Smith) for an authentic eighteenth-century journal of the misery in Philadelphia that could befall runaways or individuals mistaken for runaways; it reveals what Franklin was up against in the autumn of 1723.

3   *"The first Thing"*: FW, 272.

3   *"a tolerable genius"*: R. Campbell, *The London Tradesman*, 123.

4   *"grew in a little"*: *ABF*, 1354.

6   *"If a Philadelphian in 1728"*: James Parton, *Life and Times of Benjamin Franklin* (1864 ed.), 1:209.

7   *"Poor Richard, I repeat"*: Ibid., 1:228.

8   *"But this obstacle"*: *PBF*, 1:311.

9   *"There is, however"*: Ibid., 350.

9   *"Having received much"*: *PBF*, 2:3.

10 *"An Almanac, how soon cast aside"*: *GM*, 1749, 19:40.

11 *"I take notice"*: *PBF*, 4:220.

CHAPTER II: THE PARTY BEGINS

12 *"Philosophy is"*: Benjamin Martin, *The General Magazine of Arts and Sciences* (Jan. 1755), quoted in John Millburn, *Benjamin Martin: Author, Instrument-Maker, and 'Country Showman,'* 73.

12 *"as Dr Spencer, who was"*: *ABF*, 1452.

12 *"not very expert"*: Ibid., 1452.

12 *"some account of the use"*: Ibid., 1453.

13 *"phenomena, so surprising"*: *HAWD*, 194.

13 *"Even Poland"*: Ibid., 194.

13 *"I supped"*: Duchesse of Bedford to Duke, 1746, published in Mary Borer, *An Illustrated Guide to London 1800*, 209.

14 *"The electric shock itself"*: Joseph Priestley, *The History and Present State of Electricity* (3rd ed.), xv.

15 *"Could one believe"*: *HAWD*, 194.

15 *"fiery intellect"*: *ESEC*, 263.

15 *"If there be but one"*: Richard Sheridan, *The Rivals* (Act II, scene 1), 820–821.

17 *In the severe moral*: See David H. Fischer's *Albion's Seed* for description of Pennsylvania sexuality, 498–502.

18 *Thales . . . suggested . . . amber . . . possessed*: Alfred Still, *Soul of Amber*, 7.

18 *"wonderful attracting power"*: Plato quoted in Duane Roller and Duane H. D. Roller, *The Development of the Concept of Electric Charge*, 543.

18 *"everything subject to our senses"*: Gilbert quoted in Ibid., 549.

19 *"He was the first"*: *HAWD*, 193.

19 *there were two electricities*: Geoffrey Sutton, *Science for a Polite Society*, 298–299.

19 *"I own I thought"*: Thomas Woolrich to B. Wilson, May 5, 1747, BL, 30,094 Wilson Papers.

20 *"Are there animal spirits"*: *HAWD*, 195.

20 *"Error, Sir, creeps"*: Laurence Sterne, *Tristram Shandy*, 168.

20 *"as surprising as a miracle"*: *HAWD*, 197.

20 *"For my own part"*: *PBF*, 3:118–119.

CHAPTER III: THE EQUIPMENT

22 *"I think it a great pity"*: John Freke, *An essay to shew the cause of eletricity* (3rd ed.),
     136.
23 *turnspit and a philosopher:* Bishop of Norwich quoted by De Morgan by Milburn,
     Benjamin Martin, 45.
24 *"As I see that this"*: Musschenbroek quoted and translated in *ESEC,* 313–314.
26 *"the electrical equivalent"*: Ellen Kuhfeld, interview.
29 *Andreas Cunaeus: ESEC,* 313–314.

CHAPTER IV: THE GENIUS OF NATIONS

The sources for Nollet's life drawn on in this chapter include: Jean Torlais, *Un Physicien au siècle des lumières, L'Abbé Nollet;* Heilbron's biography in *Dictionary of Scientific
Biography;* Jean-François Gauvin, "Abbé Nollet's Instrument-Making Trade . . ."; Isaac
Benguigui, *Théories Électriques Du XVIII Siècle;* and Rames Bahige Maluf, *Jean An-
toine Nollet and Experimental Natural Philosophy in Eighteenth-Century France.* The
Watson sources include: R. Pulteney, *Sketches of the Progress of Botany in England;* unpublished letters in the British Library; the fascinating Bulloch's Rolls at the Royal
Society Library, which reported the Cumberland visit; interviews with Dee Cooke of
the archive of the Society of Apothecaries; John Byrom, *Selections from the Journals and
Papers of . . .* ; the biography in *DNB;* the biography by Heilbron in *Dictionary of Scientific Biography;* and the L. F. Abbot oil portrait of Watson at the Royal Society.

32 *"For several Years"*: Nollet, "Part 5. of a Letter . . . ," *PT,* 47:1.
38 Main sources for Cumberland are *DNB; GM, 1746;* Rex Whitworth, *William
     Augustus, Duke of Cumberland: A Life;* Morris Marples, *Poor Fred and the Butcher;*
     Peter Anderson, *Culloden Moor and the Story of the Battle;* and Evan Charteris,
     William Agustus, Duke of Cumberland: His Early Life and Times (1721–1748).

CHAPTER V: UNIVERSAL CURE

41 *"I do not exaggerrate"*: C. G. Kratzenstein, *Abhandlung von dem Nutzen der Elec-
     tricität.* In *C. G. Kratzenstein, professor physices experimentalis Petropol.* Trans. and
     ed., Egil Snorrason, 38.
42 *"was the first"*: Ibid., 34.
42 *"This idea"*: Ibid., 40.
42 *"What reward"*: Krüuger quoted in Park Benjamin, *A History of Electricity: The
     Intellectual Rise in Electricity,* 501.
43 *"Her modus operandi"*: Byrom, 2:459.
43 *the presence of Queen Anne:* Boswell, 31.

44   *Nollet journeyed: ESEC*, 289, 354.
44   *"that not only"*: Winkler translated and quoted by Watson, "An Account of Professor Winkler's Experiments relating to Odours," *PT*, 47 (1751), 231.
45   *"Must we conclude"*: Ibid., 240.
45   *"a vast number"*: Watson, "A Letter from Mr. William Watson F.R.S.," *PT*, 46 (1750), 352.
45   *"a canonized Saint"*: Ibid., 355.
45   *"Great numbers"*: *PBF*, 3:284.
47   *"These appearances"*: *PBF*, 7:299.

CHAPTER VI: SUNDAY

49   *"We rub our Tubes"*: *PBF*, 3:134.
50   *known as a 'Hand'*: In interview with John Heilbron and e-mail with Simon Schaffer early in this research I was alerted to the mix of "hands" and silk-coat gentlemen in early electrical science. Schaffer sent me an electronic version of his "Experimenters' Techniques, Dyers' Hands, and the Electric Planetarium," *Isis* 88, 2 (Sept. 1997). Schaffer's fascinating account deals with the Kentish dyer Stephen Gray, who brought his manual touch to producing electricity. More than sixty years earlier, the blacksmith who invented the electrical friction tube, Otto von Guericke, had advised that the best results were achieved by an experimenter with "hard, horny hands." In static electrics, the dry, work-hardened hand of the tradesman may have outperformed the soft fleshy hands of gentlemen whose sensitive palms would perspire and leak the electrical charge away. But also the tradesmen had the kind of knowledge not expressible in language or mathematics, depending on "a light nice hand." This skill played a part in the rise of the tradesmen Watson, Nollet, and Franklin.
51   *"My house was"*: *ABF*, 1453.
52   *"rough minutes"*: *PBF*, 3:169.
52   *"American electricity"*: Ibid., 132
52   *"which we looked upon"*: Ibid., 3:126–127.
52   *"wonderful effect"*: Ibid., 127.
52   *"We suppose, as"*: Ibid., 131.
54   *"having only the middle"*: Ibid., 131.
55   *"All is reduced"*: Ibid., 131.
55   *"We say B"*: Ibid., 131–132.
55   See Sibum, "The Bookkeeper of Nature": 238.
56   *"To electrise plus"*: Ibid., 132.

CHAPTER VII: AMONG GENTLEMEN

59   *"Him wot prigs"*: Samuel Pegge.

59   *"without any prefaces"*: Thomas Sprat, *The History of the Royal Society*, 2nd Part, sect. xx, in *Eighteenth Century English Literature*, Geoffrey Tillotson et al., ed., 28.

61   *"Anyone who can"*: W. H. Auden, *Restoration and Augustan Poets*, Introduction, xxii.

63   The source of the Wilson materials is the typescript of his unpublished autobiography now at the Heinz Archive of the National Portrait Gallery at London.

65   *"This pamphlet contains"*: *GM*, 16 (June 1746), 291.

65   *"most generous . . . drawn up . . . a great many"*: letter in *GM*, 16 (July 1746), 355–356.

66   *"a man in a state of nature"*: Laurence Sterne, *Tristram Shandy*, 235.

67   See the marvelous Hogarth oil portrait of Martin Folkes at the Royal Society.

68   *"When people don't"*: Ellen Kuhfeld, interview.

68   *"this report is not"*: William Watson, "Some further Inquiries," *PT*, 45 (1748), 93.

68   *"America serves for"*: Edmund Burke, "Second Speech on Conciliation with America. The Thirteen Resolutions." (May 22, 1775).

68   *"As this experiment"*: Ibid., 98.

69   *"The solution of"*: Ibid., 100.

CHAPTER VIII: NIGHT BENJAMIN

70   *"Benjamin Franklin invented"*: often attributed to Balzac, the source is his novel *A Distinguished Provincial at Paris*, nt (Peter Fenelon Collier & Son, New York, 1900), 258. A character says, "That [canard—or hoax] is our word for a scrap of fiction told for true, put in to enliven the column of morning news when it is flat. We owe the discovery to Benjamin Franklin, the inventor of the lightning conductor and the republic." The aphoristic version here appears as early as 1918 in the Yale Chronicles of America Series; see Bliss Perry, *The American Spirit in Literature*, 57.

71   *"to indulge me"*: *PBF,* 3:123.

71   *"I readily consented"*: Ibid.,124.

72   *"great and growing"*: Ibid., 125.

72   *"the duty of"*: Ibid., 125. The main sources for information on these events were Max Hall's remarkable book, *Benjamin and Polly Baker: The History of a Literary Deception;* Hall, "Benjamin Franklin's Whoppers," *Harvard Magazine* (Nov.–Dec. 1985), Discovery Section, 72A–72H; Max Hall himself in interview; Franklin's *Autobiography;* and Verner Crane's *Benjamin Franklin's Letters to the Press.*

      In all fairness to Max Hall, he differs sharply with my view that Franklin used his hoaxes for personal advantage. Hall views them as literary satire. In a note addressed to me, Hall states that Franklin the hoaxer "had a motive, not to deceive but to entertain and to poke holes in pomposity and folly, and to show up bad policies."

74   *this was payback:* See Francis Drake, *The Town of Roxbury,* also Leo LeMay's Web
     site menu for 1722–1723. A 1723 article in a Boston paper had criticized the magis-
     trates and noted "(. . . the infamous Gov. D[udley] and his family) have been re-
     markable for hypocrisy." One eighteenth-century source identified Benjamin as
     author; LeMay suggests that James Franklin may have written it. The article re-
     ferred to Paul's father, Governor Thomas Dudley, and the rest of the eminent fam-
     ily. The Franklin brother's legal problems aside, Benjamin might have also envied
     Paul Dudley, who had all the advantages that Benjamin did not. Dudley had
     wealth, social status, political power, and even received scientific honors when he
     was made a foreign member of the Royal Society in London and was published in
     Transactions. The Dudleys, father and son, were also widely known as difficult peo-
     ple. Massachusetts oral folklore told that one day Dudley senior was driving to
     Boston when he stopped and commanded a laborer to hurry back to the judge's
     home and retrieve a lawbook. The wide-eyed laborer hesitated, then enquired, "Can
     one fetch it, sir?" "Oh yes," the judge replied. "Then go yourself," the man replied.

75   *Franklin began to shake:* Franklin told of his confession at Passy to Jefferson,
     quoted in Ford, ed., *The Writings of Thomas Jefferson,* Vol. 10:120–121.

76   *The sixteen-year-old: ABF,* 1323.

76   *After the Puritan Assembly:* Ibid., 1325.

77   *Benjamin arrived:* Ibid., 1330.

77   *In 1729 masquerading:* Franklin in LeMay, ed., "A Modest Enquiry into the Na-
     ture and Necessity of a Paper-Currency," *Franklin Writings,* 119–135.

77   *In the same year:* See account in LeMay text notes, Ibid., 1474. See also Carl Van
     Doren, *Benjamin Franklin,* 95–98.

77   *In 1732: PBF,* 1:310–312.

77   *In 1747:* Franklin, *ABF,* 1411. Source for "Plain Truth" text is a facsimile of a 1747
     pamphlet as published.

77   *Beginning in 1755:* Max Hall, "Benjamin Franklin's Whoppers," *Harvard Maga-
     zine* (Nov.–Dec. 1985), Discovery Section, 72E–72F. Also Hall, *Benjamin Frank-
     lin and Polly Baker,* 91–92.

77   *In 1761:* Franklin, LeMay, ed., "The Jesuit Campanella's Means of Disposing the
     Enemy to Peace," *Franklin Writings,* 535–539.

77   *In 1763:* Franklin, LeMay, ed., "An Edict by the King of Prussia," *Franklin Writ-
     ings,* 698–703. See Hall scholarship for evidence from William Strahan the
     printer, "Benjamin Franklin's Whoppers," 72E–72F. See Franklin himself (*PBF,*
     20:438–439) for a passage concerning the edict hoax that reveals how Franklin
     was regarded by his wealthy and titled friends during the silk-coat years in Eng-
     land: they knew he was a hoaxer.

78   *In the 1770s:* Antonio Pace, *Benjamin Franklin and Italy,* 86.

78   *During the American Revolution:* Numerous works document how Franklin pre-
     sented himself in Paris. Key ones include Alfred Aldridge, *Franklin and His
     French Contemporaries;* David Schoenbrun, *Triumph in Paris: The Exploits of Ben-
     jamin Franklin;* Sainte-Beuve, *Portraits of the Eighteenh Century,* Vol. 2; and C.

Sellers, *Benjamin Franklin in Portraiture.* Wonderful and extensive nineteenth-century treatments include E. E. Hale and E. E. Hale, Jr., *Franklin in Paris,* and James Parton, *Life and Times of Benjamin Franklin,* Vol. 2. Abigail and John Adams are primary sources who record Franklin in Paris with acid pens but sharp precision. See, for instance, John writing of Franklin's "passion for reputation and fame," *John Adams Letters,* 2:367.

78   *In 1782:* Hall, "Benjamin Franklin's Whoppers," 72H.

78   *His last:* Franklin, LeMay, ed., "Sidi Mehemet Ibrahim on the Slave Trade," *FW,* 1157–1160.

CHAPTER IX: IVY-GIRLS AND HOLLY-BOYS

79   *"Let a person":* Neale, 30.

79   *"his salty year":* Carl Van Doren, *Benjamin Franklin,* 154.

80   *"There was an edge":* J. H. Plumb, quoted by Charles Goodwin "The Religion of Feeling: Wesleyan Catholicism," *His Today* 46 (Oct. 96), 4.

80   *maidservant desiring an evening:* Mrs Parker, *A Glossary of Words Used in Oxfordshire,* 120.

80   *"The philosophers are now":* Samuel Johnson, *Dictionary* 1: "Electricity," entry 1.

81   *"5. A lover":* Ibid., 2: "Spark," entry 4.

81   *"Airy, gay":* Ibid., 2: "Sparkish," entry 1.

81   *women who issued electrical fire:* "Account of a lady consumed by fire," *GM,* 16 (July 1746), 369. See also "Surprising Phenomenon of a human Body" by "J.L." in *GM,* 17 (May 1747), 220–221.

82   *on Shrove Tuesday:* Samuel Pegge, *An Alphabet of Kenticisms,* 33.

82   *"Four feet distant":* "An account of a lady consumed," *GM,* 16 (July 1746), 369.

82   *Sigaud de Lafond:* Heilbron, *ESEC,* 320.

83   *"I beheld":* The Bible, Ezekiel 1:4, 1:27, and 8:2.

83   *"We suspend":* PBF, 3:133.

84   *"We increase":* Ibid., 133.

84   *a Franklin electric party:* Mason Locke Weems, *The Life of Dr. Franklin,* 168–174.

84   *"created a Franklin":* Carla Mulford, "Figuring Benjamin Franklin," *New England Quarterly* 72 (Sept. 1999), 420.

84   During this research, every effort was made to track down the Dickinson source and information about Elizabeth Seaton, without result.

84   *of Health and Hymen:* Guy Williams, *The Age of Agony,* 190–192.

85   Louis-Léopold Boilly, oil painting, "The Electric Spark," Virginia Museum of Fine Arts.

Addendum note: As this was written, Patricia Fara's *An Entertainment for Angels: Electricity in the Enlightenment* was published with its excellent discussion of eighteenth-century social context.

CHAPTER X: DEADLY BOX

87   *"He* [Peter Collinson] *got them": ABF,* 1453.

87   *First, Watson:* See William Watson, "Some further Inquiries . . . ," *PT,* 45 (1748), 98–100.

87   *Second, Watson:* An examination of the Journal Book of the Royal Society indicates Franklin's letter was never read.

87   *The third Franklin:* The Journal Book entry for Dec. 14, 1749, records the attempt to introduce the letter, bypassing Watson, but the Society conveyed the letter to Watson to process. The Dec. 21, 1749, entry records Watson giving his response and promising to communicate it also in writing. Remarkably, Watson again spoke of the letter at the Jan. 11, 1750, meeting and took the significant step of entering his critical objections to Franklin in the Journal Book itself. See Watson's text in *PBF,* 3:457–458.

88   *"laughed at by": ABF,* 1453.

90   *"laughing fraternity":* John Hill, *A Dissertation on Royal Societies,* 25–26.

90   *"stifled": ABF,* 1453.

90   *Collinson discreetly fudged: PBF,* 3:283.

90   *Watson promised:* Ibid., 457–458.

90   *Franklin took two: PBF,* 4:7.

90   *"The members": PBF,* 3:36.

91   *the third letter:* This chronology of Franklin's science letters is based on that established by the Yale Franklin project. For issues of dating this correspondence see also I. B. Cohen, "Some Problems in Relation to the Dates of Benjamin Franklin's First Letters on Electricity," *Proceedings of the American Philosophical Society* 100 (1956), 537–542. A brief early Franklin letter concerning his gratitude to Collinson and his enthusiasm is not in this narrative; in the fourth edition of *E & O* Franklin inserted it as the first letter. Here the first letter identified is dated May 25, 1747, the letter reporting the three men/two wax cake demonstration and announcing his *plus/minus* theory (I in Bowdoin ms.). The second letter is dated July 28, 1747, the report applying his *plus/minus* theory to the Leyden jar (II in Bowdoin ms.). The third letter is dated April 29, 1749, and it includes the two jokes (III in Bowdoin ms.). The fourth letter, the one sent via Mitchell, is also dated April 29, 1749 (IV in Bowdoin ms.), and is filled with atmospheric and planetary speculations; this report was ridiculed by the members at Nov. 9 and 16 meetings of the Society. I have designated the Mitchell letter fourth for several reasons. Franklin did so, and it was the fourth installment in his thinking on electricity. In London, however, the fourth letter was read aloud at the Society meeting a month before the third. In the New World—due to shipping circumstances and Mitchell's extraordinary delay—the news of the third returned to Franklin before the news of the fourth. The brief note dated July 27, 1750 (V in Bowdoin ms.), begins, "Mr. Watson I believe wrote his observations on my last paper in haste," and responds to Watson's critique: The refuted refutes back.

Collinson had promised a personal response and "further favors" but had delayed four months before at last on April 25 sending what proved to be Watson's slighting response. Two days after Franklin answered Watson's criticisms, he next wrote the July 29, 1750, report (Bowdoin VI), the fateful letter with the sentry-box experiment.

91 *"The hot weather"*: *PBF,* 3:364–365.
91 *"Hold the picture"*: Ibid., 358–359.
92 *"To determine"*: *PBF,* 4:19–20.
93 *"Before I leave"*: Ibid., 20.
94 *"The Doctor after"*: Priestley, *History,* 216.
94 *"We have bought"*: *PBF,* 3:466.
95 *neat scale drawing:* DuSimitiere papers, Historical Society of Pennsylvania.
96 *"propose to have an observatory"*: *PBF,* 3:483.
96 *"Could there have"*: Parton, 1:289.
96 *"Mr. Watson I believe"*: *PBF,* 4:7.
97 *"Franklin thought"*: Cohen, *Franklin and Newton,* 487.
97 *"If any danger"*: *PBF,* 4:19–20.
98 *"la couverture"*: Dalibard, *Expérences et Observations,* Vol. II, 45; Dubourg, *Oeuvres,* 63.
98 *he helpfully inked in:* Schonland, 22 (Figure 3).

CHAPTER XI: THE CRUSADERS

99 *"The [Royal] Society has"*: Thomas Sprat, *History of the Royal Society: Second Part,* Section 20 in *Eighteenth Century English Literature,* Tillotson et al., eds., 28.
99 *"below the middle size"*: Kippis, *Biographia Britannica,* 42.
99 *"among the ranks . . . these businessmen"*: Lisa Jardine, *Ingenious Pursuits,* 269.
100 *"conceal thy intention"*: Collinson quoted in Condon, *Transatlantic Friends,* 50.
100 *"withdrew"*: Bulloch's Rolls at the Royal Society Library, London.
100 *"explain the cause"*: Cadwallader Colden, *An Explication of the First Causes . . . ,* iv.
101 *"I perceive that you"*: Colden, *The Letters and Papers of Cadwallader Colden,* IV:419.
101 *"had said more sensible"*: Fothergill letter March 18, 1751, edited by Corner and Booth, *Chain of Friendship,* 143.
101 *£1000 to publish:* R. Hingston Fox, *Dr. John Fothergill and his Friends,* 27.
202 Main sources for Edward Cave are John Nichols, *Literary Anecdotes of the Eighteenth Century,* *Boswell's Life of Johnson;* B. Foster, *Ye History of ye Priory and Gate of St John.*
103 *published in the first issue:* GM, 1 (Feb. 1731), Introduction.
104 *"beheld it with reverence"*: Samuel Johnson quoted in *Boswell's Life of Johnson,* 81–82.

105   *Cave was a huge man:* See Cave's portrait etched by E. Scriven from the oil painting by F. Kyte.

105   *"he had few":* Sir John Hawkins quoted in Nichols, 87.

105   *"He was watching":* Samuel Johnson quoted in Ibid., 80.

106   *"Nothing was ever":* Priestley, *History and Present State of Electricity,* 192.

106   *"Your American electrical operator . . . into some printer's hand":* PBF, 3:460.

106   *"dilatoriness":* PBF, 4:122.

107   "After the immemorial"*: PBF,* 4:126–127.

108   *on Captain Waddel's:* PBF, 4:143–145; in *PT,* 48 (1751–1752), 289–291.

109   *"was either ignored":* Heilbron, *ESEC,* 344.

109   *"It was however":* ABF, 1454.

109   *"happening":* Ibid.

CHAPTER XII: MARLY

110   *"The discoveries made":* Abbé Nollet, "An Account of a Treatise, presented to the Royal Society . . . ," *PT,* 48 (1753), 201.

111   *"The desire to please":* Father Raulet quoted in Thomas Dalibard, "Extrait D'un Mémoire De M. D'Alibard," PBF, 4:306.

111   *a new look at the background:* John Heilbron, *ESEC,* xv, sect. 2, "Buffon's Clique," 346–352. A main source for this Marly narrative is Heilbron's interpretation.

112   *"His way of reasoning":* Joseph Adrien Lelarge quoted in Ibid., 346.

112   *"happening": ABF,* 1454.

112   *"He [Franklin] asked":* Dalibard, "Avertissement" to Franklin's *Expériences et observations,* translated by Dalibard (1752 edition), 1:4. Translation supplied by Elizabeth Ihrig.

112   The account of Buffon is principally based on Jacques Roger, *Buffon: A Life in Natural History,* O. Fellowes and S. Millikin, *Buffon;* the sketch in *Dictionary of Scientific Biography;* and Heilbron's *ESEC.*

114   *to the royal dungeon:* Heilbron, *ESEC,* 347.

116   *"immediately he flew":* Dalibard, "Extrait . . . ," PBF, 4:306.

116   *"double speed":* Ibid., 306.

118   *"Each try":* Ibid., 307.

120   *"plainly perceived":* "Extract of a Letter from Paris," *London Magazine* (June 1752), 249.

121   *"One of those":* "Paris, July 7," *London Magazine* (July 1752), 327.

121   *"After all, a fly":* Buffon quoted in Heilbron, *ESEC,* 347.

121   *any reference to Delor:* Dalibard, "Avertissement" to Franklin's *Expériences et observations.* Dalibard's second edition was a different version of Franklin's reports too, one that improved on the hasty work that first caught the king's eye. Although most scholars have ignored this edition (the second edition appeared in 1756), it reveals much about how the French viewed, or wanted to view, Frank-

lin. There were significant changes. The version includes Dalibard's and Raulet's correspondence about Marly. Franklin himself would insert their un-translated accounts—with a few changes—into the 1769 version of his *Experiments and Observations*. Dalibard's version is also sprinkled with quotes from his superior, Buffon. But the real change was on a much larger scale.

In the second edition, Dalibard completely turned inside out the structure of *Experiments and Observations* and introduced a whole new architecture, changes made without warning the reader, changes made in fact in a way to disguise that these occurred if the reader didn't have the original text to compare. The fault line, predictably enough, turns out to be the sentry-box proposal. Without explanation, the second edition moves "Opinions & Conjectures," which was sixth in the original edition, up to the second spot. Equally mysterious, "Additional Papers," which was fifth, has been moved to first in the new edition. "Opinions & Conjectures" undergoes major surgery with nothing to clue the reader that changes have been made; Dalibard omits the sentry box, introduces a quote from Buffon, and ends the letter. The para-graph numbering doesn't indicate the surgery. The sentry box is then swept to the rear in Volume 2, where it is inserted in another letter, but the paragraph numbering gives the impression nothing has happened, all is seamless. Why are these changes made? One guess is that Franklin is being made over in the image of a French encyclopedist on the order of Buffon. Here his experiments, which to us seem so valuable and which start his book, are tossed unannounced to the rear of the French second edition. What goes in front is Franklin at his worst, wholesale hypothesizing about earth, air, and sea, all observations and no experiments. It's almost as if a fancy but silly French wig had been popped on his head. He is now The Man of Reason.

Franklin wasn't comfortable with this French version—he had it reversed when his ally Dubourg published a new translation twenty-five years later.

121   *"not yet quite master":* PBF, 5:186.

123   *"The Abbé Nollet":* Buffon quoted in Heilbron, *ESES*, 349.

123   *"Mr. Franklin's concussion":* G. M. Bose, letter at the British Library, BL 4443, f47. The July, 1751, date at the letter's end seems inconsistent with its content.

Chapter XIII: Lightning

124   *"The deep—":* Shakespeare, *King Lear*, IV.7:33.

124   *"I beheld Satan":* Bible, Luke 10:18.

125   *weekly editing:* One of editor Franklin's earliest references to lightning occurs in *The Pennsylvania Gazette*, June 19, 1732; it revealed that he understood that metal (pewter) conducted lightning, and it revealed his humor: "From New York, we hear, that on Saturday se'nnight, in the afternoon, they had there most terrible thunder and lightning, but no great damage done. The same day we

had some very hard claps in these parts; and 'tis said, that in Bucks County, one flash came so near a lad, as without hurting him, to melt the pewter button off the waistband of his breeches. 'Tis well nothing else thereabouts, was made of pewter."

125   *ironing boards were metal: The Pennsylvania Gazette,* July 14, 1768.

125   *In 1763:* Ibid., Oct. 27, 1763.

127   *The older spelling, "lightening": OED,* VIII:935

127   *"It is a dogma":* Thomas Aquinas quoted in Park Benjamin, *The Intellectual Rise in Electricity,* 592.

128   *"I break up lightning":* Ibid., 593.

128   *"In Munich in 1784":* Bern Dibner, *Early Electrical Machines,* 39n.

128   *"The weather has suited":* Daniel Wray quoted in D. P. Miller, "The Hardwicke Circle: The Whig Supremacy and Its Demise in the 18th-Century Royal Society," *Notes and Records of the Royal Society London* 52 (1998), 85.

128   *"If one made . . . It will go hard":* Ibid.

128   *"You may assure":* "A Letter from a Gentleman at Paris . . . ," GM 22 (June 1752), 263–264.

129   *"prepare and set up":* Watson, "A Letter of Mr. W. Watson . . . ," *PT,* 47 (1751–1752), 567–568.

129   *The schoolmaster performed it:* John Canton quoted in Ibid., 568–569.

129   *"I repeated the experiment":* Benjamin Wilson, transcript of his autobiography at NPG London.

130   *"Trifling as":* Watson, Ibid., 569.

130   *"I see by Cave's": PBF,* 4:355, dated Sept. 14 in the month when calendar change removed September's last two weeks.

130   *"in pursuance":* letter in *GM,* 22 (May 1752), 229.

131   *"I hope": PBF,* 4:355.

131   *"But if the artists":* Jane Mecom, *The Letters of Benjamin Franklin & Jane Mecom,* edited by Van Doren, 200.

131   *"He that by the plow": Poor Richard's Almanack, 1747; FW,* 1242.

132   *"Philosophy as well": Poor Richard Improved, 1753; FW,* 1276.

CHAPTER XIV: THE KITE

Main sources for this chapter include interviews with these specialists: Jay Nelson, Sr., Philadelphia, eighteenth-century lock and key authority; Michele Majer, New York, authority on eighteenth-century fashions and silk; Professor Allen G. Noble of Akron University, authority on eighteenth-century vernacular style in agricultural architecture; and Albion Bowers and James Murray of NASA Dryden Flight Research Center and Professor Michael Selig of Illinois University, authorities on aerodynamics.

Issues concerning the text of the kite tale are several. The first to notice that Franklin changed the text of his kite report for later publications was Gustav Hellman

in *Ueber Luftelektricitat 1746–1753* (Berlin: Asher, 1898). The German scholar speculated that Franklin's motive was to claim priority. Another crack in the legend appeared in the article of an American scholar who demonstrated that Franklin probably
did not fly his kite as early as June, 1752, and likely heard of the French experiment and
their version of the lightning rod before anything like a kite experiment was on the
horizon. See Abbot Lawrence Rotch, "Did Benjamin Franklin Fly His Electric Kite
Before He Invented the Lightning Rod?" *Proceedings of the American Antiquarian Society* 18 (1906), 118–123. Rotch produced two other articles: "The Lightning-Rod Coincident with Franklin's Kite Experiment," *Science* 24 (Dec. 1906), 780; and "When
Did Franklin Invent the Lightning Rod?" *Science* 24 (Sept. 21, 1906), 374–376. Alexander McAdie of Blue Hill Observatory at Cambridge, Massachusetts, produced a
landmark paper that closely examines Franklin's literary text and also closely compares
authenticated kite flights with the 1752 report and began to demolish the story. See
McAdie's "The Date of Franklin's Kite Experiment," *Proceedings of the American Antiquarian Society* 34 (Apr.–Oct. 1924), 188–205. Marcus W. Jernegan attempted to salvage
the legend after McAdie's and Rotch's articles but in the process did more damage,
calling into question Franklin's precedence over the French in erecting lightning rods.
See "Benjamin Franklin's 'Electrical Kite' and Lightning Rod," *The New England
Quarterly* 1 (1928), 180–196.

In 1938, Carl Van Doren's classic biography *Benjamin Franklin* devoted six pages to
the inconsistencies of the kite and rod announcements; he calls the kite "famous but
mysterious." His sources may have been the articles mentioned above, but he doesn't
make this entirely clear. I. B. Cohen produced a work of valuable research to celebrate
a Franklin anniversary. Uncollected in his many books, it is "The Two Hundredth
Anniversary of Benjamin Franklin's Two Lightning Experiments and the Introduction of the Lightning Rod," *Proceedings of the American Philosophical Society* 96 (June
1952), 331–366. Cohen defends the traditional Franklin kite story, devoting special effort to fending off the priority claims of Jacque de Romas.

135   *"That which deceives"*: Plato, *The Republic*, Book III:413-C.
136   *"But God, as if"*: Parson Weems, *The Life of Benjamin Franklin*, 167.
136   *"Why should he"*: Park Benjamin, *The Intellectual Rise in Electricity*, 592.
136   *"Benjamin Franklin succeeded"*: Sabine quoted in Mottelay, *Bibliographical His-
      tory of Electricity & Magnetism*, 194.
136   *"Modern Prometheus"*: Kant quoted in Brother Potamian, *Makers of Electricity*,
      119n.
137   *published in* Philosophical Transactions: *Franklin, "A Letter of Benjamin Franklin
      Esq., to* Mr. Peter Collinson, F.R.S. concerning an electrical kite." *PT,* 47
      (1751–1752), 565–567.
137   *"As frequent mention is"*: Franklin, Ibid., 567–570.
138   *"thereby the sameness"*: *PBF,* 4:367.
139   *"Keep all this to yourself"*: *PBF,* 20:327.
140   *"I have . . . seen"*: *PBF,* 4:376.

141   *If you look carefully:* More than thirty years afterward Franklin at last claimed he
      was an active agent in the kite event. See his *Autobiography*, 1455: "I will not swell
      this narrative with an account of that capital experiment, nor of the infinite
      pleasure I receiv'd in the success of a similar one I made soon after with a kite at
      Philadelphia, as both are to be found in the histories of electricity." Of course, he
      gracefully strikes a warm-fuzzy note of delight, all the while refusing to answer
      requests such as Musschenbroek's for more specific detail. He also pluralizes pri-
      mary source support, citing "*histories*." There was only one (Priestley's).

141   *of bifocal glasses:* letter to George Whatley, Aug. 21, 1784, in *FW*, 1104–1110.

141   *"Description of":* Franklin, "Description of an Instrument for Taking Down
      Books from High Shelves," Jan. 1786, Ibid., 1116–1118.

141   *Lastly concerning text:* The kite text does not survive written in Franklin's hand.
      There are two early versions, one printed in *The Pennsylvania Gazette* and a copy
      now at the Royal Society written in Peter Collinson's hand. There are some puz-
      zles. The Yale Franklin project has done some fascinating sleuthing regarding the
      Collinson copy. That document is dated October 1, a date that doesn't seem to fit
      other evidence from Franklin's correspondence and transatlantic shipping times.
      The Yale scholars suggest that "conceivably, Collinson's pen slipped when he
      wrote 'Octo: 1,' as it occasionally did in referring to other Franklin letters." There
      is an addendum on the bottom of the copy, perhaps printer instructions: "See his
      Kite Experiment." It raises the possibility that Franklin included an illustration
      with his original transmission that was lost, ignored, or edited out in the edito-
      rial process that concluded with publication in *Philosophical Transactions* (earlier
      Franklin had apparently sent Collinson a brief essay on electrical points that was
      published in *Gentleman's Magazine* in 1750, which involved a simple diagram-
      matic illustration, perhaps in the vein of the missing kite illustration). The Yale
      scholars discovered that the ending paragraph announcing lightning rods in-
      stalled in Philadelphia is written in William Watson's hand: "The words are
      doubtless Franklin's," argue the Yale scholars. This view is shared here—the
      terms of reference are colonial; the style and word choice, Franklin's. The Yale
      suggestion is that Watson may have had Franklin's original letter at hand in the
      editorial process and added its end paragraph to a copy by Collinson destined for
      the printer. What is clear is that afterward Franklin edited this announcement in
      his later book publications, deleting two important items.

142   *Watson demonstrated:* William Watson, *Experiments and Observations*, 14–15.

142   *At Marly:* Dalibard, "Memoire," in *Expériences sur l'Electricité* (1756 edition),
      2:128.

142   *ruined Watson's:* Watson, "A Letter of Mr. W. Watson," *PT*, 47 (1751), 568.

142   *"want of success":* Guillaume Mazeas, "Letters of the Abbé Mazeas, F.R.S. . . . ,"
      PT, 47 (1751–1752), 537.

142   *In our era:* Vladimir Rakov, University of Florida, in personal correspondence
      with the author.

144   *"Dr. Franklin, astonishing as":* Priestley, *History and Present State*, 215.

144   *humble little Le Monnier:* "Extract of a Letter from Paris," *London Magazine* (June 1752), 249.

144   *"easy manner, which anyone":* PBF, 4:366.

144   *"To demonstrate":* Priestley, *History and Present State*, 215–217.

147   *"within a door":* PBF, 4:367.

147   *third kite story narrator:* William Stuber quoted in entirety by Alexander McAdie, "The Date of Franklin's Kite Experiment," *Proceedings of the American Antiquarian Society* 34 (Apr. 9, 1924–Oct. 15, 1924), 197–198.

147   *in an open field: World Book,* Vol. F (2001).

148   *"the erection of a spire":* Priestley, Ibid., 216.

148   *"broken open":* The Pennsylvania Gazette, Nov. 1, 1750.

148   *"The latch key was":* Jay Nelson, Sr., Philadelphia, telephone interview, Oct. 5, 1999.

150   *How do you keep the key:* Kuhfeld has pointed out that "if the key is at the junction of silk and hemp, its weight could keep water from flowing on silk" (see her sketch). The experiment was tried. This setup sharply constricted the control of the kite-flier.

151   *a ten-inch square:* Michelle Majer, New York, telephone interview, 1999.

151   *called it a Bruschttuch:* David Hackett Fischer, *Albion's Seed,* 551.

152   *"The visit of a Quaker evangelist":* Ibid., 544.

152   *"If thou art clean":* William Penn quoted in Ibid., 546.

152   *"As late as 1788":* Brissot de Warville quoted in Ibid., 551.

153   *a Dutch hay barrack:* Alan G. Noble, University of Akron, telephone interview, 1999.

153   There's no proving Franklin *never* flew his kite. It will always remain possible. But this experiment he presented as convenient and likely turns out to be dauntingly inconvenient.

      I did fly kites to write this book. I tried to loft a pre-Eddy kite; the sticks were cedar; the airfoil, thin silk with dimensions near thirty by thirty inches with the bows tied to the stick-ends—as Franklin directed—resulting in an area about twenty-four by twenty-four inches; an aluminum knitting needle stood in for his rod on top; a quarter pound of steel (an eye-bolt) represented the eighteenth-century key; the tail was roughly four feet of cotton rags tied together; and the kite line was twine. It never got off the ground at windspeed 15–20 miles per hour. I later flew a contemporary kite—a much lighter item with plastic foil, plastic sticks, and fishing line serving as kite line. I did not attach the rod atop or the tail beneath. I simply tried to loft the quarter pound chunk of metal. In 15–20 mile per hour wind, the kite couldn't lift it. The opportunity did serve to try Ellen Kuhfeld's suggestion. The metal was suspended partly by the wind on one side and partly by me on the other. My wife held a large picture frame as a stand-in for a window frame. When I tried to keep the key safely on my side of the picture frame and "dry" and not let the line brush against the frame, especially with the reduced handling caused by the dangling key, there came the sudden realization: *He-really-didn't-do-this.*

The kite event is an equation with no terms defined. Franklin's only measurement is to say the rod on top is "a foot or more above the wood." The aerodynamics expert Michael Selig calculated a simple equation for me based on a twelve by twelve inch kite at different wind speeds. At 15 miles per hour he calculated the lift would move the quarter pound. My kite wouldn't, but Selig saw it as feasible. The NASA aerodynamics authorities Albion Bowers and Jim Murray also saw it as feasible, but these authorities also pointed out the uncalculated weights to be lifted, the metal atop the kite, the twine—especially once it was wet, and the lengthy pre-Eddy tail sodden with water. The porosity of the kite material was also an issue; the more porous the fabric, the less the lift. Silk is not a bad choice, but paper would be better—Franklin's tradeoff was that silk wouldn't wet, then tear as paper might in a storm. When a Franklin associate later thought of flying the kite, his plan was to *oil* the silk for less porosity.

Afterward, experimenters to be introduced in later chapters addressed these problems. Working likely with direct input from Franklin, Joseph Priestley commissioned a kite five feet four inches wide (length might have been seven to nine feet at least) to get the job done, but never flew it. The authentic kite-flier Jacques de Romas at Nerac, France, reported that his kite was three feet wide and seven feet five inches high. No one followed Franklin's direction to use a small silk handkerchief or breast-cloth.

We can never know for sure about Franklin's kite. There is always the possibility that the equation includes gale force winds for the unspecified wind. But the estimate here is that the lift that pulls up the key is Benjamin Franklin's imagination.

153   *experiments foiled by moisture:* Tiberius Cavallo, Jan. 4, 1776, experimental notes in *A Complete Treatise of Electricity*, 4th ed.

154   *"Nature might have":* Mazeas, unpublished letter, Nov. 19, 1752, BL 30.094, f77, British Library.

154   *flying Electric Twine:* Cavallo, Ibid., 28.

154   *Benjamin Wilson's work:* John Smeaton, *GM,* 42 (Jan. 1747), 15.

154   *"Those of our readers":* PBF, 4:510.

Chapter xv: Death at St. Petersburg

The main source for the account of Rikhman's life is G. K. Tsverava, *Georg Vil'gel'm Rikhman, 1711–1753.* Other sources used include John Heilbron, "Georg Wilhelm Richmann," in *Dictionary of Scientific Biography;* A. A. Eliseev, *G. V. Rikhman;* and Boris Menshutkin, *Russia's Lomonosov.* The death accounts draw upon these books and "An Account of the Death of Mr George Richmann," *PT,* 44 (1755); "An Account of the Death of Georg Richmann," *The Pennsylvania Gazette,* Mar. 5, 1754; "A Particular Account of the Death of Mr Professor Richmann . . . ," *GM* (July 1755), 312–313; and Charles Rabiqueau, "Lettre sur la Mort de M. Richmann." Sources for Rikhman's science include Rikhman, "De electricitate in corporibus . . . ," *Commentarii* 14 (1744–1746); "De indice electricitatis . . . ," *Novi Commentarii* 1 (1747–1748); and Eliseev et al., eds., *Trudy po Fizike*, a collection of Rikhman and some Lomonosov texts translated from Latin to Russian.

The transliteration in previous English texts has been exclusively *Richmann*. There are several transliteration standards, including distinct American and English transliterations. Here, the Russian transliteration is used, *Rikhman*.

157   *"A physical experiment":* Lichtenberg, *The Lichtenberg Reader*, 78.

157   *"sparkles in the dark":* Tsverava, 96. Tsverava suggests the experimenting at St. Petersburg was initiated by a letter from Euler announcing a Berlin Academy essay contest on the topic of electricity, and he points to an Aug. 24, 1744, meeting designating Rikhman to work on electricity. But Tsverava notes that other Russian historians state that the Empress Elizaveta set Rikhman to experimenting from a desire to be entertained by watching sparkles. In light of the dismal funding, it doesn't seem likely that the interest of the German transients was enough to secure Rikhman promotions, significant funds for equipment and books, and freedom from Nartov's harassment. Rikhman's advancement suggests support from the empress. Both versions are likely true: they do not contradict.

158   *mercilessly harassed Rikhman:* Ibid., 56–57.

158   *teetering on the verge of collapse:* Ibid., 57.

159   *the presses:* Rikhman, "De indice electricitatis . . . ," *Novi Commentarii* 4 (1752–1753), 301–340. According to Benz the volume did not appear until 1758.

159   *in the first London edition:* Tsverava, Ibid., 116. Surprisingly, Rikhman had much better access to Franklin than many of the international experimenters, including the member of the Royal Society who gave the presentation speech in London for Franklin's Copley. Rikhman acquired Franklin's *Experiments and Observations* and apparently his *Supplement* in first edition. He received them from Daniel Dumaresk, a minister of the Anglican Church in St. Petersburg and an honorary foreign member of the St. Petersburg academy, who on trips to London acted as a purchasing agent. Dumaresk also supplied Rikhman with new literature from England, including Pope's *Essay on Man*; Rikhman, skilled enough in English to appreciate humor and satire, translated the first of Pope's "letters" into German (Tsverava, 53).

159   *"Franclinus, naturalis":* Rikhman, Ibid., 323.

160   *"Even in these times":* Rikhman quoted in Heilbron, *ESEC*, 352.

160   *"My cousin has passed":* Tsverava, 126–127.

161   Main sources for Lomonosov include Tsverava, Chapter 6; the Menshutkin biography; G. E. Pavlova and A. S. Fedorov, *Mikhail Vasilievich Lomonosov: His Life and Work*; and telephone interview with David Griffiths, Professor at the University of North Carolina at Chapel Hill.

162   *". . . it thundered":* "An Account of the Death of Mr. George William Richman," *PT*, 44 (1755), 62.

163   *"faint rumbling":* Lomonosov's account in *Trudy po Fizike,* 546.

164   *pathophysiology of lightning:* Leigh Dayton, "Secrets of a Bolt from the Blue,"
       New Scientist 140 (Dec. 18, 1993), 16.

164   *"flashover":* Ibid., 16.

165   *"There were not":* "An Account of the Death of Mr. George William Richman,"
       Ibid., 65.

165   *"to float":* Ibid., 63.

165   *"a vapor, in different rays":* Ibid., 63–64.

165   *"It was such":* Ibid., 63.

165   *"I may indeed":* Ibid., 66.

166   *"I consider it":* Lomonosov quoted in Benz, *The Theology of Electricity,* 32.

166   *"At one o'clock":* Ibid., 32.

166   *. . . panting and weeping":* Ibid., 33.

167   *"Otherwise Herr Rikhman":* Ibid., 33.

168   *"It is concluded":* "An Account of the Death of Mr. George William Richman,"
       Ibid., 67.

170   *"hurt and full of blood":* "An Account . . . ," *The Pennsylvania Gazette,* Mar. 5, 1754.

170   *Lomonosov's diagrams:* See sketch in Rikhman's loose, elegant drawing style re-
       produced in *Trudy po Fizike,* 320. It's a version of the installation before he in-
       troduced "natural" electricity. See later formal diagram of the device serving
       lightning science, reproduced in a later *GM* article (July 1755, 312).

172   *"left few visible . . . so far corrupted":* "An Account of the Death of Mr. Georg
       William Richman," Ibid., 68.

172   *"From this terrible event":* Tsverava, 140.

173   *"Can you imagine":* Chernyshev quoted in Ibid., 140.

173   *Afterward Lomonosov:* Lomonosov, *Trudy po Fizike,* 546.

174   *"cast some paces":* "An Account of the Death of Mr. Georg William Richman,"
       Ibid., 64.

174   *"My deceased husband":* Tsverava, 137.

175   *"Prize proposed":* "Prize proposed by the Imperial Academy . . . ," *GM,* 24 (June
       1754), 281.

CHAPTER XVI: MAKING AMENDS

177   *"They [the Royal Society]":* ABF, 1455.

178   *"Dr Wright":* Ibid., 1455.

178   *Peter Collinson who was:* The Journal Book of the Royal Society indicates
       Collinson attended the Council meetings leading up to and debating the
       award and announcing it on St. Andrews day (Nov. 8, 15, 20, 30); he was vir-
       tually absent the rest of the year. Watson attended all Council meetings that
       year except the grand St. Andrews Day meeting, when the award was given,
       Nov. 30.

180 *oddest presentation speeches:* Earl of Macclesfield, *PBF,* 5:126–132.

180 *a printer from the Maryland colony: GM,* 23 (Nov. 1753), 539.

180 *Denny took Franklin aside: ABF,* 1456–1457.

181 'The Tatler *tells us": PBF,* 4:466–467.

181 *Abbé Nollet heard . . . an international warning:* Nollet quoted in *GM* (1753), 430–431.

182 *"I have seen": PBF,* 5:112.

182 *"The new doctrine of lightning": PBF,* 5:221.

183 *A mentally defective Philadelphian:* See J. F. Sachse, *Benjamin Franklin as a Free Mason,* 49–72, for an extended account published in 1906. An excellent recent summary is H. W. Brands, *The First American: The Life and Times of Benjamin Franklin,* 150–154.

185 *The Russian scholar:* Eufrosina Dvoichenko-Markoff, "Benjamin Franklin, the American Philosophical Society, and the Russian Academy of Science," *Proceedings of the American Philosophical Society* 91 (1947), 250–251.

CHAPTER XVII: FRANKLIN'S POINT

Main sources for this chapter include interviews with: Kari Diethorn, Chief Curator, National Park Service, Independence National Historical Park, Philadelphia; Edward Battison, New York, authority on the history of colonial ironwork; Don Burbidge, Charleston, John Lining specialist; and the late Mike Wister, direct descendent of the family that claims early priority in use of the lightning rod.

186 *"There are some":* Voltaire quoted in Richard Anderson, *Lightning Conductors,* 249.

186 *"How to secure":* Franklin, *Poor Richard's Almanack, 1753;* in *FW,* edited by LeMay, 1278.

188 *"Soon lightning rods":* Nick D'Alto, "A Stroke of Genius," *Weatherwise* (May/June 2002), 27.

188 *"Here it [the lightning rod]": PBF,* 9:52.

188 *On July 2, 1768:* Sources include F.O. Vaille and H.A. Clark, *The Harvard Book,* 65–66 and David Wheatland, *The Apparatus of Science at Harvard 1765–1800,* 147.

188 *Dalilbard . . . hundred lightning rods: PBF,* 4:310. See Heilbron, *ESEC,* 349n, that Franklin deleted this sentence from the reprint in his *Experiments and Observations.*

188 *Franklin . . . drain away . . . or conduct: PBF,* 6:98–99.

189 *"has now generally lapsed":* Benjamin Vaughan, "Hints for the preservation of the New Academy Hall from lightning," manuscript B V46p in the Benjamin Vaughan Papers at the American Philosophical Library.

189 *"Professor von Yelin":* Oliver Lodge, *Lightning Conductors,* 18.

190   *"We find that we"*: PBF, 9:55.

190   *"erected an iron rod"*: PBF, 5:69.

190   *nine feet above his roof*: PBF, 19:247.

191   *"I was pleased"*: PBF, 4:364.

191   *no lightning rods on Pennsylvania buildings:* An examination of two decades
      of the journal of the academy trustees and the daybooks and ledgers (some
      recorded by Franklin) now in the archive of the University of Pennsylvania
      reveal no lightning rod authorization, installation, or funding. The minutes
      of the Pennsylvania Assembly likewise offer not a shred of evidence that
      lightning rods were installed. A marked contrast is the magnificently docu-
      mented and explicit record of the Maryland Assembly resulting in the rod
      affixed to their statehouse steeple, an authentic eighteenth-century installa-
      tion that survives to this day. See Maryland State Archives Home Page
      www.mdarchives.state.mdus/stagser/s1259/121/5847/html/.

191   *"eight shillings"*: Trustees minutes, Pennsylvania Academy, Jan. 1753.

192   *The drawing of the Academy:* DuSimitiere papers, Historical Society of Pennsyl-
      vania.

192   *not show a lightning rod:* It is arguable that earlier artists did not depict the
      rod, deeming the mundane attachment as beneath the grand dignity of the
      building. Also, the lightning rods might have been installed *within* the walls.
      If so, the attendant risk was that moisture enclosed behind the wall panels
      and within cracks in mortar would cause the iron to corrode and crumble at
      its attachments, increasing the risk that the incomplete rods surrounded by
      mortar would have become—by 1787 when the Founders assembled
      beneath—a shrapnel bomb waiting to be discharged by a bolt. Likely the rod
      wasn't there.

192   *"rods and wires"*: Ezra Stiles quoted in Leo LeMay, *Ebenezer Kinnersley:
      Franklin's Friend,* 91.

192   *to the 170-foot point:* No one knows for sure the dimensions of the steeple on
      the State House in the 1750s. The decaying structure was torn down in 1771.
      A temporary spire took its place until 1828, when the replacement was fin-
      ished. The second steeple was intended to duplicate the first, but the archi-
      tect had never actually seen the old steeple. According to Kari Diethorn, the
      current steeple reaches 168 feet 7 1/4 inches. The height of the authentic
      eighteenth-century chimney stack was 61 feet 6 3/4 inches. The most
      authentic and detailed drawing of how the early building appeared is one
      printed later by Thomas Man, Philadelphia, 1774. Working from a scale
      based on the chimney and proportion in the drawing, the old steeple calcu-
      lates to be about 171 feet 4 inches. The numbers in this text for the chimney
      and steeple are likely quite close to what was the fact.

193   *"It was in this house"*: Charles J. Wister, *The Labour of a Long Life: a Memoir
      of . . . ,* 33.

193   *A sense of fear:* Some lightning rod histories depict a battle between the forces

of enlightenment and those of benighted religion. Several published sermons from the era offer up meaty quotes to accent such narrations. But the evidence is very mixed. Very often churchmen were the strongest supporters of lightning rod installation. At the Hapsburg court, it was the monk Procop Diviš who proposed to the emperor that he install lightning rods on the palace at Vienna. It was the scientists of His Majesty's science academy who frightened the emperor away from the idea, and a quarter century passed before any of the great buildings in the empire had lightning rods installed. The priest Father Beccaria at Turin crusaded for the adoption of lightning rods. Pope Benedict XIV ordered lightning rods installed on ecclesiastical buildings. Very often, those opposed to the new technology were what London called the *rabble*. In East Europe, for instance, as a result of drought, which the local peasants blamed on Diviš's innovations, one night they descended on his parish house and broke his lightning rod to pieces.

193   *only invention from eighteenth-century:* See the anonymous J.B.N.'s "Accidents from Lightning" in *Notes and Queries* (Aug. 25, 1860) for evidence of a folk culture of lightning-protection that dates much earlier. In England and in the ancient world, it was believed that a cottage covered with houseleek was protected from lightning. The home covered with a web of vines rooted in the earth curiously resembles the Faraday cage, William Faraday's nineteenth-century lightning-rod protection from high voltage descending.

Chapter xviii: The Tally

195   *"CLUB—An assembly":* Samuel Johnson, *Dictionary of the English Language.*

196   *advocate for lightning rod use:* Two nineteenth-century sources (Anderson, *Lightning Conductors,* 36) claim Watson erected the first lightning rod in England on his "Payneshill cottage." No eighteenth-century confirmation has been found. It is inconsistent with Watson's two residences, Lincoln's Inn Field and Bath in season. The possibility remains.

196   *"So early as in February":* Watson, "An Account of a Treatise," *PT* 52 (Dec. 1761), 338.

196   *A number of reliable witnesses:* Franklin quoting Kinnersley in Jan. 21, 1762, letter to David Hume, *PBF,* 9:21.

198   *"happy competing with Franklin":* Barrière, *L'Acadèmie de Bordeaux* (translated by McFadden), 187.

198   *"John Lining":* The story of Lining and his version of Franklin's lightning science must be approached with caution. It is here relegated to an endnote, but appears in traditional histories as a main pillar of narrative. There are four crucial documents: (1) Lining's report in the *South Carolina Gazette,* 21 May 1753, 4; (2) Lining's second letter about the kite addressed to the Royal Society, 14 Jan. 1754, at the British Library, BL 4443 f130; (3) the same letter revised at London

and published in *Philosophical Transactions*, 48, part two (1754), 757–764; (4) Franklin's lightning-experiment letter dated to Lining in May of 1754 but published nine years after Lining's death in *Experiments and Observations*, 4th ed., 1769, 319–328.

In 1753, Lining reported in the *South Carolina Gazette* that he had flown an electric kite. His account was read before the Royal Society in 1754 and published in *Transactions*. Lining was a Scottish-born physician who previously published metabolism studies in the *Transactions* and wrote an early paper on yellow fever. Here—in addition to Franklin—was another colonial report of a man simply sending up a kite. By implication, if Lining did, Franklin did. Lining reported doing so several times with "remarkable success, before many spectators."

But to look closely at his letter sent to Crane Court is to see problems with the context and with his understanding of electrical science. First, the letter's transmission. Lining sent a brief account in 1753. The Society bounced it back with a series of questions. Come again, said the London experts. Clarification is not the issue in this polite era; witness the Society sharply questioning Bose concerning his halo and also Winkler concerning electrically transmitted odors. This is more about suspicion.

Lining, however, answers, after some delay (in an unpublished portion he apologizes that during his delay they may have forgotten the questions). To begin, Lining describes the kite; he mentions that the string was hemp and offers, "A silk line, except it had been kept continually wet, would not conduct the electricity." This is stunning: A new entrant in the field of electrical science in the year 1754 is advising the Society experts that silk does not conduct electrical energy. We are in the presence of a true innocent. Elsewhere in the paper— by this date Lining has seen an account in English of Rikhman's death—he confesses, "I am at a loss to know what the electrical needle was." He is unaware of the electrometer. The physician is not familiar with the literature in electrical science.

The Society pointedly asked if lightning had flashed when he flew his kite. Apparently not. Lining's prose is cloudy on the topic; he had mentioned "an appearance of a thunderstorm" and "the awful noise of thunder, before expected," but what develops, he meant the sky looked as if it *might* thunder. Ah. Lining explains: "The quantity of lightning extracted from the cloud [by the kite], or rather its atmosphere, proved sufficient to prevent any thunder in town that afternoon." Franklin had debated whether the lightning rod conducted the occasional bolt down to earth or if it silently drained away electrostatics from above and prevented the bolt. Ultimately, he decided both. Here Lining presents the kite as lightning prophylactic. One kite will do to protect Charleston.

When Lining deals with the relevancy of Rikhman's death to his own experiment, he asks the Society if the professor's device had been grounded. "For, if it had," he explains, "there is then more danger attending these experiments than I imagined." This, of course, is Franklin's response to the death: The device should have been grounded. Today, we know Franklin—and Lining—were wrong to claim that grounding ensured the experimenter's safety. You can stand next to a grounded pole and get killed by what scientists today term lightning splashover; significant numbers of lightning fatalities claim their victims near trees and poles planted in the earth. But it gets worse in Lining's letter. What is this business assuming that if his kite experiment is grounded, he's safe? The point of the electric kite is that it is *not* grounded. Likewise, the sentry box. If his kite was grounded, he couldn't have elicited the snaps he reported.

There are other oddities. Lining published his first account of the kite in his local newspaper; Franklin had pursued the same unusual scientific venue to announce his electric kite. The *South Carolina Gazette* had started out a Franklin franchise. To go too far pursuing Franklin's secret Free Mason connections and how they helped his career in Philadelphia and later his diplomacy in France gets close to paranoid. The secrecy that shrouds the Masons discourages further probing. But it's worth noting that Franklin and his Philadelphia associates in electrical science were all very active Free Masons, as was the publisher of the Carolina paper, and so was Dr. Lining. We can't know for sure that Lining didn't fly an electric kite, but we are virtually certain that he backed out of this experimental arena and never returned, pleading the cause of his subsequent inactivity as "gout, which perhaps prevented my meeting with the same unhappy fate as professor Rikhman." The Royal Society inserted Lining's answer and the report on Rikhman's death side by side in *Philosophical Transactions*.

Lining's name is also attached to one other standard plank in Franklin narratives. This item gets inserted in chronologies as a 1749 event. In a letter addressed to Lining dated 1755, Franklin explained how his lightning science developed. He looked back and excerpted this passage from his notebooks: "Nov. 7, 1749. Electrical fluid agrees with lightning in these particulars: 1. Giving light. 2. Color of the light. 3. Crooked direction. 4. Swift motion. 5. Being conducted by metals. 6. Crack or noise in exploding. 7. Subsisting in water or ice. 8. Rending bodies it passes through. 9. Destroying animals. 10. Melting metals. 11. Firing inflammable substances. 12. Sulphurous smell. The electric fluid is attracted by points. We do not know whether this property is in lightning. But since they agree in all the particulars wherein we can already compare them, is it not probable they agree likewise in this? Let the experiment be made." These notes are a gem, a masterpiece in the history of scientific prose. At the end Franklin introduces that last brief sentence. The jolt of the command. It's a real battle cry. But it's also a battle cry he did not heed. If his dates are authentic, he waited for three years. In fact in 1749, he was in complete charge of the erection of a Philadelphia steeple.

In fact, this letter to Lining did not appear in either manuscript or print until 1769, mysteriously surfacing when Franklin was busy publishing his own fourth edition of *Experiments and Observations,* which included historical deletions. Priestley summarizes the passage and quotes three sentences in his history of 1767. What is the date of the letter's composition? There is no manuscript version of this letter. None showed up in Charleston, but that's not startling, for all the Lining letters have vanished, although as this was written an effort was made to find them. The notebook that Priestley cited has never surfaced anywhere. In London, there's no Franklin copy of his letter used by the printer. Nor has Franklin's own copy ever surfaced.

Arguably, this letter is after-the-fact business. In the 1740s when Franklin was trying to gain recognition at the Society, why would he have suggested that William Watson stand under a metal pole in a thunderstorm and follow the suggestion, offering Watson only one argument in support, the observation that both lightning and powerful discharges from Leyden jars had been known to leave the victim blind? What does the eloquent twelve-item list twenty years afterward contribute? It shores up a joke as science. It gives a serious context to a proposal that earlier had precious little.

Here, it is offered that the beginnings of the letter date only to interviews with Priestley in 1766 and that the year of composition for the letter to Lining is the year it first appeared: 1769.

198   *Loammi Baldwin:* William Morse, "Lectures on Electricity in Colonial Times," *NEQ* 7 (June 1934), 374.

198   *Musschenbroek:* reported by Mottelay, *Bibliographical History . . . ,* 320.

198   *dapper Tiberius:* See description of his electric kite experiments never performed when lightning threatened in Tiberius Cavallo, *Complete Treatise of Electricity,* 4th ed., 9.

198   *"reported nothing essentially new":* PBF, 14:260.

199   *written by Father Beccaria:* Beccaria letter dated April 2, 1767, in the Canton Papers at the Royal Society Library.

199   *"I have not lately":* PBF, 9:126.

199   *Ensconced in London:* The traditional histories measure the extent of Franklin's scientific triumph in the last half of his century by claiming that the career of his opponent Abbé Nollet sank into oblivion. "His [Nollet's] influence was on the wane," writes Cohen, "and more and more members of the Académie Royale des Sciences became Franklinists," leading Cohen to assert that by 1773, Nollet's debate "was merely an echo from the grave."

If you look at the dates in Nollet's life, it's different. Most of his awards and honors came after Franklin appeared on the scene. In 1757, for instance, the Académie Royal des Sciences appointed Nollet a *pensionnaire* to fill the vacancy created by the death of his mentor Réamur, an honor attendant with salary (in London at the Society, you paid to be a member; at Paris, you could be paid). The Abbé was awarded by the Crown with the post of preceptor in science to the royal children in 1758. Between 1753 and 1761, he gathered in three distinguished professorships at Navare, La Fere, and Mezieres. These appointments graced him with significant incomes, but flyweight responsibilities. In our era, fascinating evidence from scholars R. W. Home (*Electricity and Experimental Physics in Eighteenth-Century Europe*, 1992), David Sturdy (*Science and Social Status: The Members of the Académie des Sciences*, 1995), and Geoffrey Sutton (*Science for a Polite Society: Gender, Culture, and the Demonstration of Enlightenment*, 1995) offer evidence of the Abbé as an electrical scientist triumphantly reigning in France throughout his lifetime. Although the Abbé received income as the titular head of two monastic orders, the greater part of Nollet's income derived from his science. "By 1765," concludes David Sturdy, "he [Abbé Nollet] was earning 13,900 livres a year through teaching and the Académie." He was spending it, too. Although officially the Abbé was attached to two monastic orders, no one seems to have ever spoken to him about a life of religious self-denial. The Abbé maintained three residences. He acquired and furnished lavishly a country estate at Mons-sur-l'Orge about twenty miles south of Paris. He kept a fashionable apartment in Paris. As the trusted scientific adviser of Louis XV, he had been given an apartment in the Louvre, although this was later changed to Versailles (post–1752) in order that the Abbé could be nearby to His Royal Highness. In his personal employ were two servants, a cook, a coachman, a housekeeper, and a gardener. When Nollet needed transportation, he had his choice among an array of three personal vehicles. Rare books, expensive scientific apparatus, several real estate holdings, paintings, gold, and silver swelled his investment portfolio.

There is no other electrical scientist in the eighteenth century whose income from science approached this. And the income didn't diminish, but rather increased during the decades he debated Franklin. The Abbé also had a splendid publishing career, authoring technical and popular scientific works. Unlike Franklin, who had to settle for a vanity-press arrangement with Cave, Abbé Nollet had Paris publishers bidding for his books. In 1766, Nollet sold the rights to two of his electricity books to the publisher Durand for a stunning 8,000 livres, spiced with several additional perks from the publisher including free books. On the heels of this success, in 1768 he sold the rights for his physics book to appear in three volumes for 15,000 livres. Another mark of influence—and a profitable one—was selling electrical and other scientific devices to complete the *cabinet de physique* in wealthy homes. Scholar Geoffrey Sutton has pointed out that the illustrations in his best-selling books are the machines he sold and that he also put his own images in these scientific illustrations—just as Franklin created a Poor Richard and Ned Cave a Sylvanus Urban—in his market niche the Abbé established himself as a trademark. In the last year of his life, Nollet led the winning majority in a landmark vote on membership strata at the Académie Royale des Sciences, crushing the Dalembert forces, triumphant to the end.

The sources of the Abbé-in-decline narrative are not public ones open to debate and refutation, but exist at the whispering level of private letters traded among Benjamin and his friends, and in the century beyond were elevated to history set-pieces. A favorite of the Franklin histories is a scene described by Collinson to Benjamin. The hero is an anonymous "nobleman," sympathetic to Franklin's science. Testing an unidentified Franklin hypothesis in public, "the Abbé and his creatures put on grave looks and shook their heads intimating things did not succeed—this put the nobleman quick out of temper and on a nice inquiry and observation found out the juggle and contrivance, gave them their due in high language and published the base and juggling intention all over Paris." No search has unearthed evidence of such a public humiliation of the Abbé in Paris. (In *ESEC, 359*, Heilbron notes that Delor had hinted at duplicities in Nollet's experiments and that Nollet requested an enquiry by a panel of experts from the Académie, who tested his experiments and "unanimously attested to their veracity"—Delor's defeat may have been imaginatively transformed by Collinson in private correspondence to Franklin as a defeat for Nollet.) Nollet had an international reputation as a reliable experimenter. Indeed, as the next ten years demonstrate, he was perfectly capable of devising cogent experiments for his debates with Franklin.

In his *Autobiography* Franklin claimed that in France by 1770 only two elderly *philosophes* supported the two-fluid theory of electricity. In our era, the scholar R. W. Home chronicles some landmarks in the single-fluid versus double-fluid debate in eighteenth-century France. There were debates at the Paris academy, but Nollet emerged thumpingly triumphant over the Franklinist Jean-Baptiste LeRoy. LeRoy's pro-Franklin articles vanished from later editions of Diderot's influential *Encyclopédie*. Once Dalibard had published his 1754 edition, Franklin's book went out of print in France for fifteen years. By 1762, Dalibard writes Franklin that the two-fluid opposition is so strong, it has forced him to "renounce electrical experiments almost entirely." The two Franklinist experimenters Dalibard and Delor, who deserved some recognition for Marly, never gained membership in the academy—nor was Franklin made an honorary foreign member until 1772, two years after Nollet's death. As late as 1772 when LeRoy reads a paper before the Paris academy, he apologetically takes time out to define *plus* and *negative* electricity, because as LeRoy complains, so few members understand it.

Even the English scientists failed to back Franklin with a single-fluid consensus. His defenders included the middle-folk scientists, John Canton the schoolmaster and William Henley the linen draper. But Watson transmitted sympathetic translations of Nollet's letters to the Society. The two-fluid theory didn't die in London after Benjamin settled there. In 1759, Robert Symmer became fashionable with his own theory of two *positive* energies based on the bizarre discovery that a pair of stockings, one black and one white, worn on the same leg displayed no electrostatics, but when removed, as they were pulled apart, released astonishing electrical energies. According to a report, her Highness Queen Caroline immersed herself in the study, perhaps for the sake of science lending her own royal leg. And as late as 1785, when the London instrument-maker George Adams, Jr., published the second edition of *Essay on Electricity*, the tradesman judiciously provided sections on both dual and single electricities, leaving his customers to make their own choices.

Historian of science R. W. Home has made a fascinating distinction about how Benjamin Franklin was received in Europe: "The success of the lightning experiments of 1752 made Franklin's name a household word throughout the learned world … but the merits of Franklin's electrical theory were by no means so universally recognized at this early period."

199   *academy at Berlin never:* Stephan Fölske, archivist at the Berlin-Brendenburgische Akademie der Wissenschaften, reports that Franklin was never made a member of the Berlin academy.

200   *how the Council had voted:* PBF, 14:342.

200   *Old Petrus van Musschenbroek, the grand:* PBF, 8: 329–333.

201   *Euler devoted two letters:* Euler, *Letters to a German Princess,* 2: letters 36 and 37.

201   *"Having regard to all":* commissioners quoted in I. B. Cohen, "The Two-Hundredth Anniversary of Benjamin Franklin's Two Lightning Experiments and the Introduction of the Lightning Rod," *Proceedings of the American Philosophical Society* 96 (June 1952), 363.

Chapter xix: The Making

205   *"Such a career":* Woodrow Wilson, Introduction, in Franklin's *Autobiography* (1901), vi.

205   *"tiny gray eyes":* See portrait by Rembrandt Peale at American Philosophical Society Library.

206   *"the most hasty":* Priestley, *Memoirs,* 34.

206   *"The academy did not":* Ibid., 36.

207   *"little employment":* Priestley, Ibid., 47.

207   *"When Dukes or noble":* R. Dodsley quoted in A. F. Scott, *Every One a Witness,* 235.

208   *"Dr. Franklin's principles":* Priestley, *History and Present State of Electricity,* 193.

208   *"Dr. Franklin's discoveries":* Ibid., 192.

208   *"Well deserving … ":* PBF, 14:312

209   *"One that sat near":* Ibid., 327.

209   *fear of getting killed:* Timothy Priestley quoted in F. W. Gibbs, *Joseph Priestley,* 28.

210   *"In some cases":* I. B. Cohen, *Benjamin Franklin's Experiments,* Introduction, 149.

210   *in 1749 the Schuylkill:* Sources on the ferry over the broad, floodplain river include Joseph Jackson, *Encyclopedia of Philadelphia,* 650, and Thomas Pownall, "Thomas Pownall's Description … ," *Pennsylvania Magazine of History and Biography,* 18 (1894), 212.

211   *Myth fit Franklin:* Twentieth-century academic historians of science have not been immune to myth when narrating the tale of points versus knobs. Witness this retelling of the event.

In 1772, after the Purfleet powder magazine was hit by lightning, the English Board of Ordnance had asked a group of Royal Society eminences including Franklin to recommend lightning protection for the structures. Among other issues, the committee debated pointed lightning rods versus blunt lightning rods and ruled in favor of Franklin's recommendation of points, over the opposition of Benjamin Wilson. As colonial and Crown relations deteriorated, George III, carried away by the political climate, decided the preference of the rebel Franklin must be wrong and had knob-ended conductors put on Purfleet armory and Kew Palace. The tale continued with King George face to face with Sir John Pringle, president of the Society, asking him to rubberstamp the second decision. Sir John then pointed out "the laws of nature were not changeable at Royal pleasure." The infuriated king forced Sir John to resign the presidency.

Not longer after the ruling in 1774, this anonymous verse epigram started circulating in the newspapers.

> While you, great George, for safety hunt,
> And sharp conductors change for blunt,
> The nation's out of joint:
> Franklin a wiser course pursues,
> And all your thunder fearless views,
> By keeping to the *point*.

It's a satisfying story, the forces of monarchy versus those of democracy, stupidity versus scientific intelligence.

But the reality, it turns out, was altogether different. The story of Pringle's resignation was in fact apocryphal. In a biography of Pringle written by Andrew Kippiss, a friend and contemporary, Kippiss asserted that the cause of Pringle's resignation was ill health due to an accidental fall; Kippiss "never heard from him any suggestion of the kind that has been mentioned." Other aspects of the tale ring equally false. George III had no power at the Royal Society. The king had no mechanism for leveraging Pringle out of office, nor is there any evidence that he tried to do so.

Remarkably, after pointed lightning rods were attached according to Franklin's directions at Purfleet, the armory was struck again by lightning on May 15, 1777. Some Franklinist histories minimize this by pointing out there was only minor damage—the powder was not ignited—but at a powder arsenal, is there really any such thing as a little lightning accident? George III, as any administrator might have done, took a second look and decided to try knobs instead of points. Today, in light of contemporary lightning science, we know that the controversy was a tempest in a teapot, that neither points nor knobs at the end of lightning conductors have significantly greater effect on lightning discharges. But it dates from the era when Franklin began defending his philosophical turf. Van Doren in his Franklin biography has devoted one paragraph to Purfleet, using a sentence to make clear the armory was struck by lightning after pointed rods were attached. In Cohen's history of Franklin's lightning science, he devotes seven pages to the Purfleet story but fails to mention the armory was hit a second time. This version was handed on to later historians who retold the tale complete with apocryphal rebels-versus-Loyalist flourishes and the omission of the second lightning strike.

A Journey from London to Dover, 1787, by Thomas Pennant extracted in *The Port of London Authority Monthly* (Mar. 1929) gives an account of the second lightning strike at Purfleet (162–163). See Heilbron for scholarly skepticism concerning Pringle's resignation (*ESEC,* 382n). Cohen's version reappears in Dudley Herschbach, "Ben Franklin's 'Scientific Amusements,'" in *Harvard Magazine* 98 (Nov.–Dec. 1995), 36–46. A recent scientific response by atmospheric physicist Charles Moore to the issue of points versus knobs is reported in Jeff Hecht, "Putting It Bluntly: Lightning Conductors Work Best Without Sharpened Points," in *New Scientist Magazine* 166 (27 May 2000), 10.

211   *"I was trying to kill a turkey":* Paul Zall, *Benjamin Franklin Laughing,* 107.

212   *Franklin rose to mythic stature:* An excellent discussion of the growth of Franklin's myth in America in the late eighteenth century and throughout the nineteenth century is Carla Mulford's "Figuring Benjamin Franklin in American Cultural Memory," *New England Quarterly,* 415–443.

212   *bird that upon death:* Max Hall, "Benjamin Franklin's Whoppers," 72A.

212   *"Dr. Franklin's electrical rod":* John Adams in Mulford, Ibid., 415.

Addendum note: When the Franklin kite myth is celebrated, there often surfaces a standard sub-myth, one that Franklin did not invent and nourish. Even today, Web sites and periodicals loft the myth that after Franklin's triumph, two other scientists died flying electric kites. The purveyors link it to a don't-try-this warning.

Extensive research done here found no evidence for these kite-flying deaths. The tale—when pursued—has the elusiveness of urban folklore. Contact was made with a magazine that had commemorated the Franklin story, mentioning the two dead kite operators. What were the sources? The editors didn't know—the employee responsible had since passed away. Possibly the inspiration was two vague, yet provocative sources from the eighteenth century. "In Germany," wrote G. C. Lichtenberg, "no Franklin has as yet discovered the conductor, although many a city and township has its Rikhman, who had to forfeit his own life for his presumption" (*Lichtenberg's Visits to England,* 13). Commenting in 1765 on deaths related to rod experiments, Procop Diviš mentioned "several people—among them the famous Professor Richmann of Petersburg—have been killed by lightning during such experiments" (quoted in Benz, 34). Research turned up no eighteenth-century evidence for these assertions. As this was written, Professor Rakov of the University of Florida involved in similar searches had found no evidence. In interview, John Heilbron pointed out that Lichtenberg's assertion was more likely literary flourish than sober account.

Late in this search, discovery was made of a human fatality resulting from electric kite experimentation (*Monthly Weather Review*, Oct. 1919, quoted in Ivan Brunk, "Lightning Death during Kite Flight," *Weatherwise*, Dec. 1958, 204–205). The man was not a scientist but a laborer, a sort of twentieth-century Coiffier employed by the U.S. Weather Bureau in an era when it used kites for extensive atmospheric research. His name is Charles H. Heckelsmiller. He was killed on Aug. 28, 1919, near Ellendale, North Dakota. He was not holding the kite line but standing nearby, and was killed by lightning splashover as surely as he would have been had he been holding the short silk ribbon Franklin advised the experimenter to grasp.

CHAPTER XX: BOLT OF FATE

215 *"Franklin had lain"*: Hilliard d'Auberteuil quoted in Aldridge, *Franklin and His French Contemporaries*, 43.

217 *the celebrated Edward Gibbon:* Gibbon's published letters from that year fail to mention the incident, raising the possibility it is apocryphal.

217 *"L'Electronique Ambassedeur"*: Nick D'Alto, "A Stroke of Genius," *Weatherwise* (May/June 2002), 28.

218 *"Only the person"*: de Cröy quoted in Lever, *Marie Antoinette*, 124.

221 *"Truth is"*: Franklin quoted in M. Lenoir letter in Stevens, *B. F. Stevens's Facsimiles of Manuscripts in European Archives Relating to America 1773–1783*, Vol. 18 (1648).

221 *"Ah, it is not"*: Benjamin Rush, "Excerpts from the Papers of Dr. Benjamin Rush," *Pennsylvania Magazine of History and Biography*, 27–28.

221 *"He showed himself"*: Capefigue quoted in Hall and Hall, *Franklin in France*, 141–142.

223 *In Italy, a professor:* Antonio Pace, *Benjamin Franklin and Italy*, 86.

224 *"101 livres"*: Charles Sellers, *Benjamin Franklin in Portraiture*, 97, quoting Franklin MSS (H.S.P.), 7, 8.

225 *"This Franklin of 1767"*: Sainte-Beuve, *Portraits of the Eighteenth Century*, 2:356.

225 *"Never contradict"*: Sarah Randolph, *The Domestic Life of Thomas Jefferson*, 318.

226 *"I have at she"*: WBF, 8:110.

226 *"The clay medallion"*: PBF, 29:613.

226 *"Franklin's interest"*: See Sellers, 78, 128, 366.

228 *"He has a passion"*: John Adams in diary, May 10, 1779, *Diary & Autobiography of John Adams*, 2:367.

228 *"The game of chess"*: BFP, 29:754.

228 *"The game becomes"*: Ibid., 754.

CHAPTER XXI: CHECKMATE

229 *"This is the civilest"*: PBF, 30:514.

229 *"not to be too much discouraged"*: PBF, 29:755.

230   *"at every street corner":* Felix Nogaret quoted in Charles Sellers, *Benjamin Franklin in Portraiture,* 137.

232   *"My wife has":* Ibid., 164.

232   *"His venerable":* Elkanah Watson, *Men and Times of the Revolution; Or, Memoirs of Elkanah Watson,* 89–90.

232   *"The portrait of":* Ibid., 89.

233   *"I should have taken":* E. L. Vigée-Le Brun, *The Memoirs of Mme. Elisabeth-Louis Vigée*-Le Brun, *1755–1789,* 170.

233   *"Firmly assure":* Louis XVI quoted from Duc de Croy, *Journal in Edit IV,* 78, in Van Doren biography of Franklin.

Epilogue

235   *"As having their":* Franklin, *The Letters of Benjamin Franklin & Jane Mecom,* edited by Van Doren, 57.

235   *"'Tis time I should":* Ibid., 236.

236   *The inscription reads:* Franklin art-directed his own tombstone. See *Codicil* to *Last Will and Testament* in *WBF,* 10:508.

237   *"not to form any":* *WBF,* 10:496.

Bibliography

"Account of a Lady Consumed by Fire." *Gentleman's Magazine* 16 (July 1746), 369.

"An Account of Mr Watson's Treatise on Electricity." *Gentleman's Magazine* 16 (June 1746), 291–292.

"An Account of the Death of Mr. George Richmann." *Philosophical Transactions* 44 (1755), 61–69.

Adams, John. *Diary and Autobiography of John Adams*. Ed. L. H. Butterfield. Cambridge: Harvard University Press, 1962.

Aldridge, Alfred Owen. *Franklin and His French Contemporaries*. New York: New York University Press, 1957.

Anderson, Peter. *Culloden Moor and the Story of the Battle*. Inverness: William MacKay, 1920.

Anderson, Richard. *Lightning Conductors: Their History, Nature, and Mode of Application*. London: E. & F. N. Spon, 3rd ed., 1885.

Anisimov, Evgenii V. *Empress Elizabeth: Her Reign and Her Russia 1741–1761*. Gulf Breeze, FL: Academic International Press, 1995.

Asimov, Isaac. *The Kite That Won the Revolution*. Cambridge: Houghton Mifflin, 1963.

Balzac, Honoré de. *A Distinguished Provincial at Paris*. New York: Peter Fenelon Collier & Son, 1900.

Barrett, C. R. B. *History of the Society of Apothecaries*. London: E. Stock, 1905.

Barrière, P. *L'Académie de Bordeaux: Centre de Culture Internationalle au XVIII Siècle (1712–1792)*. Bordeaux: Éditions Bière, 1951.

Bart, John Barrow. *Sketches of the Royal Society and Royal Society Club*. London: Murray, 1849.

Batcheler, Penelope H. *Independence Hall Historic Structures Report, Architectural Data Section: Part II Portion The Central Hall and Tower Stairhall*. Philadelphia: Independence National Historical Park, 1989.

Beccaria, Giovanni Battista. Letter to RS 2 April 1767. Canton Papers, Royal Society Library, London.

——. *A Treatise upon Artificial Electricity*. London: J. Nourse, 1776.

Becker, Carl. "Franklin's Character." In *Benjamin Franklin: A Collection of Critical Essays*. Ed Brian Barbour. Englewood Cliffs, NJ: Prentice Hall, 1979.

Bell, Walter George. *Fleet Street in Seven Centuries*. London: Sir Isaac Pitman, 1912.

Benguigui, Isaac. *Théories Électriques Du XVIII Siècle*. Genève: Geogr, 1984.

Benjamin, Park. *A History of Electricity: The Intellectual Rise in Electricity*. New York: John Wiley, 1898.

Berkeley, Edmund, and Dorothy Smith Berkeley. *Dr. John Mitchell: The Man Who Made the Map of North America*. Chapel Hill, NC: University of North Carolina Press, 1974.

Benz, Ernst. *The Theology of Electricity*. Trans. Wolfgang Taraba. Allison Park, PA: Pickwick Publications, 1989.

Bing, Franklin C. "John Lining, an Early American Scientist." *The Scientific Monthly* 26 (Mar. 1928), 249–252.

Borer, Mary Cathcart. *An Illustrated Guide to London 1800*. London: Robert Hale, 1988.

Boswell, James. *Boswell's Life of Johnson*. Ed. G. B. Hill, rev ed. L. F. Powell. Oxford: Oxford University Press, 1934.

Bowen, Catherine Drinker. *The Most Dangerous Man in America: Scenes from the Life of Benjamin Franklin*. Boston: Little Brown, 1974.

Brands, H. W. *The First American: The Life and Times of Benjamin Franklin*. New York: Doubleday, 2000.

Brett-James, Norman G. *The Life of Peter Collinson*. London: Privately printed, 1925.

Bridenbaugh, Carl, and Jessica Bridenbaugh. *Rebels and Gentlemen: Philadelphia in the Age of Franklin*. Oxford: Oxford University Press, 1965.

Brinitzer, Carl. *A Reasonable Rebel: Georg Christoph Lichtenberg*. Trans. Bernard Smith. New York: MacMillan, 1960.

Brunet, Pierre. "Les Premieres Recherches Experimentales sur la Foudre et L'Electricite Atmospherique." *Lychnos* (1946–1947), 117–148.

Brunk, Ivan W. "Lightning Death During Kite Flight (Or Radiosondes Are Safer)." *Weatherwise* (Dec. 1958), 204–205.

Burnby, J. G. L. *A Study of the English Apothecary from 1660 to 1760*. London: Wellcome Institute for History of Medicine, 1983.

Byrom, John. *Selections from the Journals and Papers of John Byrom, Poet, Diarist, Shorthand Writer, 1691–1763*. Ed. Henri Talon. London: Rockliff, 1950.

Campbell, R. *The London Tradesman. Being A Compendious View Of All the Trades, Professions, Arts . . . .* London: T. Gardner, 1747.

Charteris, Evan. *William Augustus, Duke of Cumberland: His Early Life and Times (1721–1748)*. London: Edward Arnold, 1913.

Chipman, R. A. "An Unpublished Letter of Stephen Gray." *Isis* 49 (1954), 33–40.

Clark, Sir George. *A History of the Royal College of Physicians*. Vol. 1. Oxford: Oxford University Press, 1964.

Clark, Ronald W. *Benjamin Franklin: A Biography*. New York: Random House, 1983.

Cohen, I. Bernard. "Introduction." In *Benjamin Franklin's Experiments. A new edition of Franklin's Experiments and Observations on Electricity*. Ed. I. B. Cohen. Cambridge: Harvard University Press, 1941.

———. "Benjamin Franklin and the Mysterious 'Dr. Spence': The Date and Source of Franklin's Interest in Electricity." *Journal of the Franklin Institute* 235 (1943), 1–26.

———. "The Two Hundredth Anniversary of Benjamin Franklin's Two Lightning

Experiments and the Introduction of the Lightning Rod." *Proceedings of the American Philosophical Society* 96 (June 1952), 331–366.

———. "Some Problems in Relation to the Dates of Benjamin Franklin's First Letters on Electricity." *Proceedings of the American Philosophical Society* 100 (1956), 537–542.

———. *Franklin and Newton.* Cambridge: Harvard University Press, 1966.

———. *Benjamin Franklin's Science.* Cambridge: Harvard University Press, 1990.

Colden, Cadwallader. *An Explication of the First Causes of Action in Matter; And of the Cause of Gravitation.* London: J. Brindley, 1746.

———. *The Letters and Papers of Cadwallader Colden.* New York: New York Historical Society, 1920.

Condon, Adrienne. *Transatlantic Friends: The Correspondence of Peter Collinson (1694–1768) and John Bartram (1699–1777).* Dissertation, University of South Florida, 1996.

Cooper, Mary Ann. "Lightning Injuries: Prognostic Signs for Death." *Annals of Emergency Medicine* 9 (Mar. 1980), 134–138.

Craig, Steven R. "When Lightning Strikes: Pathophysiology of Lightning Injuries." *Postgraduate Medicine* 79 (Mar. 1986), 109–124.

Crane, Verner W. *Benjamin Franklin, Englishman and American.* Baltimore: Williams & Wilkins, 1936.

———. *Benjamin Franklin's Letters to the Press, 1758–1775.* Chapel Hill, NC: University of North Carolina Press, 1950.

———. *Benjamin Franklin and a Rising People.* Boston: Little, Brown, 1954.

Dalibard, Thomas François. "Expériences et Observations sur le Tonnerre, Relatives à celles de Philadelphie." Printed in *Expériences et Observations sur L'Electricité faites à Philadelphie en Amérique par M. Benjamin Franklin.* Paris: 2nd ed., 1756, 99–125; cited from *Papers of Benjamin Franklin,* Vol. 4, 302–310, in translation made for this book by Chantal McFadden.

D'Alto, Nick. "A Stroke of Genius." *Weatherwise* (May/June 2002), 22–29.

Dayton, Leigh. "Secrets of a Bolt from the Blue." *New Scientist Magazine* 140 (18 Dec. 1993), 16.

D.D. "A Short View of Mr W's Treatise on Electricity . . . ." *Gentleman's Magazine* 16 (June 1746), 291–292.

Dibner, Bern. *Early Electrical Machines: The Experiments and Apparatus of Two Enquiring Centuries (1600–1800) That Led to the Triumphs of the Electrical Age.* Norwalk, CT: Burndy Library, 1957.

Drake, Francis S. *The Town of Roxbury.* Boston: Municipal Printing Office, 1908.

Dunsheath, Percy. *A History of Electrical Engineering.* London: Faber and Faber, 1962.

Dvoichenko-Markov, Eufrosina. "Benjamin Franklin, the American Philosophical Society, and the Russian Academy of Science." *Proceedings of the American Philosophical Society* 91, 3 (Aug. 1947), 250–259.

Enestroem, Gustaf. *Verzeichnis der Schriften Leohard Eulers.* Leipzig: B. B. Teubner, 1910, 1913.

Euler, Leonhard. *Letters of Euler to a German Princess on Different Subjects in Physics and Philosophy.* Trans. Henry Hunder. London: H. Murray, 1795.

Fara, Patricia. *An Entertainment for Angels: Electricity in the Enlightenment.* Cambridge: Icon Books, 2002.

Faraday, Michael. *Experimental Researches in Electricity.* London: 1838.

Fay, Bernard. *Franklin: The Apostle of Modern Times.* Boston: Little, Brown, 1929.

Fellows, Otis, and Stephen Millikin. *Buffon.* New York: Twayne, 1972.

Figuier, Louis. *Les Merveilles de la Science.* Paris: Furne, Jouvet, 1868.

Finn, Bernard S. "An Appraisal of the Origins of Franklin's Electrical Theory." *Isis* 50 (1969), 362–369.

Fischer, David Hackett. *Albion's Seed: British Folkways in America.* Oxford: Oxford University Press, 1989.

———. *Paul Revere's Ride.* Oxford: Oxford University Press, 1994.

Ford, Paul Leicester. *A List of Books Written By Or Relating to Benjamin Franklin.* Brooklyn, NY: Privately printed, 1889.

Fortune, Brandon, and Deborah Warner. *Franklin & His Friends: Portraying the Man of Science in Eighteenth-Century America.* Washington, D.C.: Smithsonian National Portrait Gallery, 1999.

Foster, B. *Ye History of ye Priory Gate St. John.* London: William Pickering, 1851.

Fothergill, John. *Chain of Friendship: Selected Letters of Dr. John Fothergill of London, 1735–1780.* Cambridge: Harvard University Press, 1971.

Fox, R. Hingston. *Dr. John Fothergill and his Friends: Chapters in Eighteenth Century Life.* London: MacMillan, 1919.

Franklin, Benjamin. *Plain Truth or, Serious Considerations on the Present State of the City of Philadelphia and Province of Pennsylvania* (facsimile edition). Philadelphia: 1747.

———. "A Letter of Benjamin Franklin, Esq; to Mr. Peter Collinson, F.R.S concerning an electrical Kite." *Philosophical Transactions* 47 (1751–1752), 565–567.

———. *Expériences et observations sur l'électricité faites a Philadelphie en Amérique, par Benjamin Franklin.* Traduites de l'anglois. Paris: Chez Durand, 1752 (Bakken Library).

———. *Expériences et observations sur l'électricité faites a Philadelphie en Amérique, par Benjamin Franklin . . . .* Traduites de l'anglois . . . par M. d'Alibard. Paris: Chez Durand, 1756 (Bakken Library).

———. *Oeuvres de M. Franklin, Docteur ès Loix, membre de l'Académie Royale des Sciences de Paris . . . .* Traduites de l'anglois . . . par M. Barfeu Dubourg. Paris: Chez Quillau l'ainé et al., 1778 (Bakken Library).

———. *The Writings of Benjamin Franklin.* Ed. Albert Henry Smyth. New York: MacMillan, 1905–1907.

———. *Experiments and Observations on Electricity.* Ed. I. Bernard Cohen using text from 5th ed (1774) edited by Franklin. Cambridge: Harvard University Press, 1941.

———. *The Papers of Benjamin Franklin.* Ed. Leonard Labaree, Ellen Cohn, et al. New Haven: Yale University Press, 1959–2002.

————. *The Autobiography. Benjamin Franklin Writings.* Ed. J. A. Leo LeMay and P. M. Zall. New York: Library of America, 1987.

Franklin, Benjamin, and Jane Mecom. *The Letters of Benjamin Franklin & Jane Mecom.* Ed. Carl Van Doren. Princeton: Princeton University Press, 1950.

Freke, John. *An essay to shew the cause of electricity . . . .* London: W. Innys, 3rd ed., 1752.

Gauvin, Jean-François. "An 18th Century Entrepreneur: Abbé Nollet's Instrument-Making Trade . . . ." *Bulletin of the Scientific Instrument Society* 57 (1998) 21–25.

Gibbs, F. W. *Joseph Priestley: Revolutions of the Eighteenth Century.* New York: Doubleday, 1967.

Goodwin, Charles. "The Religion of Feeling: Wesleyan Catholicism." *History Today* 46 (Oct. 1996), 44–50.

Grendel, Frédéric. *Beaumarchais: The Man Who Was Figaro.* London: MacDonald and Jane's, 1977.

Hackmann, W. D. *Electricity from Glass: The History of the Frictional Electrical Machine 1600–1850.* Alphen aan den Rign, Netherlands: Sijthoff & Noordhoff, 1978.

Hahn, Roger. *The Anatomy of a Scientific Academy: The Paris Academy of Sciences, 1666–1803.* Berkeley: University of California Press, 1971.

Hall, A. Rupert. "'Gravesande, Willem Jacob." In *Dictionary of Scientific Biography.* Ed. Charles Coulston Gillispie. New York: Scribner, 1970.

Hall, Max. "Benjamin Franklin's Whoppers." *Harvard Magazine* (Nov.–Dec. 1985), Discover Section, 72A–72H.

————. *Benjamin Franklin and Polly Baker: The History of a Literary Deception.* Pittsburgh: University of Pittsburgh Press, 1990.

Haller, Albrecht von. "An historical account of the wonderful discoveries made in Germany, &c. concerning Electricity." *Gentleman's Magazine* 15 (April 1745), 193–197.

Harris, Sir William Snow. *On the Nature of Thunderstorms . . . .* London: J. W. Parker, 1843.

Haycock, David and G.S. Rousseau. "Voices Calling for Reform: The Royal Society at Mid-Eighteenth Century—Wartin Folkes, John Hill, and William Stukeley." *History of Science,* 37 (Dec. 1999), 377–403.

Heathcote, N. H. deV. "Franklin's Introduction to Electricity." *Isis* 46 (1955), 29–35.

Hecht, Jeff. "Putting It Bluntly: Lightning Conductors Work Best Without Sharpened Points." *New Scientist Magazine* 166 (27 May 2000), 10.

Heilbron, J. L. "G. M. Bose: The Prime Mover in the Invention of the Leyden Jar." *Isis* 57 (1966), 264–267.

————. "Kleist, Ewald Georg Von." In *Dictionary of Scientific Biography.* Ed. Charles Coulston Gillispie. New York: Scribner, 1970.

————. "Nollet, Jean-Antoine." In *Dictionary of Scientific Biography.* Ed. Charles Coulston Gillispie. New York: Scribner, 1970.

————. "Richmann, Georg Wilhelm." In *Dictionary of Scientific Biography.* Ed. Charles Coulston Gillispie. New York: Scribner, 1970.

————. "Watson, William." In *Dictionary of Scientific Biography.* Ed. Charles Coulston Gillispie. New York: Scribner, 1970.

———. "Franklin, Haller & Franklinist History." *Isis* 68 (1977), 539–549.

———. *Electricity in the 17th and 18th Centuries.* Berkeley: University of California Press, 1979.

———. "From Horsehair to Lightning Rods." *Nature* 401, 6751 (9 Sept. 1999), 329.

Hellman, Gustaf. *Ueber Luftelektricitat 1746–1753. Neudrucke Von Schriften Und Karten Uber Meteorologie Und ErdMagnetismus.* Vol. 11. Berlin: Asher, 1898.

Herschbach, Dudley R. "Ben Franklin's 'Scientific Amusements.'" *Harvard Magazine* 98 (Nov.–Dec. 1995), 36–46.

Hibbert, Christopher. *Versailles.* New York: Newsweek Books, 1972.

Hill, John. *A Dissertation on Royal Societies in Three Letters . . . .* London: John Doughty, 1750.

Home, R. W. *The Effluvial Theory of Electricity.* New York: Arno Press, 1981.

———. *Electricity and Experimental Physics in Eighteenth-Century Europe.* Hampshire, UK: Ashgate Publishing, 1992.

Huang, Nian-Sheng. *Franklin's Father Josiah: Life of a Colonial Boston Tallow Chandler.* Philadelphia: American Philosophical Society, 2000.

Jackson, Joseph. *Encyclopedia of Philadelphia.* Harrisburg, PA: National Historical Association, 1933.

Jacquet de Malzet, Louis Sebastien. *Precis de l'electricite, ou, extrait experimental & theoretique des phenomenes electriques.* Vienne: J.T. de Trattnern, 1775.

Jernegan, Marcus W. "Benjamin Franklin's 'Electrical Kite' and Lightning Rod." *The New England Quarterly* 1 (1928), 180–196.

Jex-Blake, Arthur John. "Death by electric currents and by lightning." The Goulstonian lectures for 1913. London, 1913.

Johnson, Samuel. *A Dictionary of the English Language . . . .* London: Printed by W. Strahan for J. and P. Knapton et al., 1755.

Kaiser, Cletus J. *The Capacitor Handbook.* New York: Van Nostrand, 1993.

Kelley, Joseph J. *Life and Times in Colonial Philadelphia.* Harrisburg, PA: Stackpole Books, 1973.

Kippis, Andrew. *Biographia Britannica.* London: 1824.

Kratzenstein, C. G. *Abhandlung von dem Nutzen der Electricität.* 2nd ed. (Halle, 1745). In *C. G. Kratzenstein, professor physices experimentalis Petropol.* Trans. and Ed. Egil Snorrason. Odense: University of Odense, 1974, 25–50.

Krider, E. Philip. "Atmospheric Electricity and the Heritage of Benjamin Franklin." *Benjamin Franklin: Des Lumières a Nos Jours.* Lyon: Université Jean-Moulin, Etudes Anglaises 95, 1991.

LeMay, J. A. Leo. "Franklin's 'Dr. Spence': The Reverend Archibald Spencer (1698?–1760), M.D." *Maryland Historical Magazine* 59 (1964), 199–216.

———. "The Text, Rhetorical Strategies, and Themes of 'The Speech of Miss Polly Baker.'" In *The Oldest Revolutionary: Essays on Benjamin Franklin.* Ed. Leo LeMay. Philadelphia: University of Pennsylvania Press, 1976.

———. *The Canon of Benjamin Franklin 1722–1776: New Attributions and Reconsiderations.* Newark: University of Delaware Press, 1986.

———. "The American Aesthetic of Franklin's Visual Creations." *Pennsylvania Magazine of History & Biography* III (Oct. 1987), 465–499.

———. "Franklin." www.english.udel.edu/lemay/franklin/html.

Lever, Evelyne. *Marie Antoinette.* New York: Farrar, Straus, & Giroux, 2000.

Lichtenberg, G. C. *The Lichtenberg Reader: Selected Writings of Georg Christoph Lichtenberg.* Ed. and Trans. Frantz H. Mautner and Henry Hatfield. Boston: Beacon Press, 1959.

———. *The World of Hogarth: Lichtenberg's Commentaries on Hogarth's Engravings.* Trans. Innes and Gustav Herdan. Boston: Houghton Mifflin, 1966.

———. *Lichtenberg's Visits to England as Described in His Letters and Diaries.* Ed. and Trans. Margaret Mare and W. Quarrel. New York: Benjamin Blom, 1969.

———. *The Waste Books.* Trans. R. J. Hollingdale. New York: New York Review of Books, 2000.

Lining, John. "Extract of a letter from the ingenious Dr. Lining of Charles Town . . . ." *Gentleman's Magazine* 23 (1753), 431.

———. *South Carolina Gazette,* 21 May 1753, 4.

———. "Extract of a Letter from John Lining, M.D. of Charles Town . . . ." *Philosophical Transactions* 18 (1754), 757–764.

———. Letter to the Royal Society. 14 Jan. 1754. BL 4443, f130, British Library, London.

Lodge, Sir Oliver. *Lightning Conductors and Lightning Guards.* London: Whitaker, 1892.

Lopez, Michel. "La caracterisation de l'electricite dans la foudre au XVIIIeme siecle par Thomas-Francois Dalibard, un physicien francais meconnu." 7 June 2001, inri.online.fr/dali.html.

Lyons, Henry. *The Royal Society 1660–1940.* Cambridge: Cambridge University Press, 1944.

Maluf, Rames Bahige. *Jean Antoine Nollet and Experimental Natural Philosophy in Eighteenth Century France.* Dissertation, University of Oklahoma, 1985.

Marples, Morris. *Poor Fred and the Butcher.* London: Michael Joseph, 1970.

Maryland State Archives. "Protecting the State House from Lightning: The Franklin Lightning Rod." *Maryland State Archives Home Page,* 1 Nov. 1999, www.mdarchives.state.mdus/msa/stagser/s1259/121/5847/html/lightrod.html.

Mazeas, Abbé. Letter dated 19 Nov. 1752. BL 30.094, f77, British Library, London.

———. "Letters of the Abbé Mazeas, F.R.S. to the Rev. Stephen Hales, D.D., F.R.S concerning the Success of the late Experiments in France." *Philosophical Transactions* 20, 91.

———. "Observations upon the Electricity of the Air . . . ." *Philosophical Transactions* 48, pt. 2 (1754), 377–384.

McAdie, Alexander. "Some Kite Experiments During Thunder-Storms." *The Electrical World* 20, 13 (24 Sept. 1892), 191–192.

———. "Protection from Lightning." Washington, D.C.: U.S. Weather Bureau, 1895.

———. "The Date of Franklin's Kite Experiment." *Proceedings of the American Antiquarian Society* 34 (Oct. 1924), 188–205.

McClellan, J. E. *Science Reorganized: Scientific Societies in the 18th Century*. New York: Columbia University Press, 1985.

McEachron, K. B., and Kenneth G. Partrick. *Playing with Lightning*. New York: Random House, 1946.

McFait, Ebenezer. "Observations on Thunder and Electricity." *Essays and Observations Physical and Literary. Read before a Society in Edinburgh . . .* 1 (1754), 189–196.

Mendelsohn, Everett. "John Lining and His Contribution to Early American Science." *Isis* (1960), 278–292.

Menshutkin, B. N. *Russia's Lomonosov*. Princeton: Princeton University Press, 1952.

Middlekauff, Robert. *The Glorious Cause: The American Revolution, 1763–1789*. New York: Oxford University Press, 1982.

———. *Benjamin Franklin and His Enemies*. Berkeley: University of California Press, 1996.

Millburn, John R. *Benjamin Martin: Author, Instrument-Maker, and 'Country Showman.'* Leyden, Netherlands: Noordhoff, 1976.

———. *Adams of Fleet Street, Instrument Makers to King George III*. Aldershot, UK: Ashgate Publishing, 2000.

Miller, D. C. *Sparks, Lightning, Cosmic Rays*. New York: Macmillan, 1939.

Miller, David Philip. "The 'Hardwicke Circle': The Whig Supremacy and Its Demise in the 18th-Century Royal Society." *Notes & Records of the Royal Society* 52 (1998), 73–91.

Moraley, William. *The Infortunate*. Ed. Susan Klepp and Billy G. Smith. University Park: Pennsylvania State University Press, 1992.

Morgan, Edmund. *Benjamin Franklin*. New Haven: Yale University Press, 2002.

Morgan, William. *Memoirs of The Life of The Rev. Richard Price*. London: R. Hunter, 1815.

Morse, William Northrop. "Lectures on Electricity in Colonial Times." *New England Quarterly* 7 (1934), 364–374.

Morton, Larry, and Jane Wess. *Public & Private Science: The King George III Collection*. Oxford: Oxford University Press, 1993.

Morus, Iwan Rhys. "The Sociology of Sparks: An Episode in the History and Meaning of Electricity." *Social Studies of Science* 18, 3 (Aug. 1988), 387–417.

Mottelay, Paul Fleury. *Bibliographical History of Electricity & Magnetism chronologically arranged*. London: Charles Griffin, 1922.

Mulford, Carla. "Benjamin Franklin and the Myths of Nationhood." In *Making America/Making American Literature: Franklin to Cooper*. Ed. A. R. Lee and W. M. Verhoeven. Amsterdam: Rodopi, 1996.

———. "Figuring Benjamin Franklin in American Cultural Memory." *New England Quarterly* 72, 3 (Sept. 99), 415–443.

Muller-Hillebrand, D. "Torbern Bergman as a Lightning Scientist." *Daedalus. Tekniska museets arsbok* (1963), 35–76.

Musschenbroek, Petrus van. *The Elements of Natural Philosophy*. Trans. John Colson. London: J. Nourse, 1744.

Mylius, Christlob. "Extract of a Letter from Mr. Mylius of Berlin, to Mr. W. Watson, F.R.S . . . ." *Philosophical Transactions* 28 (1753), 559.

N., J. B. "Accidents from Lightning." *Notes and Queries* 110, Second Series, 243 (25 Aug. 1860), 145.

Neale, John. *Directions for Gentlemen Who Have Electrical Machines*. London: 1747.

Needham, John Turberville. "A Letter from Paris Concerning Some New Electrical Experiments Made There." London: C. Davis, 1746.

Nichols, John. *Literary Anecdotes of the Eighteenth Century*. Ed. Colin Clair (reprint). Carbondale, IL: Southern Illinois University Press, 1967.

Nollet, Abbé. "Part of a Letter from Abbé Nollet, of the Royal Academy of Sciences at Paris, and F.R.S. to Martin Folkes Esq; President of the same, concerning Electricity." *Philosophical Transactions* 47 (1747–1748), 1–8.

———. "Extracts of Two Letters of the Abbé Nollet F.R.S. to Mr. William Watson, F.R.S. relating to extracting Electricity from Clouds." *Philosophical Transactions* 20, 92 (1751–1752), 553–556.

———. Letter to William Watson. 6 June 1752. Trans. W. Watson. L&M Collection, Royal Society Library, London.

———. *Lettres sur l'électricité, dans lesquelles on examine les dernieres découvertes . . . .* Paris: Guérin & Delatour, 1753.

———. "An Account of a Treatise, presented to the Royal Society, intitled *Letter Concerning Electricity* . . . extracted and translated from the French, by Mr. William Watson F.R.S." *Philosophical Transactions* 48 (1753), 201–216.

Nollet, Abbé, and Jean Jallabert. *Theories Electriques Du XXVLIII Siecle: correspondance entre L'Abbé Nollet et le physicien Genevois Jean Jallabert*. Ed. Isaac Benguigui. Geneva: Georg, 1984.

"The Oath of a Freeman of the Company of Apothecaries." Manuscript. Society of Apothecaries of London, nd.

Olsen, Kirstin. *Daily Life in 18th Century England*. Westport, CT: Greenwood Press, 1999.

Oswald, John C. *Benjamin Franklin Printer*. Garden City, NY: Doubleday, Page, 1917.

Owen, George E. *The Universe of the Mind*. Baltimore: Johns Hopkins University Press, 1971.

Pace, Antonio. *Benjamin Franklin and Italy*. Philadelphia: The American Philosophical Society, 1958.

Parker, Mrs. *A Glossary of Words Used in Oxfordshire*. London: nd, in English Dialect Society Series C Original Glossaries.

Parton, James. *Life and Times of Benjamin Franklin*. New York: Mason Brothers, 1864.

Pavlova, G. E., and A. S. Fedorov. *Mikhail Vasilievich Lomonosov: His Life and Work*. Moscow: Mir Publishers, 1984.

Pegge, Samuel. *An Alphabet of Kenticisms*. London: 1736, reprint in English Dialect Society Series C Original Glossaries.

Pennant, Thomas. "A Journey from London to Dover, 1787." Extract in *The Port of London Authority Monthly* (Mar. 1929), 161–163.

Pennsylvania Archives: Eighth Series: Votes and Proceedings of the House of Representatives of the province of Pennsylvania. Harrisburg: 1931–1935.

Pepper, William. *The Medical Side of Benjamin Franklin.* Philadelphia: W. J. Campbell, 1911.

Perry, Bliss. *The American Spirit in Literature.* New Haven: Yale University Press, 1918.

Piggot, Stuart. *William Stukeley: An Eighteenth-Century Antiquarian.* New York: Thames and Hudson, 1985.

Porter, Roy. *London, a Social History.* Cambridge: Harvard University Press, 1995.

Potamian, Brother F.S.C., and James Walsh. *Makers of Electricity.* New York: Fordham University Press, 1909.

Pownall, Thomas. "Governor Thomas Pownall's Description of the Streets and the Main Roads about Philadelphia, 1754." *Pennsylvania Magazine of History and Biography* 18 (1894).

Priestley, Joseph. *The History and Present State of Electricity, with Original Experiments.* London: J. Dodley et al., 1767.

———. *Memoirs of Dr. Joseph Priestley. Written by Himself.* Reprint from 1809 ed. London: 1893.

Pulteney, R. *Historical and Biographical Sketches of the Progress of Botany in England,* II. London: T. Cadell, 1790.

Rabiqueau, Charles. "Lettre sur le Mort de M. Richmann." Paris: 1754?

Rackstrow, B. *Miscellaneous observations, together with a collection of experiments on electricity.* London: B. Rackstrow, 1748.

Rakov, Vladimir. "Lightning Discharges Triggered Using Rocket-and-Wire Techniques." *Recent Research Developments in Geophysics* 2 (1999), 141–171.

Randolph, Sarah. *The Domestic Life of Thomas Jefferson.* New York: Frederick Ungar, 1958.

Rikhman, Georg Wilhelm. "De electricitate in corporibus producenda nova tentamina." *Commentarii* 14 (1744–1746) 299–324.

———. "De indice electricitatus et ejus usu in definiendis artificialis et naturalis electricitatis phaenomenis, dissertatic." *Novi commentarii* 4 (1752–1753), 301–340.

———. *Trudy po Fizike.* Ed. A. A. Eliseev, V. P. Zubov, and A. M. Murzin. Moscow: 1956.

Riley, Edward M. "The Independence Hall Group." *Transactions of the American Philosophical Society* 43 (1953), 7–42.

Riskin, Jessica. "Poor Richard's Leyden Jar: Electricity and Economy in Franklinist France." *Historical Studies in the Physical and Biological Sciences* 28, 2 (1998), 301–336.

Roberts, Lissa. "Science Becomes Electric: Dutch Interaction with the Electrical Machine During the Eighteenth Century." *Isis* 90 (1999), 680–714.

Roger, Jacques. *Buffon: A Life in Natural History.* Trans. S. Bonnefoi. Ithaca: Cornell University Press, 1997.

Roller, Duane, and Duane H. D. Roller. *The Development of the Concept of Electric Charge: Electricity from the Greeks to Coulomb. Harvard Case Histories in Exper-*

imental Science. Ed. J. B. Conant and L. K. Nash. Vol. 2, 543–639. Cambridge: Harvard University Press, 1966.

Romas, Jacques de. *Mémoire, sur les moyens de se garantir de la foudre dans les maisons* . . . . Bordeaux: Chez Bergeret, 1776.

Rotch, Abbot Lawrence. "Did Benjamin Franklin Fly His Electric Kite Before He Invented the Lightning Rod?" *Proceedings of the American Antiquarian Society* 18 (1906), 118–123.

———. "When Did Franklin Invent the Lightning Rod?" *Science* 24 (21 Sept. 1906), 374–376.

———. "The Lightning-Rod Coincident with Franklin's Kite Experiment." *Science* 24 (Dec. 1906), 780.

Royal Society. *Bulloch's Rolls.*

———. *Journal Book.*

Rush, Benjamin. "Excerpts from the Papers of Dr. Benjamin Rush." *Pennsylvania Magazine of History and Biography.* 19 (1905), 15–30.

Sachse, J. F. *Benjamin Franklin as a Free Mason.* Philadelphia: Privately printed, 1906.

Sainte-Beauve, C. A. *Portraits of the Eighteenth Century.* Trans. K. P. Wormeley. New York: G. P. Putnam's Sons, 1905.

Schaffer, Simon. "The Consuming Flame: Electrical Showmen and Tory Mystics in the World of Goods." In *Consumption and the World of Goods.* Ed. John Brewer and Roy Porter. London: Routledge, 1994.

———. "Experimenters' Techniques, Dyers' Hands, and the Electric Planetarium." *Isis* 88 (1997), 456–483.

Schoenbrun, David. *Triumph in Paris: The Exploits of Benjamin Franklin.* New York: Harper & Row, 1976.

Schonland, Basil. *The Flight of Thunderbolts.* Oxford: Clarendon Press, 1964.

Scott, A. F. *Every One a Witness: The Georgian Age.* London: Martins, 1970.

Seeger, Raymond J. *Benjamin Franklin: New World Physicist.* Oxford: Pergamon Press, 1973.

Sellers, Charles Coleman. *Benjamin Franklin in Portraiture.* New Haven: Yale University Press, 1962.

Shapin, Steven. *A Social History of Truth. Civility and Science in Seventeenth Century England.* Chicago: University of Chicago Press, 1994.

Sheridan, Richard. *The Rivals. Twelve Famous Plays of the Restoration and 18th Century.* Ed. Cecil A. Moore. New York: Modern Library, 1933, 793–872.

Shor, Elizabeth Noble. "Buffon, Georges-Louis LeClerc, Comte De." In *Dictionary of Scientific Biography.* Ed. Charles Coulston Gillispie. New York: Scribner, 1970.

Sibum, Heinz Otto. "The Bookkeeper of Nature: Benjamin Franklin's Electrical Research and the Development of Experimental Natural Philosophy in the 18th Century." In *Reappraising Benjamin Franklin: A Bicentennial Perspective.* Ed. J. A. Leo LeMay. Newark: University of Delaware Press, 1993.

Siegfried, Susan L. *The Art of Louis-Léopold Boilly.* New Haven: Yale University Press, 1995.

Simon, Grant Miles. "Houses and Early Life in Philadelphia." *Transactions of the American Philosophical Society* 43 (1953), 280–288.

Singer, S. *The Nature of Ball Lightning*. New York: Plenum, 1971.

Smith, Charles John and Henry George Bohn. *Historical and Literary Curiosities*. London: H.G. Bohn, 1847.

Smith, Samuel. *History of the Province of Pennsylvania*. Ed. William Mervine. Philadelphia: Colonial Society of Pennsylvania, 1913.

Snorrason, Egil. *C. G. Kratzenstein, professor physices experimentalis Petropol*. Odense: Odense University, 1974.

Sorrenson, Richard. "George Graham, Visible Technician." *The British Journal for the History of Science* 32 (1999), 203–221.

Sparks, Jared. *The Works of Benjamin Franklin . . . with Notes and a Life of the Author*. Vol. 1. Boston: Tappan, Whittemore, and Mason, nd.

Srodes, James. *Franklin: The Essential Founding Father*. New York: Regnery, 2002.

Stahlin, Karl. *Aus den Papieren Jacob von Stahlins*. Berlin: 1926.

Sterne, Laurence. *The Life and Opinions of Tristram Shandy, Gentleman*. New York: Coward, McCann, 1950.

Stevens, B. F. *B. F. Stevens's Facsimiles of Manuscripts in European Archives Relating to America 1773–1783*. Washington, D.C.: 1889–1898.

Still, Alfred. *Soul of Amber: The Background of Electrical Science*. New York: Murray Hill Books, 1944.

Stimson, Dorothy. *Scientists and Amateurs: A History of the Royal Society*. New York: Greenwood Press, 1968.

Strong-cock, Paddy. *Teague-Root Displayed: Being Some Useful and Important Discoveries Tending to Illustrate the Doctrine of Electricity*. London: W. Webb, 1746.

Struik, D. J. "Musschenbroek, Petrus Van." In *Dictionary of Scientific Biography*. Ed. Charles Coulston Gillispie. New York: Scribner, 1970.

Sturdy, David. *Science and Social Status: The Members of the Academie des Sciences, 1666–1750*. Woodbridge, UK: Boydell Press, 1995.

"Surprising Phenomenon of a Human Body." *Gentleman's Magazine* 17 (May 1747), 220–221.

Sutton, Geoffrey V. *Science for a Polite Society: Gender, Culture, and the Demonstration of Enlightenment*. New York: Westview Press, 1995.

Tanford, Charles. *Ben Franklin Stilled the Waves*. Durham, NC: Duke University Press, 1989.

Thompson, Peter. *A Social History of Philadelphia's Taverns, 1683–1800*. Dissertation, University of Pennsylvania, 1989.

———. *Rum Punch and Revolution*. Philadelphia: University of Pennsylvania Press, 1999.

Tillotson, Geoffrey, et al. Ed. *Eighteenth-Century English Literature*. New York: Harcourt Brace, 1969.

Tolles, Frederick B. "Benjamin Franklin's Business Mentors: The Philadelphia Quaker Merchants." *William and Mary Quarterly* 60–69.

————. *James Logan and the Culture of Provincial America*. Greenwood, CT: Greenwood Press, 1957.

————. *Meeting House and Counting House: The Quaker Merchants of Colonial Philadelphia 1682–1763*. New York: Norton, 1963.

Torlais, Jean. *Un Physicien au Siecle des Lumieres: L'Abbé Nollet 1700–1770*. Paris: Sipuco Press, 1954.

Troyat, Henri. *Catharine The Great*. Trans. Joan Pinkham. New York: Dutton, 1979.

Trustees of the Pennsylvania Academy. *Day Book Belonging to the Trustees of the Academy. 1749–1789*. University of Pennsylvania Archives, Philadelphia.

————. *Minutes of the Trustees of the Academy. Journal A*. University of Pennsylvania Archives, Philadelphia.

Tsverava, G. K. *Georg Vil'gel'm Rikhman, 1711–1753*. Leningrad: Nauka, Leningrad otdnie, 1977.

Tunbridge, Paul. "Franklin's Pointed Lightning Conductor." *Notes & Records of the Royal Society* 28 (1974), 207–219.

Uman, Martin A. *All About Lightning*. New York: Dover, 1986.

Vaille, F.O. and H.A. Clark. *The Harvard Book: a Series of Historical, Biographical, and Descriptive Sketches*. Cambridge: Welch, Bigelow, 1875.

Van Doren, Carl. *Benjamin Franklin*. New York: Viking, 1938.

Vigée-Le Brun, Elizabeth Louise. *Memoirs of Madame Elizabeth Louise Vigée-Le Brun*. Trans. Gerard Shelley. London: John Hamilton, 1926.

Walpole, Horace. *The Last Journals of Horace Walpole*. Ed. Dr. Doran and A. F. Steuart. London: J. Lane, 1858.

Waring, Joseph Ioor. *A History of Medicine in South Carolina 1670–1825*. Charleston: South Carolina Medical Association, 1964.

Warner, Sam Bass. *The Private City: Philadelphia in Three Stages of Its Growth*. Philadelphia: University of Pennsylvania Press, 1987.

Watson, Elkanah. *Men and Times of the Revolution; Or, Memoirs of Elkanah Watson*. New York: Dana, 1856.

Watson, John. *Annals of Philadelphia and Pennsylvania, in the Olden Time*. Philadelphia: Pennington and Hunt, 1844.

Watson, William. *Experiments and Observations Tending to Illustrate the Nature and Properties of Electricity*. London: C. Davis, 1746.

————. *A Sequel to the Experiments and Observations*. London: C. Davis, 1746.

————. "A Collection of the Electrical Experiments communicated to the Royal Society by Wm. Watson . . . ." *Philosophical Transactions* 45 (1748), 49–92.

————. "An Account of the Experiments made by some Gentlemen of the Royal Society, in order to measure the absolute Velocity of Electricity . . . " *Philosophical Transactions* 45 (1748), 491–496.

————. "Some further Inquiries into the Nature and Properties of Electricity . . . ." *Philosophical Transactions* 45 (1749), 93–120.

————. "A Letter from Mr. William Watson, F.R.S. to the Royal Society, declaring that he as well as many others have not been able to make Odours pass thro'

Glass by means of Electricity; and giving a particular Account of Professor Bose at Wittemberg his Experiment of Beatification, or causing a Glory to appear round a Man's Head by Electricity." *Philosophical Transactions* 46 (1750), 348–356.

———. "An Account of Mr. B. Franklin's Treatise . . . ." *Philosophical Transactions* 47 (1751), 202–210.

———. "A Letter of Mr. W. Watson, F.R.S. to the Royal Society, concerning the electrical Experiments in England upon Thunder-clouds." *Philosophical Transactions* 47 (1751-1752), 567–570.

———. "An Account of Abbé Nollet's Treatise concerning Electricity . . . ." *Philosophical Transactions* 48 (1753), 201–216.

———. "An Account of Professor Winkler's Experiments relating to Odours passing through electrised Globes and Tubes . . . ." *Philosophical Transactions* 48 (1753), 231–241.

———. "An Answer to Dr. Lining's Query, relating to the Death of Professor Richmann." *Philosophical Transactions* 48 (1753), 765–772.

———. "An Account of some extraordinary Effects, arising from Convulsions." *Philosophical Transactions* 50 (1758), 743–745.

———. "Some Observations relating to the Lyncurium of the Ancients . . . ." *Philosophical Transactions* 51 (1759), 394–398.

———. "An Account of a Treatise in French presented to the Royal Society, intitled 'Lettres sur 'l Electricité,' by the Abbé Nollet . . . ." *Philosophical Transactions* 52 (1761), 336–343.

Weems, Mason Locke. *The Life of Dr. Franklin.* New York: 1815.

Weigley, Russell F. Ed. *Philadelphia: A 300-Year History.* New York: W. W. Norton, 1982.

Weld, Charles. *A History of the Royal Society with Memoirs of the Presidents.* London: John Parker, 1848.

Wesley, John. *The desideratum: or, Electricity made plain and useful. By a lover of mankind, and of common sense.* London: W. Flexney, 1760.

Westfall, Richard. "Stephen Gray." heep:lles.rice.edu/ES/humsoc/GalileoCatalog/Files /gray.html; November 11, 2000.

Wheatland, David P. *The Apparatus of Science at Harvard 1765–1800.* Cambridge: Harvard University Press, 1968.

Whittaker, E. T. *A History of the Theories of Aether and Electricity.* London: 1910.

Whitworth, Rex. *William Augustus, Duke of Cumberland: A Life.*

Willard, Sterne R. *A Little Revenge: Benjamin Franklin and His Son.* Boston: Little, Brown, 1984.

Williams, Guy. *The Age of Agony: The Art of Healing ca 1700–1800.* Chicago: Academy Publishers, 1986.

Wilson, Benjamin. *Memoirs.* Transcription manuscript. Heinz Archive & Library, National Portrait Gallery, London.

Wilson, Robert. "Dr. John Lining." Typescript of unpublished manuscript presented
to the Robert Wilson Medical History Club, 2 Dec. 1926. Ms. 457, Archive
Medical University, South Carolina Library, Charleston.

Wilson, Woodrow. "Introduction." In *The Autobiography of Benjamin Franklin*. New
York: The Century Co., 1901.

Wister, Charles J. *The Labour of a Long Life: a Memoir of Charles J. Wister*. German-
town, PA: 1866.

Wright, Esmond. *Franklin of Philadelphia*. Cambridge: Harvard University Press,
1986.

Zall, Paul M. *Ben Franklin Laughing*. Berkeley: University of California Press, 1980.

———. *Franklin on Franklin*. Lexington: University Press of Kentucky, 2000.

NOTE

Acknowledgment is made to the descendents of Benjamin Wilson. The author made
every effort to contact them asking permission to quote from the typescript of the
manuscript that mysteriously surfaced at the National Portrait Gallery, London. The
same is true for the descendents of Wolfgang Taraba, whose translation of
Lomonosov is here quoted. Special thanks to John Heilbron for permission to quote
his translation of Musschenbroek.

INDEX

PUBLICAFFAIRS is a publishing house founded in 1997. It is a tribute to the standards, values, and flair of three persons who have served as mentors to countless reporters, writers, editors, and book people of all kinds, including me.

I. F. STONE, proprietor of *I. F. Stone's Weekly*, combined a commitment to the First Amendment with entrepreneurial zeal and reporting skill and became one of the great independent journalists in American history. At the age of eighty, Izzy published *The Trial of Socrates*, which was a national bestseller. He wrote the book after he taught himself ancient Greek.

BENJAMIN C. BRADLEE was for nearly thirty years the charismatic editorial leader of *The Washington Post*. It was Ben who gave the *Post* the range and courage to pursue such historic issues as Watergate. He supported his reporters with a tenacity that made them fearless, and it is no accident that so many became authors of influential, best-selling books.

ROBERT L. BERNSTEIN, the chief executive of Random House for more than a quarter century, guided one of the nation's premier publishing houses. Bob was personally responsible for many books of political dissent and argument that challenged tyranny around the globe. He is also the founder and was the longtime chair of Human Rights Watch, one of the most respected human rights organizations in the world.

. . .

For fifty years, the banner of Public Affairs Press was carried by its owner Morris B. Schnapper, who published Gandhi, Nasser, Toynbee, Truman, and about 1,500 other authors. In 1983 Schnapper was described by *The Washington Post* as "a redoubtable gadfly." His legacy will endure in the books to come.

Peter Osnos, *Publisher*